The Politics of Attention

The Politics of Attention

How Government Prioritizes Problems

Bryan D. Jones
Frank R. Baumgartner

The University of Chicago Press
Chicago and London

The University of Chicago Press, Chicago 60637
The University of Chicago Press, Ltd., London
© 2005 by The University of Chicago
All rights reserved. Published 2005
Printed in the United States of America

14 13 12 11 10 09 08 07   2 3 4 5

ISBN: 0-226-40652-0 (cloth)
ISBN: 0-226-40653-9 (paper)

Library of Congress Cataloging-in-Publication Data

Jones, Bryan D.
    The politics of attention : how government prioritizes problems / Bryan D. Jones,
    Frank R. Baumgartner.
        p.   cm.
    Includes bibliographical references and index.
    ISBN 0-226-40652-0 (cloth : alk. paper)—ISBN 0-226-40653-9 (pbk. : alk. paper)
    1. Political planning—United States.   2. United States—Politics and
    government—Decision making.   3. Government information.   4. Objectivity.
    I. Baumgartner, Frank R., 1958–   II. Title.
    JK468.P64J65   2005
    352.3′3′0973—dc22

                                                                    2005007414

CONTENTS

This book is the outcome of a long-run collaborative project that began in the late 1980s, and in many respects is an extension and elaboration of ideas we originally explored in *Agendas and Instability in American Politics* (University of Chicago Press, 1993). It is firmly based in the belief that policy change is driven not only by the seemingly unchanging aspects of politics—institutions, fixed preferences, resources—and not just by the shifting nature of the policy debate, but by a complex interaction among elements of each. It is committed to a more or less standard conception of bounded rationality as the decisional underpinning of the analysis. It is unyielding in its demand that good measurement is a prerequisite for good quantitative political science.

Here, however, we move to a distinctly different perspective than we have used before for viewing the interactions between institutions and ideas. We adopt a comprehensive perspective, covering the full range of policy topics addressed by the U.S. national government across a long historical time span. We focus on only a single part of the process, however: how information is used, and how attention is allocated to policy topics. If policy debates matter, then information matters. Viewing political systems as information-processing instruments yields insights and allows comparisons not possible with other approaches. Further, the extremely large scope of our empirical project allows us to study these processes in new ways.

Information always involves a sender, a message, and a receiver. To date, most studies of information in political science have centered on its reliability, its validity, or the conditions under which it will be communicated. None of these perspectives examines the responses of the receiver of the information, yet that is exactly what is necessary in the study of the performance of governments. How do governments respond with policy to incoming information? What aspects of the complex, multifaceted, and dynamic environment do policy makers select for scrutiny and action? These are the key questions we pose.

There are two great issues in the processing of information in politics: under what conditions it will be supplied, on the one hand, and how it will be interpreted and prioritized, on the other. The traditional economic view of information is that it is simply another "good" that will be supplied if the price is right. If someone needs information, they pay "search costs" to have someone else (an expert in the field, for example) supply it. Surely in politics that is part of the story, but it cannot be the whole story. In governmental settings, a failure to supply information means policymakers may rely on information supplied by a competitor. Moreover, American governmental institutions include an explicit realization that, even when government agencies are responsible for producing information, organizational cultures can yield one-sided estimates. Hence, policymakers have routinely established independent and competing sources of information. For example, Congress has its own bureaucracy to estimate budgets and policy impacts—the Congressional Budget Office and the Government Accountability Office. If congressmen trusted the executive branch, they would rely on the Office of Management and Budget. Trust is not what the system of separation of powers is all about. Rather, competing and independent sources of information abound in the American political system. This is both by constitutional design and by the nature of a complex pluralistic society.

In fact, there is so much information in the U.S. political system that winnowing through it is more of a problem than finding more of it. Unlike in economics, where buyers may need to search for information, in politics, governmental decision makers often have large amounts of information literally thrown at them by those clamoring for policy change (or defending the status quo). Whether the information stems from government agencies that collect it routinely, from media or academic analysts who may study the background of many different policy problems, or from interest groups, citizens, corporations, and others outside of government who may want to influence a current debate, information is plentiful in politics. The information ranges from rock-solid to poor in quality, and from neutral to heavily biased in perspective. In short, there may be many flaws in the nature of the information that abounds in politics, but scarcity is not typically an issue.

The major consequence of all this is that policymakers are constantly bombarded with information of varying uncertainty and bias, not on a single matter, but on a multitude of potential policy topics. The process by which information is prioritized for action, and attention allocated to some problems rather than others, is called *agenda setting*. Agenda setting can be viewed as a process by which a political system processes diverse incoming information streams. Somehow these diverse streams must be attended to, interpreted, and prioritized. We address these aspects of information processing in this book.

In *Agendas and Instability*, we addressed both information supply and prioritization, though we did not use those terms. We argued that the pluralistic American political system allowed many often competing policy images to survive simultaneously, ready to expand at the right moment. The "right moment" was governed by attention indexed by changes in the perceived validity of a competing policy image. The traditional elements of the American political system and its complex set of policy subsystems act as a drag, creating large-scale inefficiencies in how information is used. Policy subsystems are often based on extremely incomplete models of the policy issue at hand. Essentially, they filter out many relevant bits of information (those bits of information judged to be "irrelevant" to the dominant paradigm, as when environmental issues were once ignored in the search for more agricultural production, in the case of pesticides, or scientific "progress" in the area of civilian nuclear power). These subsystems can insulate policymakers from competing information, or from new information that does not correspond with their vision, understanding of the policy, or goals.

Like water running downhill, new information has a way of finding its voice through the complex interplay of competing venues, however. While this process is by no means guaranteed, we showed in that earlier book many examples of when these cozy arrangements and were successfully challenged. The strength of the existing arrangements meant that when a policy subsystem was disturbed, policy punctuations occurred. Information is at the core of these processes. But information is not used efficiently in politics. Rather, there are powerful psychological, political, and institutional forces that support the prevailing arrangements and are resistant to new information. The policymaking system ignores some bits of information, while giving others disproportionate attention and credence. This is inevitable in all complex institutions, because the process has its roots in the inefficiencies of human cognition itself. It is time that we develop a full theory of how human cognitive processing interacts with policymaking institutions, and that is what we attempt to do here.

In this book, we address how information is used in politics, and we focus on how it is prioritized. Why do policymakers focus on some information while ignoring or discounting other bits of information that collectively deemed to be less relevant? We demonstrate the information-rich nature of the political system and discuss its implications, but we do not assess here how the system became that way. We have explored the connection between information supply and pluralism in at least one setting—congressional committees—elsewhere (Baumgartner, Jones, and McLeod 2000) and continue this exploration in a related project. But, as we shall see, trying to understand how the American political system detects uncertain and ambiguous signals pouring in from many diverse sources, interprets those signals, and prioritizes them for policy action is plenty to occupy us in this book. Other projects, which we continue, will address related issues.

In working through our theory of information processing in politics, we have accumulated numerous debts. First, we appreciate the Political Science Division of the National Science Foundation for its steadfast support of various phases of this project, and especially several directors of the division and our program officer there, Frank Scioli. (Some of the material in this book is based on work supported by the National Science Foundation under grant no. 0111443; any opinions, findings, conclusions or recommendations expressed in this material are those of the authors and do not necessarily reflect the views of the National Science Foundation.) Second, we owe a big debt to the graduate students who collaborated with us on this project, many of whom have gone on to productive careers during the long course of this project, who displayed the best virtues of patience, hard work, and generally good humor. Several were coauthors on some of the articles that we have drawn from in various places in this book. They all bear mention: Jens Feeley, who superbly managed the Policy Agendas Project during the last several years; Valerie Hunt, Tracy Sulkin, Heather Larsen, Erin de la Mare, and most recently Sam Workman, at the University of Washington; James True, Michael MacLeod, and Jeff Talbert at Texas A&M—all were valuable contributors to the project. At the University of Washington, several generations of Center for American Politics and Public Policy Undergraduate Research Fellows helped us collect, code, and manage the datasets. Finally, we appreciate those friends and scholars who read all or parts of the manuscript in one form or another. These include Jeff Berry, Kevin Esterling, John Kingdon, Beth Leech, Christine Mahoney, John McCarthy, John Padgett, Mark Smith, Bat Sparrow, Jim Stimson, Tracy Sulkin, John Wilkerson, Walter Williams, and others who, due to our own limited memories and attention spans, we are certainly omitting here. We owe a special debt of gratitude to Jim Stimson, who not only gave the manuscript a careful critical review, but also suggested a new computer simulation to supplement those we had done, and even wrote the code for that simulation.

At several points in the book, we have integrated analyses originally presented in articles published previously. In all cases, these have been extensively rewritten and updated with the most recent data we have available to us. Nevertheless, we are indebted to our collaborators, and they bear special mention. In particular, we appreciate the collaboration over the years with James True, whose knowledge of U.S. budgeting and appreciation of punctuated equilibrium have contributed immeasurably to the theory of budgeting that is central to our work. We also appreciate the willingness of Jim, Mike MacLeod, Tracy Sulkin, and Heather Larsen, all of whom collaborated on papers that have been redrafted for this volume, to allow us to incorporate that work into this volume.

Readers of this book may be struck by its extremely large empirical scope. We have been fortunate to work together for more than fifteen years now. During this time, with the support of those mentioned above, we have organized the creation and development of some massive and comprehensive indices of the activities of the U.S. national government. These data collection projects continue. For the first time, they allow us to address some issues, such as the overall distribution of policy change, that have never been addressed before in American politics. This means that our analyses will appear unfamiliar to many readers. They are based neither in case studies of particular policy processes nor in standard regression-style causal approaches, but rather in graphical and stochastic methods sensitive to the complex interactions and dynamical processes common in politics. We hope that our readers will appreciate the more comprehensive perspective that these many years of work have allowed us to take.

How Government Processes Information and Prioritizes Problems

On Monday, July 28, 2003, Republican senator James Inhofe of Oklahoma, chairman of the Committee on Environment and Public Works, rose to deliver a speech to the Senate on global warming. He began by stating, "One very critical element to our success as policymakers is how we use science." He went on to claim that environmental extremists dismiss science as "irrelevant" because they are "prophets of doom who peddle propaganda masquerading as science in the name of saving the planet from catastrophic disaster." The senator continued: "The evidence is overwhelmingly in favor of those who don't see global warming posing grave harm to the planet and who don't think human beings have significant influence on the climate system." Inhofe ended his speech by saying, "Over the past two hours, I have offered compelling evidence that catastrophic global warming is a hoax. . . . Natural variability, not fossil fuel emissions, is the overwhelming factor influencing climate changes; . . . no meaningful warming has occurred over the last century; and climate models predicting dramatic temperature increases over the next 100 years are flawed and highly imperfect" (Inhofe 2003).

Senator Inhofe certainly has a point: Scientific information is very often distorted, ignored, misused, and cited selectively in the heat of political debate. And of course when one side does this type of thing, we can expect the other side to respond in kind. Just as he accused his opponents of distorting the facts in support of their agenda, his statements can be seen in a similar vein. They are clearly "propaganda masquerading as science," although his distortion serves the purpose of saving America from "an agenda of energy suppression" (as he might put it). Almost all of the evidence he cited as supporting his claim to sound science is either misleading or outright wrong. Prevailing evidence clearly supports the thesis of global warming since the mid-1800s, and there is ample evidence that humans have influenced the climate cycle—though there is scientific debate on this point (Alley 2000; Mayewski and White 2002).

It is indeed true that the earth's climate is highly cyclical, and climatologists must take great care in separating natural cycles and trends from human-caused (or at least more recent) changes. Moreover, Inhofe is on target with his critique that the Kyoto Treaty on Global Warming will do little (he says "nothing") to lower the earth's temperature through setting greenhouse gas emission targets. Inhofe's claim that predictive climate models "are flawed and highly imperfect" is entirely correct. But his conclusion, that his position that no meaningful warming has occurred in the last century is "supported by the painstaking work of the nation's top climate scientists," is not just misleading. It is not true.

Such misuse of information is quite common in politics, and it's been done on all sides of the climate debate. Luckily for all of us, we are not dependent on a single source of information in any complex policy debate. Information matters, even though it enters the political process imperfectly, policy advocates and government officials often attempt to distort it, and there is no guarantee that all relevant pieces of information will enter the political debate on any given subject. But the policy process, and government in general, is rife with information, and this provides a critical but often overlooked dynamic in politics.

The Role of Information in Political Systems

This book is about how political systems, and in particular the American political system, process information in producing public policies. It may seem strange to use a "J'accuse" speech full of distortions and misleading accusations by an energy-state politician with an axe to grind as a starting point for this exploration. Yet through his severely selective use of evidence and downright fabrications, surely Inhofe has scored a major point: many environmentalists have consistently overstated the scientific consensus, and made an even greater leap by implying that lowering greenhouse emissions is both possible and effective. They, too, are sinners.

Thoughtful observers may abhor Inhofe's methods. Indeed, calm people may, with just cause, reject the whole debate as "politics as usual." Many people are turned off by politics because of these types of distortions. We do not have this reaction. Rather, we want to understand how information is used, and how it can be used, in government. Government includes elected officials representing constituencies that will lose jobs if certain policies are enacted. Of course officials distort the facts. In some ways, that is their job; they were elected to protect the interests of their constituents. Others have different beliefs, and they fight for what they believe serves their interests or the public good. The key question is not how one actor behaves (or misbehaves) but how the entire system of government makes use of the conflicting and often ambiguous information thrust upon it by scientists, advocates, and others. We are not cynical or pessimistic about the ability of the American political system to process information, but neither are we complacent. The political process, with its complex machinery of government and its associated interest groups, communities of professionals in scores of policy domains, and tight links to other social and economic actors, processes massive amounts of information. It does so imperfectly and in fits and starts, with no guarantee of proportionality (indeed, with little likelihood of proportional response to new information). We spend the rest of this book explaining how the government processes information, and why that matters. Along the way, we develop a new theory of policy change, one based on disproportionate information-processing in policymaking that integrates seemingly discredited old theories of incrementalism with the theory of punctuated equilibrium.

Policymakers, interest groups, media outlets, and government agencies all have vested interests, ideological blinders, short attention spans, and self-interested motivations, so how is information incorporated into public policy? Scientists and engineers often abhor the political process because it is not "objective." The prevailing view of politics among most citizens and many political scientists is profoundly cynical: politics is simply the struggle among interests, and interests win because they have resources. We don't disagree with this (though we think it is vastly overstated), but we add to this a different focus. We note in the pages to come a litany of other human limitations that interfere with sound decision making. Yet we see information as providing a profound dynamic element to the political process, and we see the pursuit of democratic politics as essential to the processing of information in public policymaking. Just as important, the effective processing of information is necessary for the conduct of democratic government. They are as intertwined as the strands of DNA's double helix. Like it or not, we can't understand government and how it operates without understanding how it processes information, including how it distorts information.

In this argument we are far more optimistic about American democracy than the prevailing tone of cynicism would lead many to be. Citizens—many in the academy, the so-called think tanks that hype propaganda as scientific studies; most in the media; and a certain senator from Oklahoma who seems to think that distortion by the other side is wrong, but not so bad when done by his side—by actions or words all communicate that cynicism. And we continue our claims, laid out a decade ago, that a dynamic view of American politics leads not to "gridlock" and inaction (or, in the modern terminology, dominance by "veto groups"), but to destruction of prevailing elite "systems of limited participation" and to dynamic, if punctuated and uncertain, change (Baumgartner and Jones 1993). We are not Pollyannas with a naive belief in progress. Our optimism is tempered by today's harsh and unforgiving politics and the seeming failing of the American political system to focus on our own well-thought-out priorities. But it is buoyed by our study of history: democratic political systems respond to information. President Abraham Lincoln summarized it best when he commented that you can fool all the people some of the time, and some of the people all of the time, but you can't fool all of the people all of the time.

Overview of the Argument

The primary purpose of this book is to move toward placing information processing at the heart of the study of American politics and public policy. We do not stop with exhortation; we use the Policy Agendas Project datasets to develop a full set of empirical results from this approach. In the process, we show how an appreciation of the ways political systems cope with vague, ambiguous, and uncertain signals from the environment can integrate two great enterprises in the study of American politics: policy process approaches and institutional analyses. We do so by focusing not primarily on the preferences and procedures of the institutions, and not on the specifics of particular public policies, but on how institutional procedures constrain policy reactions to the flow of information. Compared to standard institutional analyses, our approach is dynamic. Compared to standard public policy process studies, our scope is comprehensive.

In developing this line of argument, we solve a long-standing problem facing the study of decision making in public policy: why no model of choice has been put forward to replace the discredited incremental theory. In incrementalism, policymakers were supposed to make small adjustments on past actions. But incrementalism had a "hidden assumption": that the information causing the small adjustments was processed proportionately (we show that the information flow itself does not have to be well behaved; only the processing of it need be so). Several studies recognized and pointed to problems with this assumption, but only two came anywhere close to solving the problem:

Larkey's (1979) idea of "error accumulation" in budget decisions, and Padgett's (1980, 1981) stochastic process studies of budgetary change. We build on those insights and show here that a model of *disproportionate information-processing*, based on how the cognitive limits of decision makers and formal and informal arrangements of groups of decision makers affect the dynamic processing of information, solves the problem by integrating incrementalism into a broader theory of political choice. Incrementalism was not wrong; indeed we show that it was probably understated by its proponents. But it is far from the full story. It must be combined with a theory of punctuated equilibrium to reach its full potential.

Disproportionate information-processing leads to a pattern of extreme stability and occasional punctuations, rather than either smooth adjustment processes or endless gridlock. It subsumes the punctuated equilibrium model of policy change, which we developed more than a decade ago (Baumgartner and Jones 1993). The term *punctuated equilibrium* was popularized by the work of paleontologists Niles Eldridge and Steven Gould (1972). We were not the first to employ the metaphor; it has been used loosely in political science to refer to reactions to large-scale crises in the environment (and occasionally more rigorously; see Carmines and Stimson 1989). We argued instead that punctuations in policy outcomes reflected an interaction between change in the environment and reverberations inside the political system. In particular, we took the traditional static notion of policy subsystem, in which specialized interest groups, congressional committees, and federal agencies responsible for implementing policies interact to find an equilibrium of interests, and added a dynamic. The dynamic is an appeal by the disfavored side in a policy subsystem, or those excluded entirely from the arrangement, to broader political processes—Congress, the president, political parties, and public opinion. This mobilization could act to destroy or radically alter the prevailing and powerful arrangements among privileged interests.

There were already key scholarly works on this mechanism (Jones 1975; Redford 1969); we added the important component of *policy image*. We argued that destroying or altering a subsystem of interests required changing the image of the policy prevailing outside the subsystem. We also noted that *policy venues* are typically not fixed in the U.S. political system and that shifting images are often linked with aggressive venue-shopping by protagonists shut out of the old venues. Venues resisting change resist new images; however, nothing stops policy entrepreneurs from seeking new venues more receptive to the new policy images, and in the U.S. system jurisdictions are often in dispute.

It is only a small step from the notion of policy image to a theory of information processing, but it is not a simple one. The reason is that *information* implies something firm, while *image* seems squishy. The trick is to see information as ambiguous (subject to differing interpretations), not just uncertain (subject to high variance). We see information as possessing dimensionality; each dimension is associated with an interpretation. Each dimension or interpretation is weighted—more or less prevalent and persuasive, more or less relevant to the decision, central or tangential to understanding the policy. In the extreme, many dimensions are effectively ignored (assigned a weight of zero), only later to be "discovered" by policymakers who should have known about them all along. Nuclear power in the 1950s was viewed through the lens of "atoms for progress," but by the 1960s it had become associated with environmental danger, workplace safety, and the fear of nuclear proliferation. Somehow over time the weights on these competing interpretations changed. They changed partly because of the facts, and partly because of the political arguments put forth by opponents of nuclear power. When images shift, punctuations can occur; image shifts are part of disproportionate information processing. Over the long term, it is sometimes surprising in retrospect how important elements of policy debate can be virtually ignored for very long periods of time. While specialists are often aware of them, they simply do not gain attention compared to other dimensions of the debate.

Of course, the American political system is not processing just one issue at a time. It juggles numerous issues simultaneously. Most issues most of the time are far from the national political agenda, far from the front page of the newspaper, relegated to the various communities that exist in all areas of public policy, and subject to subsystem equilibrium processes. If and when these issues have won the attention of the primary policymaking institutions, errors have often accumulated, and punctuations must occur to "catch up" with changing reality. While institutions can parallel process numerous policy matters simultaneously, the processing system is imperfect, and these imperfections lead to punctuations.

Finally, institutions add "drag" even beyond what the information-processing approach sketched above implies. Political institutions impose costs on the process of coming to collective choice by requiring supermajorities within institutions and collaborations among them. These decision costs do not lead invariably to gridlock, as the existing institutional literature implies. Nor do they require a change in political party (or legislative/presidential preferences) to produce major punctuations, although this is clearly one major source of change. Any flow of information can overcome the institutional friction inherent in the American political system, but either it must be very intense objectively or it must reverberate around the system via the interpretative arguments that political actors make. That is, an image change, born either of strong external signals or of internal debate (or both), must occur. And that completes the integration of policy change theories, punctuated equilibrium, and static institutional analyses.

In the rest of this chapter, we introduce the fundamental idea of information processing in policymaking; give an overview of the major features of our approach; and show how we plan to integrate incremental decision making, punctuated equilibrium, and institutional analysis within the theory.

Information Processing

Information processing may be defined as collecting, assembling, interpreting, and prioritizing signals from the environment. A *signal* is simply some detectable change in what is happening "out there." All signals are characterized by *uncertainty* (we can't always be sure something out there has actually changed) and *ambiguity* (we can't be certain what the signal means). As a consequence, it is never fully clear that there has been a relevant change in the policymaking environment. Moreover, objective changes in the environment—signals—must be distinguished from attention to these signals. Signals are information, but when we become aware of signals, they become "news." In politics, as in communication theory, signal detection is critical to future action.

Signals may be misinterpreted once they are detected, because of uncertainty or bias. Not only are many signals unclear (that is, subject to differing possible interpretations, not self-evident), but those who interpret signals are often biased. They may have professional training that leads them to focus on one issue rather than another, an ideological bias, an economic interest, or a political position that makes them support one outcome rather than another. In politics and in public policy, most who are involved care about the outcomes; they are not and should not be expected to be "neutral." Some mischaracterize signals because of conscious or unconscious bias, and others may do so purposefully for strategic reasons. In sum, there are many reasons to question not only the accuracy of signals but the ways in which signals get interpreted through the policy process. Decision makers, like all people, often ignore important changes until they become severe or until policy entrepreneurs with an interest in the matter highlight such changes. The fact that decision makers filter signals through their attentiveness, assimilate information in a biased manner, and generally act as bounded rationalists, means that they cannot be expected to respond proportionately to the strengths of incoming informational signals. That is, they have great difficulties in matching a response to the strength of a signal.

This concept of *disproportionate information-processing* is critical to this book, and we develop a full theory of how this works in policymaking. There is no one-to-one correspondence between the severity of a signal and the response of a government. At first glance, one might be tempted to assume that governments respond to signals when they cross a threshold, at which time they cannot be ignored. While threshold effects are clearly part of disproportionality, they do not tell the whole story. Governments are quite capable of overrreacting to vague or ambiguous signals, as the case of the George W. Bush administration's attack on Iraq based on the claim of "weapons of mass destruction" indicates. Further, attention to a problem almost always consumes precious agenda space; thus, a crowding effect can occur, prioritizing problems unintentionally. The same signal, at the same level of intensity, could lead to action when few issues crowd the agenda, while it would not when the public agenda is more congested. This implies that the threshold itself is contingent. Finally, signals do not generally interpret themselves. Interest groups, policy entrepreneurs, think tanks, political leaders, and mobilized citizens all may attempt to spin the issue. Because of its electoral coalition, one party may be more sensitive to an issue than another party; the party in power matters in responsiveness to mobilizations. So again the threshold is contingent—this time on the extensiveness of mobilization.

While at times decision makers must search for the information they need in making policy, just as often they are inundated with information. In this case, how they sort through, interpret, and prioritize information is critical, more so than how they search for it. Partly, this is a consequence of past policymakers establishing the tools for acquiring information. The Central Intelligence Agency, the Defense Intelligence Agency, the Office of Management and Budget, the Congressional Budget Office, and the Government Accountability Office are all agencies whose primary responsibility is the production of information for policy. But information is freely supplied by interest groups, public policy think tanks, officials from agencies that are not directly involved in the information business, state and local government agencies with experience in the area, university professors and other researchers, and citizens. As a consequence, there are two primary issues with incorporating information into the policymaking process. The first concerns the supply of information, and the second concerns how that information is prioritized through the political process, given that it is supplied.

Supplying Information

When will information relevant to the policy process be supplied? From one point of view, information may be seen as a scarce and valuable good, one that is not supplied without remuneration. If policymakers need estimates of the intentions of foreign countries, they set up agencies with paid professional staffs to study and report on the problem. Similarly it is common for Congress to delegate information-gathering functions to specialized committees and subcommittees, which make recommendations to the chamber. The "payoff" is some deference by the chamber to the committee (Krehbiel 1991). In short, policymakers delegate the collecting and assembling of information to others more expert in the particulars.

That leads to an assumption that information is generally in short supply on matters of public policy. Only experts provide information, and they do so only if compensated. This corresponds with classic economics-based understandings of "search" and "information" costs. But that cannot be the whole story, for the assumption that information is undersupplied in politics flies in the face of the clamoring diversity of information that characterizes modern America. Information on policy matters is supplied by interest groups, think tanks, political parties, bureaucratic agencies, and congressional committees. Oversupply rather than undersupply seems to be the problem. Policymakers generally report that they are bombarded with information of varying quality; they are not normally in the position of having to seek it out. As Richard Hall (1996:90) notes, "policy-relevant information is abundant, perhaps embarrassingly rich, on Capitol Hill. Interest groups, Congressional Research Service, Government Accounting Office, various administration reports, preprinted hearing testimony, studies conducted by academics, think tanks, and policy analysts in and out of government" supply it.

This does not mean that the issue of supply is solved. The structure of a political system can induce increases in the supply of information. Our earlier study of congressional committee jurisdictions indicated that overlapping jurisdictions in which committees mutually interfered with one another led to breakdowns in informational monopolies, thereby increasing the supply of information available for policymaking (Baumgartner, Jones, and MacLeod 2000). In general, we strongly suspect that pluralist, nonhierarchical systems produce more information than unitary, hierarchical systems, such as those envisioned in many conceptions of delegation to experts. That information may be less reliable (but the question of bias is open), and it will be more difficult to prioritize, because it comes from diverse sources. But there will likely be more of it. Finally, ebbs and flows of information may occur, stimulated

by the perceptions of participants that policymakers are open to this information. In fact, James Madison and his colleagues seemed to have understood this as well, since the separation of powers and federal system they devised seem perfectly designed to generate multiple independent sources of
information.

Prioritizing Information

The general oversupply of information in politics, for whatever reason,
leads to what Herbert Simon (1983, 1997) referred to as an *information-rich*
world where evaluating information in light of existing goals is more important than searching for new information. For the rest of this book we pursue Simon's insight, focusing on how policy information is detected, filtered,
winnowed, and prioritized, putting the question of supply in abeyance for
the present.

In his speech on climate change, Senator Inhofe offered no new information. He was engaged in the time-honored process of prioritizing the information available by offering an "interpretation," a "spin," or perhaps a
"distortion," depending on one's point of view. In democracies, this process
of weighting and prioritizing the available evidence is at least as important as
the acquisition of evidence. Even if evidence were neither uncertain nor ambiguous, the process of prioritization would still be necessary. In a world in
which individuals as well as policymaking institutions have limited capacities to process issues, paying attention to problems prioritizes them.

Prioritizing in information-poor environments requires search, while
prioritizing in information-rich environments requires winnowing. That is,
when we lack information we need to set up a system for searching for what
we need. When there is lots of information available, we need to find ways to
plow through all the signals bombarding us, decide what is relevant and what
is not, and estimate the quality of the information. These are vastly different
tasks, requiring very different approaches.

In either case, a decision maker needs two kinds of information: an understanding of the problem and knowledge of the possible solutions. Most
formal approaches to decision making treat the problem as if it is given, and
the issue focuses on how one chooses among the available solutions. If search
is required, it is invariably directed at the solution space. If one needs a car,
then one searches among the various alternatives. If the country needs a political leader, a voter chooses among those presented by the political parties.
If the economy is weak, governmental leaders debate whether a stimulus is
needed, and if so what kind.

But how does a person (or a government) choose what problem to address? In the case of a single individual, we generally assume that he or she knows when to begin searching for a new car. But why would one expect a government to know what problems to address and in what order to address them, and only debate solutions? There must be some prior process by which problems are detected and prioritized. A pretty good beginning assumption is that the desires of citizens to have their problems addressed (including the desire *not* to spend money on someone else's problem) are infinite. Indeed, this is just the economist's assumption that demand is infinite restated in political terms. Of course, not all people will express their desires to government, because such expression has costs. But encouraging free expression is a very good way for democracies to do business, because it functions to identify problems (in information-processing terms, to detect signals). Moreover, politicians, to the extent that they wish to be elected, have clear motivation to raise issues that will resonate with citizens, hence pushing them into the public problem space.

In short, it is a very good bet that public problem spaces—the set of issues that government is called upon to address—are information-rich, not information-poor. If so, then the first issue for government is to prioritize problems, not to cycle through possible solutions. And prioritizing somehow means winnowing—dropping from consideration for the time being problems that can wait. Of course, in the real world of policy choice, solutions are pushed forward simultaneously with problems in a confusing cacophony, but that does not make the distinction any less valid.

The Index Construction Problem

Central to the prioritization problem is how decision makers react to information from numerous sources. In effect, information from multiple sources and about diverse issues must be combined and weighted in making a policy choice. We refer to this as the *index construction problem*. The index construction problem is two problems in one. The first problem is how to decide which of many competing problems to address with public policy action. The second is how to weigh and combine the various sources of information that affect the particular problem chosen for action. Some combination of source reliability and importance of the message is necessary, across all sources and messages. But how should a decision maker weigh the various sources and messages?

For example, should a president focus on reforming education, creating jobs, ensuring better health care availability, fighting terrorism, enhancing the arts and humanities, reforming entitlements, or focusing global attention on human rights and religious freedom? All of the above, naturally. And to many other issues that press for his attention. There are scores of potential issues from which to choose, and each involves uncertain and ambiguous information. Which educational reforms will work? At what cost? With what side effects? How best to create jobs? Does invading Iraq enhance or threaten our national security? Will privatization solve the Social Security funding shortfall? It is one thing to select some social problems that deserve to be addressed but quite another to adopt a set of policies that will simultaneously reflect the relative importance of all the possible social issues that demand attention, be effective, and minimize unintended negative consequences of the policies themselves. And despite all this we want government to attend to the same issues that the public thinks are important (and, as we show later, government does so).

Interpreting Signals

Even when a signal is detected and is elevated to a high priority, its full meaning is often debated. Policymaking means attempting to solve problems based on flows of information. That statement immediately raises the questions of what problems, problems for whom, what information, and how to use (or misuse) that information. These are, in effect, questions about how a political system understands and prioritizes the situations it faces. Information is not neutral in its effects on the interests and well-being of citizens. If advocates of a point of view distort information, or if they are just better at highlighting the aspects of a complex situation that benefit them, they are more likely to succeed in getting the policies they want from government. Raising anxieties or manipulating enthusiasm can lead to support for a point of view.

Information has "color." It raises emotions. Political information has bright colors. The simple concept of "problem" adds color to "signal" or "information about a situation," and, indeed, much of politics involves getting people to see a "situation" as a "problem" by adding color. While a situation can be described objectively, a problem is essentially subjective. People translate "situations" into "problems" when they think the situation is relevant to their well-being. The raising of emotions in politics is essential to the prioritization of problems, because emotion governs the allocation of attention. As a consequence, the strategic manipulation of emotions in politics is an essential part of the process of detecting and weighting the importance of signals.

Uncertainty and Ambiguity

Information is very seldom some sort of neutral fact. Almost any "bit" of information is subject to interpretation, and any information that has consequences for humans is subject to debate. Uncertainty and ambiguity are relatives, often confused with each other, but they are not identical twins.

Every policy decision involves uncertainty, and usually lots of it. Most information, as almost everybody understands, is uncertain. It is characterized by a probability of being correct. Statisticians have shown that pure rational analysis must proceed according to different rules when information is uncertain—the "probability calculus"—than when information is certain. In particular, the probable gain from a choice must be weighed against the risks associated with the choice. An outcome may not occur even employing the best solution possible. Further, every decision involves some risk that the information it was based on was wrong. Imperfect information compounds uncertainty.

The effects of reducing greenhouse gases in the earth's atmosphere on global climate change are obviously uncertain. Climatologists are pretty sure that regular climate cycles affect today's period of warming, and for the most part they think that human activities, in particular the burning of fossil fuels, contribute to that warming. But they are less certain when it comes to the precise combination of each, and even less certain that a reduction in the burning of fossil fuels will lead to a reduction in the warming trend. They are even uncertain whether the effects of warming will lead to continued warming or a catastrophic collapse of temperatures in the North Atlantic, leading to a European "deep freeze" (Mayewski and White 2002). On this, as in many important topics of political debate, there is no shortage of uncertainty.

Further, information is almost always ambiguous. That is, it is subject to differing interpretations or perspectives. Some perspectives are comparable, but in many cases they are incommensurate. A tax cut stimulates the economy, but in a progressive tax system any cuts will go disproportionately to the wealthy. How does one compare the effects on the overall economy with distributional justice? Different people may make different value judgments about the worth of these two elements of a trade-off, even if they agree fully on the facts. Demanding increased pollution controls improves the health and general quality of life around a factory, but how does one weigh that against the lost jobs and income that may result from the costs of pollution control? Different people bear the costs and reap the benefits from the action. But factory owners are quite willing to impose costs on others, and only politics can change this. So ambiguity and conflicting perspectives are essential parts of politics. Politics is not only about information and how it should be interpreted. Often it involves straightforward conflicts of interest, competing and incommensurate goals. In such situations information can be both ambiguous and uncertain, and those seeking a certain policy goal may focus on the uncertainty, rather than the ambiguity, of the information presented by their opponents—as did Senator Inhofe in his climate speech. That their own side often has uncertain information as well is for others to discover.

Competing interpretations of information may be thought of as *attributes* or dimensions that underlie information signals. Any interpretation is some weighted combination of these attributes. In many cases, people gravitate to an interpretation that involves only one attribute out of many that could have been chosen. Today, managing the economy centers only on the issue of growth, completely ignoring the issue of distribution—who gets what—even though in the past many great political battles centered on whether creditors or debtors were helped or hurt by government fiscal policies. We return to this point in chapter 3.

Solving Problems and Making New Ones

Once a signal is detected and interpreted, a debate about the proper solution may occur. Solving public problems is neither simple nor straightforward. Each solution may have multiple implications for the problem and various "side consequences" going beyond the first problem and potentially creating new issues to deal with. These unintended consequences can add benefits or costs to other social groups, creating new supporters, new opponents, and more ambiguous information about the overall impact of the policy solution chosen. And these side effects can be uncertain as well.

Not all political systems solve problems equally well, and any given political system may vary in its problem-solving capacities across time. Some people clearly benefit more than others from problem-solving activities, and the anticipation of such benefits can even drive the search for problems. (Did President George W. Bush's tax cuts of 2001 and 2003 stem from a desire to stimulate an ailing economy? Or were they a device to distribute resources to his supporters? How would we judge them if they both stimulated the economy and distributed wealth?) In such complex situations, the information we associate with a given policy is the main target of Washington spin masters. Information is neither neutral nor always objectively defined, because the aspect of the policy that is emphasized in the debate (stimulation or distribution) often determines the outcome.

As human decision makers are fallible, so too are political systems. Emotions are aroused inappropriately: short-term gains may be maximized at great long-run cost; the collectivity is sacrificed to individual greed; ideology can trump common sense. Surely all of these shortcomings, and many more, have not been avoided in America since the Second World War. Part of good decision making is anticipating problems and avoiding them, but perhaps an even larger part is correcting errors that inevitably are made. As we suggested in a previous work, political systems may best be judged by the errors they correct rather than by the errors they make (Baumgartner and Jones 2002: 306). As we will see in the chapters to come, the U.S. political system has overreacted, hesitated, and lurched its way through scores of problems over the past fifty years. It is far from perfect, or even perfectible. It does have inherent self-correcting and self-adjusting mechanisms (albeit ones that are sometimes slow to start and deplorably inefficient), as we will show.

Even in a democratic political system, government itself can become a problem, as former president Ronald Reagan was fond of emphasizing. The search for information by government officials can itself become intrusive, as any small business owner will verify, and actually limit the civil liberties of citizens, as the aggressive use of the Patriot Act by former attorney general John Ashcroft has demonstrated. It is necessary to view whole political systems, which include political parties, interest groups, and other elements of civil society (at least in democratic systems), as the keys to public information processing and problem solving. When government cannot control itself, then civil society must intervene.

In many ways, the problem-solving capacities of government get better over time—policy learning occurs. Surely we understand how to manage the economy, or the environment, or the safety of the workplace better than we did in 1930, or in 1965, or in 1980. In other ways, these capacities may be diminished. The more tasks an organization takes on, the less effective it can become in solving any one of those problems. In solving one problem, it may contribute to others. The more capacity it adds, the more it interferes with other problem-solving mechanisms in civil society. And since government does more now than it once did, we can be sure that unintended consequences of various policies are greater now than they used to be.

Bounded Rationality, Emotion, and Interests

If decision makers were infallible, then we would need no theory of them, and we could analyze information processing from a knowledge of the nature of the information and the set of rules for making decisions within a political system. That, alas, is not the case. Decision makers in politics, like elsewhere in life, are boundedly rational (Jones 2001). They are goal-oriented and strategic, and they update their beliefs about the world based on information. But they make mistakes—not just random mistakes, but systematic and repetitive ones. These include bias in the use of information, simplification and distortion in comprehending information, and cognitive and emotional identification with particular ways of solving problems. All of these biases are on display in politics every day when the argument turns to the appropriateness of a governmental remedy to a problem.

Bounded rationality, however, is more than a laundry list of failures in human decision making. Three aspects of information processing provide the basis for a model of human decision making capable of supporting our arguments: selective attention, difficulties with trade-offs, and learning. Bounded rationality assumes that humans are strategic and goal-oriented but are equipped with cognitive architectures that limit and channel their abilities to maximize. The major constraints are straightforward, centering on an exceedingly small short-term memory (or attention span), a very large long-term memory, a rule-bound system of encoding information into long-term memory and extracting it when necessary, and an emotional "governing system" to regulate attention and action.

Selective attention is far and away the most important cognitive limitation that influences political choice. Cognitive processing capacities are constrained by a "bottleneck" of short-term memory that allows us to attend to only limited elements of the environment at any given time. The limits of attention force us to deal serially with problems, leading directly to severe difficulties in comparing different courses of action. Emotion is the gateway to selective attention: when emotion is roused, attention follows.

One major consequence of the "bottleneck of attention" and its association with emotion is that people have great difficulties in assessing trade-offs among competing strategies (Simon 1996). This characteristic is manipulated regularly in politics. Trade-off calculations, so easily modeled in economic choice by indifference curves, are extraordinarily difficult for people to make. In political debates involving ambiguous information, proponents almost always "frame" the information, stressing one perspective and ignoring others. This plays to the serial processing capacity of the audience, who often quickly focus their attention on the limited perspective advocated in the debate (B. D. Jones 1994).

In addition, the manner in which people encode and recover information affects political choice. Information is coded into long-term memory via rules, and the application of rules to new situations is governed by the ability to view the new situation as analogous to the one in which the rule was learned. People come to value the rule in itself—they identify with the means—and often apply the rule in situations where it is not fully applicable, rather than searching for more appropriate strategies to follow. In the study of military strategy, this tendency is recognized by the aphorism that "generals are always fighting the last war."

This means that learning is not Bayesian—in the face of new information, people do not drop learned behavior that they value intrinsically, according to Bayes' rule, which in a rational but uncertain world would govern how people react to new information. Instead, they update with difficulty, sporadically and episodically. In politics, partisans defend their president even though the signals all point to failed policy choices. Changes may come, but they come grudgingly. Proponents who fought long and hard to get a new policy implemented or a new agency created do not suddenly admit mistakes; they resist, resist, and resist until either they are outmaneuvered or the evidence simply overwhelms them. In politics, information is not neutral; it creates winners and losers. People prefer to be seen as winners and do not like to admit when they are wrong.

Bounded rationality leads to disproportionate information-processing. Signals are ignored, responses are delayed, and ineffective strategies are deployed. The whole story is not delay, however—people are clearly capable of overreaction and rushes to judgment. In fact, our model of how information is used leads to a model of delay, then overreaction. Once evidence or pressure accumulates indicating that some new dimension deserved more attention, the system often overresponds to this in turn.

The General Punctuation Hypothesis

Things get even more complex when we put fallible decision makers facing uncertain and ambiguous flows of information together with other decision makers holding differing preferences and values in a policymaking system. Add yet another complexity: the decision makers occupy different roles in the system, some having more institutional power than others.

Political scientists understand reasonably well the effects of the set of rules that govern decision making in political systems. We know that different election results, and different configurations of preferences for policies, stem from different electoral arrangements. Systems of separated powers yield different results than parliamentary systems. Constitutions can be designed to retard change and slow the translation of mass passions into policy action, as in the

U.S. system, or they can be designed to reflect public opinion in intricate detail, as in modern parliamentary systems.

What is less recognized is the first principle of behavioral organization theory: formal organizations, like the Roman god Janus, face two ways. They allow people to escape their cognitive and emotional information-processing bounds, but, being constructed by humans, they also fall prey to the same limits that affect human information-processing capacities. Formal organizations, such as governments, allow the coordination of individual behaviors toward the accomplishment of a collective end. When they operate properly, they also allow the combining of diverse preferences and viewpoints to come to a decision. What is less noted is that organizations can be designed to allow for the correction of errors that humans invariably make. The key notion is feedback. Firms that make products that are unwanted or inferior may be driven out of business. Political parties that make policies that don't satisfy voters can lose control of government.

In appropriately designed markets and democracies, feedback is available for course corrections before disaster strikes. Firms may suffer as demand declines and profits wither, and they can adjust their product lines accordingly. Parties may lose the support of key interest groups, or find increasing support for opponents in "pulse taking" back home in the constituency. (In both cases, careful "market research" can allow leaders to avoid products or policies that will cause a problem in the first place.) A close election, or even the anticipation of a close election, may send a signal for a course correction.

Directors of firms or leaders in government may or may not attend to cues calling for changed policies, and this process may be more or less efficient. Some companies may keep close tabs on where they stand in the market, constantly adjusting to changing conditions. Some ignore powerful signals until they are forced out of business and others take their place. The system responds but the individual organisms may die. Similarly in politics, some institutions may adjust relatively continually to new demands; others may resist calls for change until they are compelled by outside forces either to change their behaviors or to go out of existence (yes, this does happen even in government). Why are powerful signals sometimes ignored, even when they often are obvious in hindsight? One reason is selective attention. Selective attention in individuals is agenda setting in politics, and the human limitations in juggling attention apply to agenda items in political systems. Comparing competing courses of action is very difficult, especially across policy domains. A political system focusing on potential terrorist attacks has trouble comparing the potential damage from these acts to the damage stemming from climate warming, or traffic accidents, or pandemic influenza. This is not only a consequence of the uncertainties surrounding these events. More Americans died in traffic accidents in the month following the terrorist attacks on September 11, 2001, than died in the acts themselves. Most would recoil with horror at the implied suggestion that we ought to take money from Homeland Security and put it into traffic safety. In effect, they reject making the implied trade-off explicit, yet rational decision making requires just such explicit calculations.

If we put together the limits of human information processing and the characteristics of democracies that encourage error correction, we get a model of politics that is very static but reluctantly changes when signals are strong enough. The system resists change, so that when change comes it punctuates the system, not infrequently reverberating through it. Even in systems with well-articulated feedback mechanisms, such as in developed democracies, change comes in bursts. Different institutions may have different capacities for change. Some are relatively efficient in reacting to new inputs; others resist change until forced by overwhelming pressures to give in. But, as we shall demonstrate empirically in the chapters to come, all institutions of government share these characteristics to some extent. It is an inevitable part of the policymaking process where there are so many potential problems and so many potential ways of responding to them.

We described this process in our earlier work on punctuated equilibrium as applying to policy subsystems (Baumgartner and Jones 1993). A set of partial equilibria characterizes policy subsystems, with each subsystem subject to destructive change if mobilization is strong enough. The "driver" of the model was attention. It was long noted that the inattention of policymakers allowed policy subsystems to flourish; we asked what happens when attention gravitates to a subsystem. The *general punctuation hypothesis* adds institutional analysis to this model.

The set of rules that constitutes the American political order affects different parts of the policymaking process differently. It is relatively easy to gain a hearing in the councils of government, but it can be extraordinarily difficult to gain satisfactory policy action. Agenda access is comparatively simple; policy commitments come hard. The implication is that agenda processes will be less punctuated than policy changes.

We make three claims, explored in detail throughout the book. First, all distributions involving human decision making exhibit patterns of stability and punctuations. Second, the operation of the formal rules that govern the policymaking process—the system of checks and balances characteristic of American democracy—also lead to punctuations. Third, the interaction among cognitive characteristics of decision making and formal rules and pro-

cedures allows us to order the severity of punctuations from the least punctuated, where formal rules are not restrictive and "veto groups" are not em-
powered, to the most punctuated, where formal procedures operate to magnify punctuations. So we will observe a greater likelihood of punctuations in
some institutions of government than in others; this is related to the efficiency
of the institutional design. But cognitive limits are ubiquitous, so we observe
the effects of these in all institutional settings.

The Disproportionality of Attention

Because of the nature of cognition and the capacities of the political systems we construct, there is no one-to-one correspondence between the severity of problems in the decision-making environment and the policy responses
of government. Information processing in politics is disproportionate; it is
disjoint and episodic; it is stasis interrupted by bursts of innovation. Immediate one-to-one responsiveness to problems is hindered not just by the obvious
set of rules requiring concurrent majorities in the branches of government.
It is hindered also by aspects of human and organizational information-
processing capacities.

A major hindrance in producing proportionate policy responses to information stems from limits on the capacity of the policy agenda. Governments,
like individuals, have limited attention spans. Focus on one issue, and you
become inattentive to others. The only way to avoid this is not to try to pay
attention to lots of things simultaneously, but rather to juggle attention, rapidly cycling through the various information flows. If you face lots of issues,
however, it will take time to cycle through them. The "shortcut" is to monitor
emotions as indicators of priorities (Marcus, Neuman, and MacKuen 2000).

The same is true for governments. Issues must be prioritized for action,
but in a world of many problems such agenda juggling has important consequences for proportionality in response. If policymakers are focused on addressing the problem of the fairness of the tax structure, they are liable to ignore deteriorations in the public health infrastructure. When they become
attentive to public health problems, they may find that large policy "fixes" are
required. While they attend to public health, problems in the management
of public lands may accumulate. And so forth. The juggling is often accomplished via emotions, usually when constituents or groups are mobilized and
angry.

Disproportionate information-processing implies policy punctuations.
Mostly, policy in a particular area is static or changes incrementally as responsible bureaus are able to adjust within the bounds of the enabling legis-

lation they operate under. But major policy advances require the intervention of the policymaking branches—the president, Congress, the courts. For reasons of politics and of agenda inefficiencies, these branches respond only sporadically to any particular problem—especially when emotions are running high.

Methods

Our study of information processing in American politics relies on a vast data-collection effort that we began more than ten years ago. That effort, which we call the Policy Agendas Project, involved assembling, managing, integrating, and coding data on congressional hearings, U.S. laws, budget authority, media coverage, and public opinion from the end of the Second World War to the end of the twentieth century. The result is a set of high-quality data sources that can be used to study the processes of policy change in a manner hitherto impossible.

The Policy Agendas Project provides a consistent and reliable set of policy content categories applied to many different archived data sets that record political change in the federal government. We have explained the philosophy and details of this approach elsewhere. (See in particular chapter 2 and the appendix of Baumgartner and Jones 2002; our Web site, http://www.policyagendas.org, also provides more information, including all the data reported in this book.) Briefly, the idea is to be able to trace changes in policy activity across diverse data sources with confidence. For the first time, we have reliable time series data on many aspects of policymaking, time series data that may be explicitly compared across data sets. For example, we have consistent and reliable information that allows us to compare the policy priorities of citizens (though a recoding of Gallup's "most important problem" polls), the attention given in Congress to those same matters (through a coding of all hearings conducted since the Second World War), and the policy responses of the federal government on those issues (though a coding of all statutes passed since the Second World War, and a weighting system for ranking these statutes according to their importance). These data allow the exploration of a whole new way of thinking about representation, and we do that in chapter 10. A description of these data sets, and our content coding system, may be found in appendix 1.

The use of this resource, harnessed to an information-processing perspective that immediately shifts the discussion toward dynamics and evolution, allows us to broach entirely new questions about American politics, public policy, and democratic governance. We are able to unify critical aspects of more recent American political development with both the statics of institutional analysis and the dynamics of political processes. Political development has insisted on the relevance of history and prior organizational arrangements to explain change; institutional analysis demands explicit consideration of the decision rules governing choice in a political system; political dynamics points to the raucous roles of parties, candidates, and voters in determining political outcomes. Just how these elements interact has eluded political scientists. While we do not claim to have all the answers, we try to demonstrate that we have lots of them, and that our approach yields the right questions as we struggle to make sense of democratic governance in America.

Most important, the ability to measure policy change with much more precision allows the systematic study of policy punctuations. Policy punctuations are unavoidable. Yet most of the time most policies are stable. If we want to understand policy most of the *time*, we study those facets of government that reinforce stability. These include the structure of American political institutions, the power of interest groups, the ideologies of elites, and the party identifications of masses. Most of the total change in public policies across time, however, comes about because of the punctuations—they happen not incrementally but in large bursts, even if there are many, many more incremental changes than punctuations. If we want to understand most of the *change*, we have to understand the punctuations. Of course, if we want to understand the entire system we need to understand both the stability and the change.

Punctuations stem from signals from outside the political system as these are variously ignored or amplified by forces within the system. Disproportionate information-processing implies that prediction based on information alone is virtually impossible. The political system operates as a "filter," sometimes dampening and sometimes amplifying any given signal. To appreciate patterns of punctuations and stability across the full range of public policies, we drop the traditional political science focus on "point prediction," the prediction of exactly when an event will occur, or even exactly how a particular external event will affect the course of a particular public policy. We need to be more sensitive to the complex set of interactions that can set off major changes. Previous studies have not done this, partly because people often want to know about the development of a particular policy issue, and partly because the large data sets we have constructed allow us to approach the question in a way others have not been able to do before.

Fortunately, tools from other disciplines are available to us to summarize characteristics of the entire system, and we use these in this book. These tools are quite straightforward but may well be unfamiliar to political scientists steeped in regression modeling. Regression modeling is well suited to descriptions of trends, for testing well-understood hypotheses, and for analyzing the functioning of a stable institutional environment, but for explanatory power it relies on point prediction. That is, to model a process over time correctly, we need to be able to specify in advance how the precise dynamics work. If we are wrong, of course we can reject and modify.

But what if we know only that a system will lead to punctuations, if we really have no a priori idea of when those punctuations will occur? This question is especially crucial in situations where many causes can bring about the same effect. In some circumstances, perhaps social movements have brought about major policy change; in others, it was elite-generated; in still others, it was developed and carried by the political parties. Large-scale policy changes are historically contingent, and to date the most successful approach to understanding them is the careful case study. Some scholars have attempted to understand the operations of American institutions by lumping policy changes across contexts—as for example, has David Mayhew (1991) in his important study of divided government using a weighting scheme for most important statutes. But these approaches are incapable of distinguishing when the important statute will be directed at voting rights and when it will be directed at environmental protection—it is by its nature insensitive to the policy context.

Another issue involves positive feedback effects (Baumgartner and Jones 2002). Straightforward linear regression fails to model correctly outbreaks of self-reinforcing positive feedback changes in the policy process. If we look at a series of policy activities, as we do for crime, social welfare, and other policy arenas, we find clear evidence of self-reinforcing changes. While it is possible to model such complex series, how does one know in advance when these interactions will occur? Looking at the series and redescribing it with regression models can be useful—by eliminating chance as a potential factor—but it does not really get us very far, because we are generally in the position of not being able to predict such positive feedback outbreaks beforehand, nor do we have a theory of when to expect them that is itself not historically contingent.

To address such issues we introduce in a systematic manner stochastic process approaches to the analysis of policy dynamics. Stochastic process approaches focus on an entire distribution of data—for example, on budgetary outputs not for a single policy or program but across the entire range of spending for the entire government over the entire postwar period. Often we can postulate serious and testable hypotheses about distributions of activities when we are at a loss to do so for particular occurrences of these activities. We find that we can make firm predictions about and observe clear patterns in the distributions of policy changes even when we cannot predict individual policies. But we can probably learn more about the characteristics and dynamics of the political system through this type of population-level analysis than through the case-study approach that has been more common in the literature (including, we hasten to point out, much of our own previous work). In sum, we develop some new ideas here and use some unfamiliar techniques to analyze a comprehensive set of data concerning the federal government's activities over a fifty-year period.

Plan of Development

In the chapters to come we examine how the American national government detected, prioritized, and responded to information across the period after the Second World War. We focus primarily on the process by which this happens rather than trace the particulars of policy development or partisan struggles through time, although much of what we have to say is directly relevant to political dynamics and policy development. We move from theories of individual choice to organizational choice to the policymaking process, developing as we go the theory of disproportionate information-processing. Then we turn to the policy process, showing that old incremental theories of policy change are wrong, but salvageable and fundamentally important. If we integrate disproportionate information-processing into the incremental model, the resulting theory of policy change subsumes both incrementalism and punctuated equilibrium. Then we show how formal rules of governance can be incorporated into the theory. Having achieved the major goal of the book, we turn to exploring how it works in particular situations—including how government translates objective indicators into policy in particular areas, how "agenda crowding" makes the process inefficient (and disproportionate), and how representation may be reconceived to incorporate not just public preferences but the priorities of the public as well.

Here is how we proceed. The first part of the book, "Information, Choice, and Government," details the mechanisms that invariably lead to policy punctuations. Chapter 2 examines the process of decision making, drawing on behavioral decision theory and cognitive science to depict individual-level processes. Then we show how organizational decision making corresponds to individual-level processes. While there are major and important differences—particularly in the extent to which organizations, including government, can process multiple streams of information and in the problems that organizations have in combining the observations, priorities, and policy preferences of the members of the organization—there are critical similarities as well. These similarities, including critically the process of attention allocation, allow us to apply a theory of cognitive information-processing to policymaking. Chapter 3 looks at how policymakers combine and prioritize multiple streams of information from multiple sources of varying reliability to detect problems and attach solutions to those problems. These chapters, together, offer a theory of organizational processing of information and link it to an individual-level understanding based on bounded rationality.

In part 2 we apply the theory to the broad political system. Chapter 4 turns directly to the policymaking process. Because information is complex, uncertain, and ambiguous, and because policy responses are contingent on prior information processing as well as on the configuration of political forces, the trace of policymaking across time is complex and contingent, defying simple interpretation. We show that no single explanation will account for U.S. public expenditures in all policy areas; rather, explanation requires familiarity with the particulars of policy histories of each policy area. If we give up that quest and simply prepare a frequency distribution of all budget changes across all policy areas for the period of the Second World War, we find that the pooled frequency distribution is highly punctuated—strong support for punctuated-equilibrium theory.

Our earlier theory of punctuated equilibrium is perhaps best known as an alternative to the seemingly discredited incremental theory developed by Richard Fenno, Charles Lindblom, and Aaron Wildavsky. In chapter 5 we show that incrementalism, far from being discredited, may actually be integrated with punctuated equilibrium to produce a full theory of information processing in politics. The incrementalists had no theory of attention allocation and information processing—or rather they assumed proportionality without realizing it. It can be shown that incrementalism must lead to a bell-shaped distribution of outputs; the finding of punctuated or leptokurtic budget distributions discredits this form of incrementalism. (*Leptokurtic* means that a distribution is statistically not normal, but has a higher central peak as well as more outliers than a normal distribution.) But if we build disproportionate information-processing into incrementalism, the resulting frequency distribution is punctuated, and we have a theory of incremental budgeting that is fully integrated with information processing in policymaking.

Chapter 6 completes the development of the theory by adding the formal rules and procedures that govern how American public policy is made. As in our general approach, we do not analyze each particular facet of Madisonian democracy for its effects. Rather, we think of these procedures as adding *decision costs* to policymaking in a manner that allows us to disentangle these effects on the severity of policy punctuations. Then we provide both static and dynamic simulations of these processes. Punctuations occur in all distributions we simulate; they range from mild to more extreme in parallel with the imposition of institutional costs, or friction.

Chapter 7 provides a strong empirical test of the theory developed in chapter 6. Whereas chapter 6 develops a simulation that explores the parameters that explain the distribution of data we observed in chapter 4, here we provide further and extensive empirical tests. Basing our ideas on the concept that different institutions of politics are closer to the input side or the output side of things, and therefore impose either few or a great number of institutional costs, we explore the level of *institutional friction*. By looking at the distribution of outcomes across data sets covering financial markets, elections, media coverage, congressional hearings, lawmaking activities, presidential orders, and budgets, we demonstrate powerfully that institutions with the higher decision costs also have the more punctuated patterns of outcomes. This shows that some institutions are much more efficient than others. All, however, demonstrate the signature patterns of punctuated equilibrium that we expect.

In part 3 we explore some critical facets of the theory. In chapter 8 we study the particulars of the translation of informational signals into policy outputs. Not surprisingly, we find different patterns even in the three areas of public policy where widely used quantitative indicators of conditions are readily available—economic policy, crime and justice, and poverty. Chapter 9 explores in some detail the "bottleneck of attention" and its effect on disproportionate policy response. Not only do particular issues rise and fall on the agenda, but the overall capacity of the system has risen and dropped over the postwar period. Capacity has not simply grown with the economy and population; agenda capacity is part of the political dynamics that influences the weighting of issues. In fact, capacity has dropped as conservatives have argued that government has grown too large, so there is nothing inevitable about the growth in the size of the government agenda; this can be reversed. Finally, chapter 10 shows how representation may be reconceived within an information-processing approach. Instead of asking whether the policy positions of citizens and the government correspond, we ask whether the issues discussed in Congress correspond to the issues that reach the highest level of concern among the public. We find that the correspondence is very high; when the public is concerned about an issue, Congress discusses it. We also find attenuated correspondence between the public's priorities and actual lawmaking. It is clear that a proper conception of representation must include an agenda-setting component.

We conclude with some comments about the nature of democratic governance. Because of the inevitable consequences of cognitive limits and institutional design, the theory of disproportionate information-processing developed here integrates punctuated equilibrium and standard incremental approaches to government. As any democratic government simultaneously assesses disparate pieces of information on different dimensions of choice, resulting policy outputs will be disjoint and episodic, and attention to critical matters will often be fleeting. Government with fleeting and shifting policy priorities may seem inefficient, and it is, compared to some ideal standard. In these inefficiencies and overreactions, however, come openness, flexibility, corrections, feedback, and innovation.

PART I

INFORMATION AND CHOICE

In the next two chapters, we develop in some detail the theory of disproportionate information-processing. While we aim to develop a theory of policy processes—basically a theory of organizations—we need a microtheory of individual information processing as a foundation. We show how a fundamental model of boundedly rational decision makers, abstracted from scientific findings from biology, psychology, and several social sciences, has important implications for how organizations, and therefore governments, process information. We first lay out the theory as it relates to an individual; then we show how it applies in organizations. Organizations differ in some respects from individuals in how they deal with information, so we avoid any type of argument that anthropomorphizes organizations. For example, organizations may have a complex division of labor that allows them to deal simultaneously with thousands of things; people can't do that. But both organizations and individuals share certain characteristics, especially how they allocate attention, which we use as a basis for our theory.

Our theory of disproportionate information-processing has three components. The first is the unavoidable juggling of numerous issues—to which issue among many should one pay attention? The second is how decision makers understand and interpret the issue of choice—the process of weighting the attributes that characterize the issue. Given that one is concerned about international security, for example, how does one understand the issue? The third is the choice of competing solutions to the problem. Even when one has decided on how to understand a complex problem, and which elements of it are most relevant, there can often be different possible solutions, each with different costs, benefits, ambiguity, and uncertainty. Of course, in organizational settings, different advocates may especially prefer certain solutions over others, since these may affect the role that they can play in the policy. In any case, there are three elements: which issues, which dimensions, and which solutions.

Each of these elements adds a measure of disproportionality to the policymaking process. They "bend" the response to new information, and they do so in complex and interactive ways so severely that it is very difficult to connect information signals to policy responses even in democratic governments. That is, neither individuals nor organizations are efficient in monitoring and reacting to new situations in the environment. Threshold effects, status quo bias, and other characteristics of bounded rationality affect how we choose which issues to pay attention to, how we understand those issues once we start to attend to them, and how we choose among possible courses of action in addressing them. We decouple these components, examining them separately, in the next two chapters. Each part of the process is prone to discontinuous and abrupt shifts at some points, even if most of the time established routines rule the day. People sometimes lurch from one topic to another, acting with surprised discovery that some new problem urgently requires their attention. We sometimes dramatically rethink our understanding of the causes of a given situation, even if we resist this most of the time. And we sometimes adopt wholly new solutions to old problems, even if again we don't typically like to do so.

Organizations do these things even more than individuals, in fact, because organizations, unlike people, can have changes in leadership. In democratic politics, elections provide one way to bring in a new set of leaders who may have a different approach to existing problems, or different priorities in addressing problems. So there are many elements of this theory to explore. In chapter 2, we lay out in full form the parallel natures of individual and organizational decision making, showing how disproportionate information-processing is inevitable at both levels. In chapter 3, we show how this leads directly to disproportionality in the policy process. These two chapters lay the foundation, then, for the empirical chapters that come in parts 2 and 3.

2

A Behavioral Model of Policy Choice

Although most public policy issues are fundamentally complex, public discussions of them are generally simple. This chapter is about the process by which complex issues get whittled down to simplified choices amenable to public discussion or individual choice. Both individuals and organizations, including governments, go through such a process. The explanation we lay out here about decision processing leads directly to our theory of disproportionate information-processing, which is the focus of chapter 3.

Consider the problem of poverty. How many different elements, facts, considerations, and dimensions of evaluation are relevant? Does poverty exist because poor people lack the work ethic? Because of discrimination? Because the welfare system has provided a perverse incentive structure? Because of a failure of the health-care and educational systems to provide opportunities for people to do well? Because of a lack of child care and a breakdown of the traditional family structure? Because of transformations of the economy that have taken away low-skilled job opportunities? Because of crime and failures of the criminal justice system? Because of the flight of jobs overseas, to Mexico, or to other regions of the United States? Because employers pay too little in many low-wage job categories and typically provide no health benefits?

There may well be truth in each of these "issue definitions" (and there are certainly more aspects of the issue than are mentioned here). How should we weight the various elements of the issue? More important, how does the political system ascribe weights to a multidimensional issue such as poverty? Liberals and conservatives certainly have their favorite aspects of the issue on which to focus, and we can bemoan the shortsightedness and bias of those with whom we disagree. But in fact, such restricted attention is inevitable.

Poverty, like most policy issues, has so many underlying dimensions that efforts to address them can never be truly exhaustive. Rather, policy responses are almost by definition partial. That is because our cognitive understanding of the issue is necessarily incomplete.

But we have played a trick on the reader—or at least we tried to. We focused on poverty without asking why one would treat poverty as a problem, anyway. Is it not simply a condition? Some people are poor, others are rich; that's just the way life is. The existence of a condition does not automatically create a political problem or an issue. And even if it is a problem, why would anyone want to discuss it when other important problems—such as terrorism, and chronic disease, and the emergence of "super-germs," and war and peace, and the decline of moral values in America, and the tax burden, and the crisis in public education, and the loss of eco-diversity, and traffic congestion, and smog, and the cost of health care, and economic malaise—may be more important? Political systems are juggling not just a collection of definitions of a single issue but a panoply of issues as well, and all of these issues have several components, just as poverty does. Not only do we have to figure out how to assess a problem once we decide to pay attention to it, but we also have to figure out which issues to pay attention to in the first place.

In this chapter we develop a model of decision making that addresses how individuals and organizations prioritize and evaluate numerous multidimensional issues. First, we consider individual decision-making processes, and then we look at collective decisions as might be made in groups, in organizations, or in government. We will show that the two processes are parallel in the most important aspects. We then turn to the dynamics of choice, that is, how individuals and organizations move from decision to decision. No decision ever starts from a completely fresh perspective; rather, people evaluate where they are going in light of where they are now. Moving from decision point to decision point traces a time path of decisions, and the change from point to point assesses how disjoint the time path is.

Our model is a *behavioral* model, in the important sense that it builds in the cognitive capacities of individuals directly. This is not true of most so-called information theories as applied in the social sciences, which deal only with the precision of signals. The key component of this behavioral model is attention shifting. Because of the extremely limited attentional capacity that people have, they must make abrupt changes as they shift from dimension to dimension for an issue. Most of the time, for most decisions, we pay little attention to the underlying issue, and we don't change our approach to the problem—we stick with the status quo. Organizations, with limited agenda capacities, behave similarly. Occasionally, however, issues force themselves to our attention—or to an organizational agenda—and at that point we may fundamentally reevaluate. Or we may not; but unless we attend to the issue, we cannot change our strategy. Choice presupposes attention. Thus, decisions when considered over time display a characteristic pattern of usually high levels of stability for most issues and occasional major change. These features of decision making are not pathologies but are inherent in how humans process large amounts of information about difficult issues.

In the next section of this chapter, we focus on a single decision. First, we go through the model as it applies to individuals; next, we show the parallels with organizational decision making. Whereas individuals are clearly limited by cognitive capacities and the number of issues they can deal with at any one time, organizations can solve many of these problems through the division of labor that allows different parts of the organization to contribute to the same decision. In spite of these advantages for organizations, both individuals and organizations share important features that characterize boundedly rational decision making.

A Behavioral Model of Individual Decision Making

How does a single decision maker process information? While there are lots of complexities, the outlines of the process can be laid out in stages. Like any stage theory, this one is a reconstruction; in reality stages blur and even merge, differing from decision to decision. Yet it is useful to organize the decision-making process in terms of four sequential stages: a *recognition stage*, in which a decision maker recognizes that a problem exists; a *characterization stage*, in which the problem comes to be understood based on the competing attributes that could define it; an *alternative stage*, in which reasonable alternatives are delineated; and a *choice stage*, in which alternatives are examined and a choice is made. Below we detail some relevant aspects of each stage. While we focus for the moment on individuals, it is apparent that organizations must go through a similar sequence.

- *Recognition stage*
  - Attend to aspects of the decision-making environment that are potentially problematic.
  - Understand the problems presented by the environment.
  - Prioritize these problems.
  - Decide which of these problems will be addressed and which can safely be ignored for the time being.

- *Characterization stage*
  - Construct a "problem space" by determining the relevant attributes of the problem focused on from the previous stage.
  - Decide the weights of the attributes—which are most relevant to the problem (highest weight), which are relatively less relevant (lower weight), and which are irrelevant (weight of zero).
- *Alternative stage*
  - Given a list of relevant attributes from the previous stage, for each attribute consider the alternative courses of action that might be useful.
  - Examine alternatives that have been used in similar problems.
  - Search for new alternatives.
  - Construct "solution spaces" to these problems consisting of the available alternatives. Each attribute may be linked with one or several potential solutions or alternatives.
- *Choice stage*
  - Decide which alternative(s) to choose.
  - Implement the favored alternative(s).

A given choice situation may lead to the implementation of several alternatives, since many problems may be identified, many attributes may be relevant to each problem, many alternatives may be appropriate solutions to the different attributes, and more than one choice may be made. While the model above is a simplification, it allows us to focus on some key elements of the process. Considering these in some detail will be helpful in understanding the typically incremental, but occasionally disjoint, nature of most decisions as they are made over time.

Recognition

In the recognition stage, many issues clamor for attention, but only one can be addressed at a time. People prioritize problems by devoting attention to them. Herbert Simon refers to attention as a "bottleneck" of conscious thought. Attention is a scarce good; directing attention at one problem means ignoring others. A person cannot simultaneously give conscious consideration to every problem facing him or her at a given time. One cannot balance one's checkbook, work out at the gym, pay attention to family, write a book, and teach a class all at the same time. An organization, on the other hand, may deal with multiple problems through the division of labor. A university can simultaneously be active in teaching multiple classes, providing recreation services, conducting research, operating a hospital, promoting public service activities and state services, and conducting an internal audit. Even in an organization, however, there comes a point when the leader of the organization must direct attention to one problem rather than another. To be sure, some individuals and some organizations may be more efficient at dealing with problems, and better able to switch quickly from one problem to the next, but at any given time, attention focuses only on a minute subset of all the issues. The scarcity of attention governs the first stage in our model.

Characterization

Once an issue becomes the focus for a problem-solving effort, we move to the characterization stage. Here attributes underlying the problem are set and weighted by importance; that is, we characterize the problem, we define the issue. What am I looking for in purchasing a new car? Prestige? Basic transportation? A demonstration of financial success? A demonstration of responsibility and modesty? A way to impress someone? Finally having a car that works, after years of junkers? Even a simple consumer choice must be characterized, and the same purchase can mean different things to different people or to the same person at different times. Of course, as we move to public policy issues and our opinions on those, the issues are generally even more complex.

How we characterize a problem implies goal setting. For example, if we define the problem of poverty as being strongly related to nutrition and educational opportunity, then some obvious solutions are implied. These differ from solutions that would be implied if we saw the issue as fundamentally related to family structure, the structure of the economy, individual motivation, personal choice, or job training. So defining or characterizing the problem has many implications, but all issues once recognized must also be characterized or understood, and typically, for a complex problem, there are many possible ways to understand the issue.

Alternatives

In the alternative stage, a causal theory is constructed or at least implied by how the problem is understood, thereby justifying some solutions. But solutions do not flow automatically from the definition of a problem. Sometimes several solutions are available even if people agree on the nature of the problem. In any case, once an issue has been characterized, then a decision maker has to choose among available solutions or alternatives suited to solve the problem. Some of these alternatives may have been used before with greater or lesser success; some may have ready-made and available implementation mechanisms; others may not have been tried before. Choosing among available solutions to a given problem is not a trivial or an obvious process.

Choice

Once a problem has been recognized and characterized, and the available alternatives scrutinized, then a choice can be made. Some alternatives may be discarded because they are not under the control of the decision maker, because they are not politically feasible, or for other reasons. The alternatives remaining after this winnowing process constitute the choice set—those alternatives from which a choice is made. Most of choice theory, rational or otherwise, has focused on this stage, almost to the exclusion of the rest of the information-processing model we have described above. In fact, the winnowing down of which problems to focus on, which attributes of those problems to weight most heavily as being relevant, and which alternatives to choose from in addressing those attributes, determines much of the decision. Of course, the final stage of the decision-making process, actual choice, can involve many complicated trade-offs. Our point is not that the last stage is trivial; rather, that earlier stages are equally important.

The combination of four stages, each of which is nontrivial for most issues, and each of which builds on the decisions made at the previous stage, means that the overall process can be exceedingly complex. In particular, the fact that decisions at one stage have strong implications for available decisions remaining at the following stages means that decisions made over time can be either highly inertial or greatly disjoint. They can be highly inertial because previous decisions are often not examined but are ratified again without much thought. They can be highly disjoint when new issues arise, when new characterizations of old issues become more prominent, when new alternatives are proposed and taken seriously, and finally, when new choices are made. Of course, new choices can be made in the absence of differences at the previous stages (that is, people can change their minds, or new evidence can lead them to a different choice even when the available problems, understandings, and alternatives remain the same). But when we consider that decisions made over time involve not only the final choice but all the stages that come before, we can see that disjoint change can be expected at least some of the time. The process of decision making, when laid

Figure 2.1. The Logic of Choice

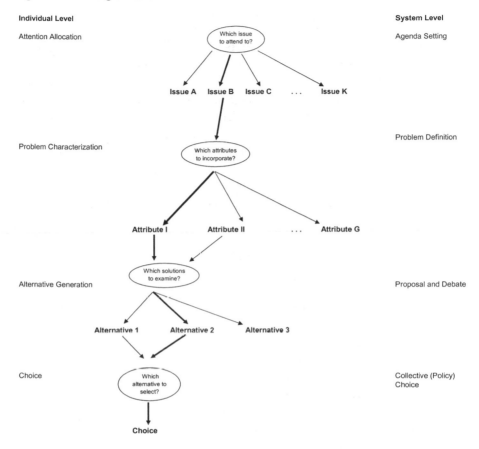

out in stages, allows both for highly inertial outcomes and for dramatic departures from previous habit.

Figure 2.1 summarizes the sequence of events in our choice model. We have discussed these stages with reference to the behaviors of an individual decision maker. Along the left-hand margin of the figure we have noted that these stages involve recognition, characterization, alternatives, and choice. Along the right-hand side of the figure we note that the analogous stages for collective decision making are agenda setting, issue definition, proposal and debate, and collective choice. We turn to that discussion next.

A Behavioral Model of Organizational Decision Making

Organizations differ from individuals in how they make decisions, of course, but the stages that we identify in figure 2.1 apply to them, with many of the same implications. The division of labor that is possible within an organization does not completely mitigate the problem of attention scarcity. Further, the complex interactions among subunits within an organization can add important new dynamics to the decision-making process that individuals do not experience. Since organizations are made up of humans, the cognitive architecture of human decision making affects how decisions are made within organizations. In figure 2.1 we laid out some terms along the right-hand margin that indicate how our decision-making model applies to collectivities. In this section, we go through each of these stages in turn as they apply to organizations, including governments.

Agenda Setting

Agenda setting is the organizational analogue to attention allocation at the individual level. Agenda setting is simply the process by which the organization comes to pay attention to some issues rather than others. One fundamental difference between individuals and organizations is that an organization can adopt a new policy choice at a given time and then create a specialized unit (agency, department, etc.) to implement this new policy; this specialized unit may go on for decades routinely implementing the policy without the issue ever appearing as part of the formal agenda again. Past decisions therefore leave a policy trace over time. In governments, there can be thousands of such policies. In sum, the parallel-processing capabilities of large organizations imply that even if agenda setting has to come first, there may be a great number of decisions routinely being made on the basis of the implementation of previous policy choices, not recent ones. Past agenda-setting activities leave policy traces in today's bureaucratic agencies, laws, regulations, and budgetary commitments.

Twenty years ago, Herbert Simon (1983) distinguished between serial and parallel capacities in processing information. Serial processing is how one processes information when attention must be focused on that single decision and no others; this is decision making *in seriatim*, or one at a time. Parallel processing capacity involves separating tasks into their component parts and assigning each one to specialized units, effectively dealing with many things simultaneously. People can do it to a limited extent, but their parallel processing capabilities are limited by the size of short-term memory. Computers can do this; some of the most powerful computers are in fact not particularly powerful individually but simply link "in parallel" great numbers of processors. Organizations can parallel process information as well, through the division of labor. The Postal Service continues to deliver the mail no matter what the Energy Department is doing; specialized functions of government allow for massive parallel processing, where literally thousands of issues are being processed, each within its own specialized community. But at some point, even large organizations capable of dealing with hundreds or thousands of different tasks at the same time must switch from parallel processing to serial processing; this is agenda setting. The bottleneck of attention that Simon described and we mentioned above applies to the agenda-setting process for organizations just as does attention allocation for individuals. While an organization can create specialized subunits to deal in parallel with separate problems, the leadership of the organization still has a limited attention span. So there is a serious bottleneck of attention; agenda setting is simply the process by which that scarce attention gets allocated.

Like all organizations, governments have a limited total capacity to direct attention at policy-relevant aspects of the environment. Organizations are able to postpone to some extent this reckoning by parallel processing and the creation of specialized departments and agencies. The congressional committee system is a good example of this ability of policymaking bodies to off-load demands, allowing them to be examined more thoroughly and protecting the chamber from information overload. If the chamber defers to the committee, then the limits of attention have in effect been circumvented.

Circumvented, but not avoided. Any controversial topic being considered for serious policy action must have some debate in the chamber; otherwise, representative government ceases to have meaning. Even routine votes take time. Because of the limits on the serial processing capacity of the chamber, there are limits on the ability of the chamber to utilize the parallel processing capacity of its committee system. This is known as a "span of control" problem in public administration, but it is intimately related to the attentional capacity of the supervising body. Devolving important decisions to organizational subunits requires that one supervise and monitor those units. Thus, there are limits to how much can be done even with extensive division of labor. Further, the creation of more and more specialized subunits creates other costs, as organizational missions may not correspond to the needs of the larger body, or as the nature of the problem evolves in ways that require coordination across specialized but unrelated subunits. So there are real costs and limits to parallel processing in organizations. We substitute the span-of-control problem, for serial processing capacity, as the limiting feature in organizational decision making. In any case, central leadership has limited attention, and these bounds can be stretched but not eliminated.

We mention the congressional committee system here only as an example; the process is quite general. The mayor of a large city devolves responsibility to his executive departments; the president devolves matters to his cabinet. Each cabinet secretary or department head similarly devolves decision-making authority to relevant subunits, and so on. But at some point, these parallel decision-making capabilities reach their limits, and major, overarching, cross-cutting decisions need to be made, affecting more than just one of these subunits. And at a minimum, the political leaders need to check to ensure that the administrative agents are acting according to their preferences. In sum, attention matters. And attention is limited.

We treat the agenda-setting stage in great detail here because setting the agenda is a complex task in organizations but is much simpler for individuals. But this still takes us only through the first stage of the process. The next stage is to determine how an issue is to be understood, or defined.

Problem Definition

There is a rich literature in political science on how political problems are defined (Rochefort and Cobb 1994; Stone 1997). While vigorous debate continues in the area, there is no disagreement that general cultural experiences and understandings often constrain how a problem is defined (Cobb and Ross 1997). Similarly, there is recognition among many studying political decision making that arguments can matter. New arguments occasionally break through the previously accepted wisdom about how a problem is to be viewed (Hinich and Munger 1994; B. D. Jones 1994; Riker 1996). In any case, whether they are determined by individuals behaving strategically, mandated by institutional rules, or affected by changing cultural mores, problems come to be defined, and these problem definitions can change over time. As in the discussion above relating to how individuals characterize problems once they've focused on them, organizations must reach some view of the nature of the problem. Different actors may promote different issue definitions, but having a sense of what the issue is about is an inherent next stage in any decision-making process. For government to adopt a new policy to address, as in our previous example, the issue of poverty, it must reach some conclusion, even a tentative one, on how it defines the issue of poverty. Otherwise, the potential solutions cannot be assessed.

Proposal and Debate

Once a problem is defined, proposals for addressing it must be generated. There is no paucity of sources for proposals, including interest groups, bureaucratic agencies, universities and think tanks, and experiences with past policy actions. Policymaking leaves a residue of appropriations, rules and regulations, and new organizations to implement new programs. These all become part of the immediate policymaking environment that legislatures and executives must at some point attend to. In particular, they become sources for proposed solutions for new problems. Bureaucracies are storehouses of previously implemented solutions generally encoded in decision rules.

General cultural understandings can influence proposal generation. For example, in the United States there is a general suspicion of government regulation as a mechanism for solving problems, and a taste for even indirect and subsidized private-sector solutions over direct governmental control. But sometimes other cultural values can conflict even with such a general one as this; take the example of public education. Because of the historical tradition of public education in the United States, the proponents of privatization have had the uphill fight in this area. Private-sector solutions are often preferred by Americans as a general concept, but not in all areas; why does one value sometimes trump another? Past practices have trumped general cultural views on government, making it very difficult for educational reformers to achieve traction, even though privatization of services and smaller government correspond to widely held cultural values. Neither cultural values nor policy inheritances uniquely determine policy proposals; both matter. In any case, the linkage between problems and solutions at the collective level is not straightforward. There are often multiple viable solutions to a given problem, and as John Kingdon (1995) has written, many political actors are more interested in making sure that "their" solution is adopted than in what problem it might be supposed to address. The third stage of a collective decision, then, proposals and debate, centers on the linkages between problems, however defined, and available policy solutions.

Collective Choice

By the time a legislature or other decision-making body votes on a proposition, a process of recognition, problem definition, and proposal generation has already occurred. In collective choice, some rule must be in force to decide the winner among alternatives. These rules generally must involve some

arbitrariness, and no rule is completely neutral in its effects. The French eigh-
teenth-century mathematician Condorcet showed that no single voting rule
works best, except in the simplest of circumstances, and that work was re-
discovered in the 1950s by Kenneth Arrow and others. By a wide margin,
however, more arbitrariness can creep into the process in the recognition,
problem-definition, and proposal-generation stages than in the choice stage.

Political scientists have studied in great detail the mechanisms of collective choice: voting rules, amendment procedures, and parliamentary mechanisms have clear importance in affecting outcomes. While these studies have
yielded great payoffs in understanding collective choice, they have come at
the cost of neglecting the earlier stages of the decision-making process. The
final stage of a decision is no more determinative of the final outcome or any
more prone to manipulation and strategic behavior than the earlier stages. In
fact, with the multistage view of the process of decision making, we simply
want to bring the reader's attention to the many uncertainties that may affect
a final choice even before the alternatives are presented for debate. Others
have shown that the outcomes of formal legislative debate can be strongly
affected not just by preferences but also by agenda control, the presentation
of alternatives, and voting rules. As important as they are, these dynamics
relate only to the last stage of the process we lay out here.

We reiterate that organizations are made up of individuals, so it should be
no surprise that many of the cognitive limitations we've noted affecting decision making at the individual level should also affect that among organizations. Formal organizations allow humans to extend their capacities—in effect, to avoid some of the limits in information processing and problem
solving imposed by human cognitive architecture. In fact, the great merit
of organizations is the division of labor that they make possible. This in
turn allows the organization to enjoy the collective contributions of hundreds or thousands of individuals, obviously with greater capacity simultaneously to attend to multiple issues than any single individual. On the other
hand, organizations fall prey to the same cognitive and emotional limitations
that individuals do in their problem-solving activities (Jones 2001:151). Because humans are the "building blocks" of organizations, the connection
between individual information-processing and organizational information-
processing is not metaphorical; it is causal.

We have laid out a model of decision making based on the somewhat arbitrary division of the process into four stages. Our use of stages is not meant
to imply that each decision necessarily progresses from one stage to the next;
often these processes are merged or come out of order. But the four stages are
logical requirements for a final decision to be made. We have presented them

as stages for clarity of exposition. These four stages apply to both individuals and, with some differences, to organizations, including governments. Let us consider now how decisions are made in sequence; in fact, this is where the most important implications of the model become clear.

The Dynamics of Choice

Choice dynamics implies information processing. Some issues are automatically reconsidered periodically, but in many cases we have some flexibility. We need not reconsider an issue unless there is some reason to do so—when there is new information about the issue. This alone gives a strong status quo bias to decision making, but there are several other aspects of human and organizational behavior that make the time trace of decision making highly inefficient.

Proportionality

Before we turn to our dynamic behavioral model, we ask how this process of reconsidering decisions across time would work in a fully rational decision-making system, that is, one hypothetically not affected by human cognitive limits. This hypothetical kind of system would be fully efficient, although uncertainty would still have to be factored into the system. There would be constant monitoring of the inputs coming in from the environment; and decisions would be adjusted in proportion to changes in the environment. Problems would be defined in direct proportion to their severities, and solutions assigned according to their efficiencies in solving the problem. This would be a fully *proportionate* process: the size of any change in response would be equal in proportion to the size of any change in the incoming signal from the environment. The movement among issues would be seamless, and any responses would be delayed only because of the costs of searching for new information and imposing a new solution. No additional status quo bias would exist.

This proportionality standard will serve as a marker from which to judge policy change in the upcoming empirical chapters of this book. We can compare the inefficiencies that stem from the operation of cognitive capacities and organizational aspects with this rational, proportionate adjustment process. The formal requirements for supermajorities inherent in U.S. institutions also add inefficiencies in comparison to a fully proportionate system, but not necessarily in comparison to a majoritarian system based on boundedly rational actors. Majorities may overreact even more than American institutions underreact.

Inefficiencies Based on Attention
and Identification with the Previous Decision

The process of attention allocation is fundamentally inefficient, in that it adds friction to the translation of informational signals into outputs. As a direct consequence, decision makers tend to respond disproportionately to new information. We show in this section how this inefficiency is unavoidable and that it is exacerbated by other aspects of human nature that add even more inefficiency to the translation of inputs into outputs.

Generally, any given decision maker (or organization) deals with many different issues almost simultaneously, as one issue bleeds into the next. Attention can be directed at only one problem at a time, but decision makers must have some mechanism for shifting attention and effort among multiple problems. So real-world decision makers often juggle multiple problems as well as multiple characterizations of each of several problems. The difficulty in handling multiple streams of information via the serial processing capacity of short-term memory led one student of human cognition to refer to the human brain as the "master juggler" (Wills 1993:268–69).

Shifting attention from topic to topic tends to be episodic, disjoint, and somewhat jarring. One minute one is watching a soccer game on TV; the next minute one realizes that one forgot to buy Mom's birthday gift. Government leaders deal one minute with a foreign policy crisis, the next with educational attainment among twelve-year-olds. Academic department heads deal one minute with research grants from the faculty, and the next with a plagiarism case. Shifting from topic to topic, and even back to a topic that has previously already been considered, can be anything but incremental.

But most of the time choice is incremental. Consider a decision maker dealing for a second time with an issue that has previously been addressed. In most situations it doesn't cross his or her mind to attend to the issue—it is "off the radar screen," as the saying goes. So most decisions are repeated through time with no conscious evaluation of why the policy or behavior is continued. One cannot make a decision without directing attention to it. But one can certainly allow the status quo to continue without much thought, and we do this all the time.

If an issue is explicitly considered, the first reaction of a decision maker might be, Is there any reason to change the way I have dealt with this in the past? If not, then repeat the previous decision. That is, we expect little reason to think that a decision maker, when dealing with a recurring issue, would change his or her decision in the absence of some threshold of unanticipated new problems or new information. So in dealing with a recurring issue, the first decision rule might be something like: if no crisis looms, or if no major new problems have emerged, then the previous choice, the status quo policy, is justified and should be repeated. In the case of an individual, it means that the issue is simply not considered further. In the case of an organization, it means that the parallel processing units within the organization (that is, specialized agencies) continue to deal with it. Leadership need not intervene. The subsystems continue to operate.

A threshold is a value for a problem-space attribute that implies policy action when it is exceeded. In a perfectly rational, full-information situation, one would reevaluate a standing decision when the improvement from re-evaluation exceeded the costs of search for a new solution, and that would result in some positive threshold before it would be worth the trouble to re-consider. But reconsidering requires attention and conscious thought, both of which are scarce and must be allocated in serial fashion—that is, when we are thinking about one problem, we cannot be thinking simultaneously about an-other. As a consequence, a behavioral model of decision making incorporat-ing serial processing results in a larger threshold than does a full-information rational model. The situation must be more dire in the behavioral model, and that generally evokes emotion.

Directly because of the constraints of serial processing, people and orga-nizations have much higher thresholds for working on a problem than would be the case in the absence of this cognitive facet. But there are other elements that cause previous decisions, status quo biases, and thresholds to loom much larger in a behavioral model of choice. These include, most importantly, an emotional attachment to the prevailing way of doing things—identifica-tion—but may also involve vested interests and simple indolence. Different institutions and different individuals may be more or less efficient in the sense of having a low threshold for reconsidering old issues, but there is nec-essarily some bias to the system because of the scarcity of attention. We pri-oritize attention to those issues that seem to require it most strongly.

Inefficiencies Based in Difficulties in Entertaining New Issue Characterizations

"Do I need to pay attention to this issue now?" Often, the answer to that ques-tion is no. In this case, the status quo understanding, issue definition, solutions, and choices remain the same by default. What if the answer is yes? This implies that something about the status quo policy or choice currently in place is worth reconsidering. Now, it could be a relatively simple matter of periodic revisitation, a routine reconsideration of the issue according to some timetable set in advance. In this case, the choice may be very simple and quickly made in favor of continuing the status quo. Or it could be that a simple change in some indicator has become apparent, and an adjustment to the policy is needed, but no fundamental rethinking is called for; this also may constitute a large proportion of choice situations.

But if things are considerably out of kilter, it may be necessary to consider a fresh characterization of the issue. New information may cause the individual to give greater weight to dimensions previously given less consideration; for example, when buying a second car after having first bought a red sports car, one might decide to be more practical. Similar choices made sequentially over time need not always be made with the same weights for each of the dimensions of evaluation. We can assign different weights to the various dimensions of choice, even completely ignore some of them, at different times if we face the same or a similar choice repeatedly over time. For organizations, new issue characterizations are often associated with the entry of new participants or a change in leadership. In governments, elections and other personnel changes can lead even an ongoing organization to reconsider and reevaluate issue characterizations.

In sum, there may be many causes for the decision maker to reevaluate a status quo policy. But the first step in the process is to pay attention to the issue. At this point, once the agenda has been set so that attention will be paid to this issue again, several things can happen. Previous decisions can be evaluated and concluded to have been made appropriately or to require only minor adjustments. But looking back at the stages of the model presented above, it is clear that several other options are possible: the issue definition may have changed; the mix of available solutions may have been altered; the preferences or the identities of the decision makers may have changed. There is often nothing more than an incremental adjustment, at best, however, unless a new characterization of the issue is adopted. Further, the very fact that the issue passed the first test, that it requires attention, may imply that the previous decision was based on a faulty issue definition. So when an issue reemerges on the agenda, one may expect some reevaluation of how it should best be characterized.

Inefficiencies in Choosing Solutions

Once attention is directed at an issue and the issue has been characterized, the search for solutions occurs. In facing any issue, people naturally consider whether the issue is similar to one they have considered in the past. Generally speaking, in forging solutions to problems, humans draw upon two resources: the previously encoded or learned responses to problems from memory and the search for solutions that have not been used before. This is known as the "preparation–deliberation trade-off" (Newell 1990). Being able to use previously learned solutions presupposes being able to classify problems and deciding when a new problem is "sufficiently similar" to understood ones that a previously learned solution will work. Using previous solutions is efficient, in the sense of not requiring further search, but it runs the risk of being inappropriate or downright wrong. The key is to know whether a previously chosen solution remains appropriate for the new issue; is the current issue really similar to an issue that may have been dealt with in the past? Or does it just appear similar at first glance?

Often, people become emotionally attached to favored solutions beyond their direct utility. Herbert Simon (1947) referred to this phenomenon as "identification with the means." This emotional association in effect "locks in" previous ways of doing things, making adoption of a new solution more difficult and less "smooth" than it otherwise would be. One major instance of this phenomenon in politics is ideology. People identify with an ideological position—"I am a conservative"—and this identification affects how they prioritize problems, construct problem spaces, and organize solutions. Changing these perspectives in a committed ideologue is difficult indeed. But cognitive lock-ins need not be limited to ideological issues. Many public policies are administered by professionals with a strong identification with the means. That is, forest rangers often have a professional identification with a certain way of managing the forests; social workers often believe in a certain way in providing welfare services. Foreign Service officers often differ from Army Rangers in their views on how to conduct foreign relations. These professional identifications often make professionals resistant to changing issue definitions or to considering or adopting new solutions to old problems, even when it may be clear to others that the status quo policies are failing. Individuals and organizations may not be readily willing to abandon their old ways of thinking. Professional identities, training, and knowledge can lead to identification with the means just as much as ideology can.

In humans, in organizations, and in public bureaucracies, there is great friction, or resistance to change, far beyond what can be explained through rational search costs. Attention, when focused on an issue, tends to stay there. During the time attention is directed at a given issue, a certain set of issue definitions, policy proposals, and choices may be justified. When change does occur, it can be dramatic, because the friction that leads to so little change much of the time has to be overcome before any serious change is possible. It takes a lot to overcome the cognitive and organizational frictions that encourage replication of the status quo.

When faced with a decision similar to a decision one has already made in the past, remembering the past decision is likely one's first heuristic shortcut. If it seemed to have worked, and if the current situation indeed appears similar to the previous one, then why not repeat the previous decision? It seems the most logical course of action. But what is the reason for reconsidering this previous decision in the first place? Issues can recur on a personal agenda for reasons that either are routine or indicate a need to rethink previous decisions, since apparently they did not work out. But one may have a tendency to muddle through, implementing old decision rules as long as they seem to work tolerably well. In sum, it may take a high threshold before one decides that muddling through is not the best option; when this occurs, then a more fundamental rethinking can occur. The resulting distribution of decisions may show the characteristic shape of adhering the great majority of the time to a strong status quo bias but occasionally involving dramatic innovations.

Among organizations similar processes go on, but they are accentuated by established organizational missions. Organizations do not simply give up their old ways of thinking about problems. Bureaucratic entities come to identify with their established ways of doing things. Sunk costs and organizational structures matter. Now, these established ways of doing things are not fully immutable. At some point, even the most hidebound bureaucracies can modernize. The point here is simply that organizations, probably more than individuals, will tend first to look for reasons why it may be appropriate to consider any new decision situation sufficiently similar to previous ones that status quo policies can be used to muddle through tolerably well. And this is not a bad approach in most cases. The same cognitive processes that are apparent among individuals also work for organizations, but these are accentuated by the fact that in many organizations employees have professional identities, if not jobs and entire self-justifications, at stake. Just as we did with individuals we would therefore expect organizations to exhibit a pattern of favoring status quo policies unless and until sufficient and substantial pressure builds up to demonstrate that these are no longer feasible. At that point, past some threshold, more fundamental restructuring and new problem definitions can come into play. Therefore, we may expect a distribution of outcomes similar to what we described for individuals above: extreme allegiance to the status quo most of the time, with occasional bursts of innovation.

Policy Inheritances and Path Dependency

Notions of organizational sunk costs and tendencies to repeat past decisions are nothing new in the study of public policy. Rose and Davies (1994) term the tendency to rely on past decisions "policy inheritances." Policies today are not made in a vacuum; they are built on previous policy decisions, which exert a heavy hand on future commitments. The general phenomenon of policies reproducing themselves through time is known as path dependency (Pierson 2000). Once a path is chosen, it tends to be followed. Moving off the path can be difficult.

It is not immediately evident why policies at one time should be so heavily influenced by policies at a previous time. Policies are designed to effect objectives; so one explanation is that the conditions that gave rise to the policies in the first place are still present. Because conditions are constant, policies stay in place. But if the conditions are the same, why continue the policies if they have not affected them? Moreover, empirical analyses of many policy commitments show that one cannot explain them easily from conditions or lagged conditions (that is, those conditions present in the past) alone. An explicit consideration of earlier policy commitments must be part of the explanation of current policy commitments. This is particularly true of government budgets.

Why is this adjustment for previous policy commitments necessary? Perhaps policies work, and because they work, they are continued. The problem here is that many would argue that policies in place for a very long time don't work very well. A vigorous debate over welfare reform in the United States illuminated both the weaknesses and strengths of the system, but the continuance of the system for many years indicates that policy inheritances go far beyond the successes of the policy. Because policy commitments represent past political victories by interest groups, and these groups fight to keep their previous victories in place, an interest-group explanation might be the key. But empirical studies of policy subsystems indicate that, much of the time, policy activity occurs in low-conflict situations. Even when conflict occurs in policy subsystems, it settles into routine channels in which participants learn from each other (Sabatier and Jenkins-Smith 1993). Continual interest-group activity to protect past gains is not vigorous enough to explain policy stability.

Another oft-noted reason for the difficulty in shifting policy direction stems from continuity of participation in key governmental positions. After all, the American system of separation of powers and different electoral cycles for the president, the House, and the Senate makes wholesale changes in government officials relatively rare. But enacting change often requires the involvement of a diverse range of policymakers. Many of these, including those in important gatekeeping positions, typically were involved in creating the earlier policy or at least in administering it. They often have a sense of ownership in the status quo policy, and convincing them to admit that their previously favored policy is now outdated or is no longer the best policy, and perhaps was a mistake in the first place, may not be an easy task. Naturally, they resist admitting past mistakes, and changing a policy in the absence of dramatic evidence of changing circumstances often comes close to admitting that the previous policy was a failure. Not all involved in implementing or enacting the previous policy will want to do that, and many of those people will still be involved in the policy at the next go-round.

Policy inheritances must be understood as organizational phenomena. New policies put in place new agencies to implement them. These new agencies and programs acquire a life of their own, as agency personnel identify with their new mission and interest-group activity centers in the new agency. Most importantly, the major political combatants abandon their attentiveness to the policy arena, treating it as a policy settlement that has solved the problem (or at least provided a satisfactory compromise for the time being). New organizations are created, and they are part of the current policy environment.

Disproportionate Information-Processing

These cognitive and organizational facets lead to a model of decision making that stresses disproportionality in response to incoming information. Generally, people do not respond in proportion to the strength of the information signals they receive from the environment, nor do the organizations they inhabit, and this is because of their cognitive architectures. Mathematician Benoit Mandelbrot put it this way: "Man tends to react either by overestimation or neglect" (1997: 280; see also Mandelbrot 1999). Similarly, governments are disproportionate information-processors. Sometimes they underrespond, not attending to the problem; at other times they overrespond. Some of this characteristic pattern of disproportionate information-processing can be accounted for by decision costs: the fact that in American political institutions "supermajority" constitutional requirements limit quick action. But much of the disproportionality comes from the process of collective allocation of attention. The roots of disproportionality are in the cognitive architecture of humans as well as in constitutional rules or institutional procedures.

Often, disproportionality plays out in policymaking as a pattern of overlooking clues in plain sight and then overreacting when attention is directed at the previously obvious clues. We need not look far for examples of systematic underappreciation of some rising policy problem and then an overreaction to that same problem. Reports from commissions studying the response of government to the events of September 11, 2001, indicate that American government officials understated or underattended to the issue of terrorism on our shores, and of course subsequent to those events many government agencies rushed to make terrorism a major priority. Proportionality would have implied a smoother process. Even given the "noise" in signal processing, it is clear that the Bush administration in its early months underappreciated the terrorist threat, even as the intelligence officials responsible for the area were very concerned (Clarke 2004).

But what agency, much less one that does not have a particular mission to focus on terrorism, would overcome its own status quo biases to make this a new priority? The National Security Council had difficulty in appreciating the nonstate nature of the al-Qaida threat, believing that the resources of a nation-state would be necessary to accomplish a major terrorist attack. Shifting attention requires a major impetus and an associated problem redefinition, and some general intelligence about possible threats would not be enough. The natural tendency is to underemphasize new threats, new ways of thinking of things, new ways to organize public bureaucracies, until and unless some significant threshold of urgency is crossed. At that point, major changes can occur. While the 9/11 terrorism example is an extreme case of such a thing, similar patterns of overresistance, then overreaction, are general characteristics of government. Crises seem necessary to drive change.

Why Thresholds Are Not the Whole Story

We've laid out a model of attention shifting and argued that this leads to severe disproportionality in policymaking. Threshold effects are an important part of this story. One might think that all disproportionality could be understood in terms of thresholds. We could assume that each problem is indexed by a measure of severity (the information), and each measure has a threshold that triggers government action. Attention would shift to a problem if the indicator exceeds its threshold. In a behavioral model such as the one we have developed here, thresholds would be much larger than in a pure rational-information model, but they might be assumed to operate similarly even if at different levels.

There are major differences, however. The first is the tendency of humans to overreact with "alarmed discovery" when a clue in plain sight is recognized. In our behavioral model, thresholds don't cause proportionality; they compound disprorportionality. Thresholds in human decision making do not work like thermostats. A thermostat keeps a room's temperature constant by turning on the heat when the temperature drops below a threshold, and turns it off when it rises above a second threshold. The range is quite narrow, so that a person would not notice the minor differences in temperature. Human decision makers, however, often hold to a prior decision far beyond its utility, because attention is directed elsewhere, or because beliefs or political ideologies are so strong that reevaluating them would be quite painful psychologically. When they are forced to change, they can be so far "behind the curve" that major adjustments are required, leading not to a smooth adjustment to events but to disjoint shifts that themselves can disrupt the system.

Second, the same facets of belief and ideology that usually lead to a strong status quo bias can lead in some circumstances to overreaction. Ideologies and beliefs, when strongly held, can motivate people to take action they would not take under calmer analysis. Third, communication matters and can account for behavior in collectives that is unimaginable in noncommunicating aggregates of people. People talking to one another can become "irrationally exuberant" (Shiller 2000) or simply follow the crowd in a cascading reaction to a minor change.

Two other well-known mechanisms undermine a pure threshold model. The first is the now-classic garbage can model. In that model, attention is triggered as much by policy entrepreneurs as by any agreed-upon threshold. The George W. Bush administration's push to attack Iraq for "weapons of mass destruction" is a case in point. It is at least the case that the threshold value for attention and action was pushed much lower after the terrorist attacks of September 11. But this sort of contingency goes much deeper. Could one imagine President Gore, or President Bradley, or President McCain, or President Buchanan, or President Nader attacking Iraq in the face of such a severe threat from al-Qaida? While one can never be certain of such "counterfactuals," certainly the probabilities would have been vastly different. In any case, as we noted above, attention to a given issue does not always tell us much about what solution will be adopted.

The second mechanism is agenda crowding. If at one point in time many issues clamor for attention on the agenda, while at another fewer issues are present (for whatever reason), then threshold values are likely to be affected accordingly. With a limited agenda-processing capacity, all other things being equal, thresholds will be lower for the case where fewer other issues are already on the agenda. Where the agenda is already full, it will be that much harder for a new issue to merit attention. Since the current "crowdedness" of the agenda is likely unrelated to the severity of any particular other problem, we can't conceive of the thresholds we describe here as fixed; they depend on the current state of affairs and can be higher or lower depending on other unrelated factors. But they always exist; they are never zero.

The most important way in which a simple threshold model is insufficient to capture the degree of discontinuity that we describe is the existence of interactions among the stages of our behavioral decision-making model. Attention to any given issue may be related to threshold effects (these may be variable thresholds, as noted above), but the model has four stages, and the decisions made in the subsequent three stages may all reinforce the disjoint nature of the process. As we noted with the case of the war in Iraq, the emergence of the issue of terrorism on the international agenda on September 11, 2001, did not determine the nature of the subsequent policies. In fact, different governments around the world have responded differently than ours, and there is little reason to suspect that another leader would have chosen the policies that President Bush followed. So the rise of a new issue is just the first step; the issue must then be characterized; solutions must be evaluated, and choices must be made. Each of these four stages is subject to interactive effects, because previous decisions at each stage can be discredited when the issue is forced again to the agenda. So disjointedness is greater than in a simple threshold model.

In sum, a strong status quo bias exists in human and organizational decision-making processes. This bias stems from a variety of cognitive and emotional mechanisms, including the friction of attention allocation, the unwillingness to sacrifice a comfortable characterization of an issue, emotional identification with a particular solution, and simple familiarity with and confidence in a particular solution. But the resulting path dependency is not inevitable—it does not have to go on forever—and when it collapses it may cascade into destructive waves of change. So disproportionate information-processing does not imply a generalized threshold effect that delays a response until problem severity reaches a critical level (whatever that critical level might be). It also means that path dependency can be broken in a wave of overreaction, either because political leaders are playing "catch up" to deteriorating indicators of a situation or because some other mechanism has resulted in a collective focus on a previously ignored problem.

Fortunately, methods are available to study policy processes for such complexities. The qualitative case study has been the tool of choice in policy studies, perhaps in large part because of the implicit recognition of these kinds of overwhelming complexities. We rely much more heavily in this book on stochastic process methods, which simply incorporate the contingencies and uncertainties into the approach, as we make clear in chapter 4.

Conclusions

This chapter has laid out a model of decision making, first at the individual level, next at the collective level, and finally in dynamic terms, as we move from one decision to the next. This process is not smooth. In fact, the disjoint nature of attention shifting as one moves from one choice to the next is one of the fundamental characteristics of the decision-making process that determines the nature of policy change.

Change tends to be either feast or famine. There is an extreme allegiance to the status quo simply because we are so overloaded with choice opportunities, problems, and complex issues that we cannot deal with any but a small fraction of the ones that probably deserve some attention. While this allegiance to the status quo may be ideological, it does not have to be. A powerful status quo bias would exist even in the absence of ideology, because it is based in human cognition and then exacerbated in organizational settings by missions and bureaucratic procedures. Coupled with famines where little change takes place come the feasts: policies can change quite dramatically, because once we decide to focus on them, we may fundamentally reevaluate not only our choice, but indeed our understanding of the issue, our weighting of the relevant dimensions of the issue, our consideration of potential solutions, and our goals in addressing the issue in the first place. Similarly, within organizations, if an issue is pushed up high onto the political agenda, typically it is because the status quo policies have been shown to be inadequate for some reason, at least in the perception of some relevant actors. So look out!

In the remaining chapters of this book, we will demonstrate the feast-or-famine nature of policy change. Here we have tried to start out with a simple explanation of the root causes of these processes: the bottlenecks of human cognitive architectures and the behavior of organizations constructed from human raw material that are so obvious in politics. The dynamics of policy-making come from how political systems process information. Understanding how information is processed in the political system allows us to understand how policies are chosen, reified, and occasionally dramatically revised.

3

The Intrusion of New Information

The things Congress does best are nothing and overreacting.

—Tom Korologos

New information carries with it the potential to shock, to disrupt, and to destabilize as it intrudes into the policy process. Indeed, the model we laid out in the previous chapter implies that either information is underappreciated by being ignored or interpreted in a benign fashion, or it stimulates overreaction, ushering in a period of "alarmed discovery" (Downs 1972). This chapter is about how a political system reacts to new information. We address two key questions: When is a change in the environment, an informational signal, recognized as relevant to a policy problem? If it is, how is the signal interpreted?

Underlying these two questions are two related processes for the recognition and interpretation of new information. We term these *issue intrusion* and *attribute intrusion*, the former to denote reaction to new or previously overlooked information, and the latter to denote the process of issue redefinition as people grapple with the meaning of this information. Issue intrusion, concerning the detection of signals in the environment, addresses the first stage of figure 2.1. To study it we develop what we call the implicit index model of attention (Jones 2001:179–84). In monitoring the environment, people must juggle numerous sources of information of varying reliability and relevance. Somehow they must combine the messages from these various sources into something relevant to action (or inaction). We refer to the process of combination as implicit index construction because its construction and use is rarely recognized or admitted explicitly. Rather, like an informal set of

norms not recognized by those who are following them, it evolves and develops over time.

In fact, neither people nor organizations typically monitor all the relevant
aspects of the environment as these relate to a given issue; they attend only
to a subset of them—the indicators that seem most relevant. If these indices
were fully comprehensive and properly weighted, then reactions to new information would be proportionate to the importance of that new information. The implicit indices that people typically use, however, generate disproportionate responses, because their incompleteness and disproportionate
informal weighting of the component parts ensure that, through "alarmed
discovery" of previously ignored (or underweighted) elements of the environment, new issues will intrude suddenly to the attention of the decision
maker. This "seat of the pants" heuristic index construction is not as good
as a fully comprehensive set of monitoring tools, and the undisciplined reweighting of index components leads to error accumulation and subsequent
"alarmed discovery."

Because it is typically impossible to develop a fully comprehensive model
for most complex issues, the implicit index model that we describe here fits
much better with observations of how people and organizations actually
function. The advantage of thinking about the process of combining messages
from diverse sources is that we will be able to show the consequences of incomplete monitoring and episodic updating on policy decisions in an information-rich world.

Just as new issues can intrude suddenly to our attention, so can new attributes of existing issues suddenly gain more importance. Attribute intrusion is basically issue redefinition. This fleshes out the middle two stages of
figure 2.1. The complexity and multidimensionality of decision making on
many public policy issues forces decision makers to use informational shortcuts such as the implicit index approach we describe. But the incompleteness
of the resulting decision-making system has a corollary. Occasionally it is disrupted by the emergence of a previously ignored dimension or an entirely
new aspect of an issue that was not part of the discussion. These new attributes are often a consequence of the disproportionate updating of the incomplete "basket" of indicators that decision makers are monitoring. The system
must scramble to incorporate the new interpretation into the process. In sum,
partiality begets stability, but also occasional destabilization.

To illustrate these dynamic disruptive processes, we examine two important policy areas—business regulation and the corporate governance scandal
of 2001–2 and the welfare reform movement of the mid-1990s. These cases illustrate the disruptive impacts of new information and fresh interpretations

on policy equilibria. Finally we show that in American politics disruption due to the "shock" of new information goes well beyond electoral mandates and the replacement of political leaders, by examining situations of major change where elections cannot have been the source of the change. No theory of political change can rely on electoral dynamics alone.

The Implicit Index Approach

In any reasonably complex decision-making environment, there are typically more sources of potentially relevant information than can simultaneously be considered, evaluated, and systematically incorporated. So people and organizations alike use heuristic shortcuts to handle the overabundance of information. One important shortcut is to pay attention to certain indicators rather than to others. These indicators are almost always imperfect; they measure social realities with error. Further, the set of indicators that people monitor is virtually always incomplete—a direct consequence of the bottleneck of attention.

This incomplete monitoring of the state of the world causes perceived reality, or "beliefs" (as understood from the indicators), to drift from the facts. Given enough time, the divergence can become substantial. Even in the short run, if an indicator that is not being monitored suddenly becomes relevant, the index of indicators actually being used will become highly misleading. Of course, it is fine to overlook indicators in the environment that are trivial or have low values. But just because an indicator has a low value at one point in time (and can therefore safely be ignored) does not mean that it will remain trivial in the future. But if it isn't being monitored, a decision maker may find out about it only when it emerges "suddenly" as a sort of crisis. If and when the new information is brought into the implicit index, the resulting updating of beliefs can be disjoint. The updated set of indicators can have similarly jarring implications for the proper response to the state of the world, such as public policy outcomes. The result will be policy punctuations.

It is important to stress that this process is virtually inevitable in any reasonably complex decision situation. Some organizations may be better at scanning their environments for potentially important trends that need to be monitored before they emerge dramatically, but no organization uses a fully comprehensive one; this would be impossible.

The manner in which decision makers process information from multiple sources is like the formal process of index construction. In making decisions, policymaking systems receive information from a diversity of sources. Somehow the participants in the system must weigh the various bits of information and come to a decision. Combining these diverse streams resembles explicit index construction, such as what economists do when they develop the index of consumer sentiment, or the Consumer Price Index. We have all sorts of indices for various social and economic trends. In economics, these take the form of stock market indices, consumer sentiment indices, price indices, etc. In politics, we have indicators of the liberal or conservative voting records of congressmen, of the military strength of nations, of their religious liberty, of tax burdens of states, and many others. For a given social problem there are often widely recognized indicators used by many to monitor the severity of the problem or the success of various policies: the unemployment rate, the poverty rate, air and water quality indicators, disease rates, crime rates, housing affordability rates, etc.

An index combines various sources of information in a way that will be more reliable than relying on a single indicator or even no explicit data at all. In effect, indexes reduce the misleading effects of random error in the measurement of a trend. Indexes are constructed so that the most important indicators within a single index are weighted more heavily than those that are less important. The processes that people or organizations go through often are implicit rather than explicit, however, and as a consequence it is subject to greater error.

In politics, a similar process of weighting various bits of information occurs, but it is typically done in an unconscious if not downright haphazard fashion. Should Congress vote for a major tax reduction? Lots of information pours in at a rapid rate, some of it being clearly relevant, some tangential, some irrelevant, and of course much of the information is conflicting. Who will benefit? What incentives will it create? What effects will it have on future government deficits? How will interest groups view it? How will voters view it? What is the president's position? And different individual policy makers of course weight different bits of information differently. Collectively, however, a decision will emerge, and it will reflect the relative weights attached to the various streams of information that are considered.

Figure 3.1 diagrams the process of implicit index construction. On the left-hand side of the diagram, numerous sources produce imperfect indicators. On the right-hand side, the decision maker, the receiver of the information, somehow combines the various indicators so that he or she can make a decision.

In reacting to information, noise (that is, random error) enters the process at two points. Noise in information processing is like static in a telephone connection. It adds to uncertainty about the meaning of the information that

Figure 3.1. The Implicit Index Model: Combining Information from Diverse Sources

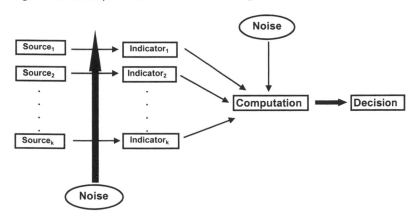

is being received but causes no long-term bias in interpretation. One point where random error enters is when the decision maker implicitly constructs indicators from the various sources of information pressing down, and the other is when the decision maker must combine the various indicators and make a decision. Weighting diverse relevant pieces of information incorrectly can be a significant source of error, just as is measuring the relevant social indicators incorrectly. Imperfect indicators may include random error, or simple "noise," but indicators can also be biased. Indeed, political information many times is biased, because it is promulgated by interest groups wishing something of value from political leaders.

Computational errors can be random noise, but they can be systematic and biased, because we do not know for sure how relevant the various indicators are to the decision at hand, or whether we have considered all the relevant indicators. Combining lots of biased indicators is far better than relying on a few biased ones, because there can be a "canceling out" of the most misleading information—so long as the biases come from all directions.[1] That is, of course, a major reason for allowing "free expression" in democratic politics. A system that leaves out the biased indicators entirely is even better, but that can be extraordinarily difficult in politics.

In any case, leaving out important indicators has very important consequences, but it is virtually unavoidable because of the limits of a decision maker's attention capacity. Biases in decision making can be overcome either

1. This can be shown statistically through the justly famous Central Limit Theorem from statistics. We will examine the consequences of this indicator combination approach in chapters 4–6.

through the incorporation of better indicators or though the incorporation of all potential indicators, even if they are biased. Including only some biased indicators (or weighting those biased indicators too heavily) clearly leads immediately to problems.

What may be less obvious is that even the inclusion of a nonbiased but incomplete set of indicators can lead to difficulties over time. Any system that monitors only part of the world must implicitly assume that the monitored parts and the unmonitored parts change in a similar manner. If they do not, then the facts and the monitored indicators will drift further and further apart. Errors will accumulate.

Implicit indices get out of kilter with reality because of limits of attention—only so many indicators can be monitored at once. But they also fall prey to the tendency of people to become attached cognitively and emotionally to abstractions—religions, political ideologies, even simple things such as teaching methods. So it is not surprising that people can become emotionally attached to particular indicators—attachment to party, for example— employing them as guides when they may not be appropriate. This adds to the difficulties of adjusting to changing circumstances. Also problematic is the fact that different decision makers can have different favorite indicators. There is lots of evidence from psychology and political psychology that people have favorite sources of information and allow their biases to color how they look at other potential sources (Gerber and Green 1999).

The organizational and public policy implications of the implicit index model are profound. The theory implies a divergence between the severity of a problem in the real world and the interpretation and response of the system to the problem. The major points of divergence occur in detecting a signal in an environment crowded with other signals about competing problems (that is, in detecting the problem in the first place) and, once a problem is detected, in combining information from diverse sources to gauge the magnitude of the problem and the most appropriate response. Each of these leads to disjoint and episodic responses to information signals from the environment. In the next sections we turn to some examples of how issues intrude and how implicit indices are updated, often dramatically changed, during this process.

Issue Interpretation

The implicit index model implies nonlinearities in the policymaking process. As a decision maker brings new indicators into the index, which is likely only if the new indicator seems urgent or pressing, dramatic changes may occur. If the indicator had previously been recognized as important and adjustments had been made in the past, a smoother set of policy changes would result. But that is not the only source of disproportionality. Nonlinearities can also arise in the process of interpreting the indicators. Indeed, the process of interpretation can be stimulated independent of any change in the policymaking environment through such well-known factors as a change in governing party control or the mobilization of interest groups.

We will examine in this section the important dynamics of how solutions become attached to problems, and how the intrusion of new interpretations or attributes characterizing an issue can change policy outputs, almost always in a disproportionate manner. As we saw in figure 2.1, collective decision making begins with deciding which issue to pay attention to. But it does not end there. Attributes, or issue definitions, can also rise or fall from attention. These two dynamics, issue intrusion and attribute intrusion, are central to our themes in this chapter.

Let us consider the dynamics of attention to various attributes of a given policy issue first. It should be clear that we are focusing here on the bottom elements of figure 2.1, laying out the logic of choice. We reproduce these bottom elements here as figure 3.2. Our theme is straightforward: attention to the attributes structuring a choice in many cases affects policy outcomes, even if we ignore for the moment those dynamics that come from paying attention to one issue rather than another.

Our issue-intrusion approach is a direct descendant of the rich literature on problems and solutions in public policy. Many theories of the policy process hinge on the idea that policy proposals and policy solutions are analytically separate and, indeed, may develop independent of one another (Cohen, March, and Olsen 1972; Kingdon 1995; Zahariadis 1999). It has become fashionable in public policy studies to note that solutions "search out" problems as policy activists try to justify their favored policies by highlighting the problems they solve. But that is not the entire story. Unless the problem accesses the public agenda, major new policy initiatives are not likely to be undertaken. Nevertheless, it is true that problems and solutions often develop somewhat independently. Problems stem from the environment, while solutions can come from new search procedures or can be drawn from organizational memory. It would be inefficient to search for solutions every time problems emerge; a more efficient approach would be to store some solutions in memory and modify them to meet current challenges.

Because solutions and problems develop independently, they can be subject to very different causal dynamics. Another way to think about this is to think of separate selection processes being applied to three different compo-

Figure 3.2. From Attributes to Solutions

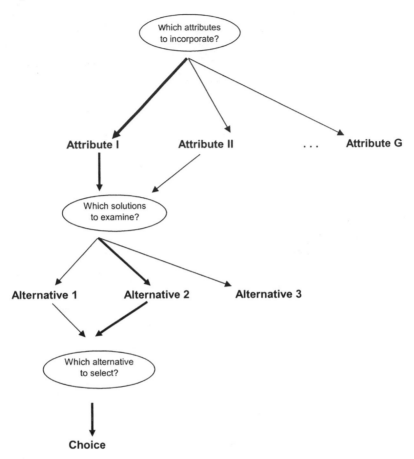

nents of the choice process. Recall that in chapter 2 we distinguished among attention allocation to issues, problem characterizations, and solutions or alternatives. Choice processes involve all three of these. As a consequence, selection processes may operate on solutions (or policy alternatives); on attributes (issue definitions); and on the allocation of attention to issues. A complete characterization of a policy proposal would need to capture all three of these aspects.

These processes may be quite different, because the environment or context for each element may be different. Choice of solutions within an alternative set occurs within the confines of policymaking institutions; hence, political parties and legislative organization are critical. Attention to issues may be driven by broader media debates. But they may also be intertwined—the emergence of a new issue may be connected to the previous emergence of a new characterization of that issue. That seems to have been the case during the mid-1990s in discussion of welfare reform. Conservatives' characterization of welfare as going to the undeserving did not particularly resonate, but the notion that the incentives were misdirected and caused decent people to do the wrong thing by paying them not to work struck a more responsive chord. So it is possible that the rise of a new attribute can lead to a rise in attention to an old issue. Remember that the stages we laid out in figure 2.1 do not have to occur in sequence.

A Model of Attribute Intrusion

Policy solutions or alternatives often may be arrayed on a line, from the greatest level of governmental effort to the least. For example, in one important case, using monetary policy in economic management, policy has centered for many years on how much to raise or lower the volume of money in circulation (with interest rates, which set the price of money, being the major tool available to policymakers). The potential solution or alternative set consists of numbers on a line—the so-called "discount rate"—from zero to some positive number. The effort would here be defined as how far away from the status quo the Federal Reserve, responsible for government's interest rate policy, would set the rate.

Clearly most of these alternatives are not considered seriously, so the realistic alternative set might consist of alternatives from a low of 1 percent to a high of 6 percent (in the past, this range would have been considerably broader). The realistic range is contingent on the nature of the problem, of course, so one can think of a rate range varying by how policymakers define the trade-offs of growth and inflation. But the point does not change: the debate is constrained to the size of the rate change, and the nature of the problem is assumed to be structured within a single dimension.

Monetary policy has not always been so consensual. For most of the history of the Republic, great political fights were waged around the distributional component of monetary policy. High interest rates were thought to benefit investors; low interest rates, borrowers and consumers. Just how and why the debate about monetary policy came to exclude fairness of the division of the social product is an interesting historical question, but here we simply note that excluding this attribute had the effect of focusing interest-rate policy to one goal: long-term growth in the economy. With distributional considerations excluded, the job of economic management through monetary policy became less contentious.

Much policy debate in less structured policy domains concerns how to characterize a policy problem rather than the solutions available once the problem is characterized. All problems may be characterized by multiple attributes, even though only a limited number of those attributes may be relevant at the time. This was the case for monetary policy in the past. It continues to characterize the issue of welfare policy. Conservative reformers argued that the welfare system that had developed in the United States undermined the work incentive, while defenders argued that the system was directed at protecting children. Which attribute was the correct one? Clearly both characterizations had merit, but then what are the attribute weights that ought to be applied in altering the system?

Attributes and Alternatives in Policymaking

Policy choices may be viewed within a spatial framework in which the points in the space represent policy solutions, and the axes or dimensions are some sort of conflict organizing system. The "conflict organizing system" in spatial theory may be viewed as a heuristic for organizing the many policy choices that confront a political decision maker. Often these axes represent ideology (particularly when the dimension is the classic left-right dimension with points arrayed along a single line).

We think of a policy as being characterized by a point in a multidimensional space. This space has two different components: the alternatives or policy solutions, and attributes or policy characterizations. In effect, the attributes provide the structure for how the alternatives are evaluated. To evaluate the effects of a policy proposal, we must know with respect to what: that is, which attributes of the issue are being evaluated? One attribute that characterizes policy is left-right ideology. A policy can be characterized by how liberal or conservative it is. But that is not the only possible characterization.

The alternative set is arrayed along a line embedded within this space. Alternatives can always be arrayed along a single line of "more or less." Let us return to the issue of monetary policy. The "more or less" aspects of the alternative set are the interest rates that the Federal Reserve sets. Even with the simplified framework of today, in managing the economy the Federal Reserve faces a trade-off. Inflation undermines long-term economic growth, but if interest rates are raised, inflation can be brought under control only at the expense of immediate economic growth. In this case, controlling inflation and promoting economic growth are the attributes of the policy—really the goals

Figure 3.3. Trade-Off Faced by Policymakers on Monetary Policy

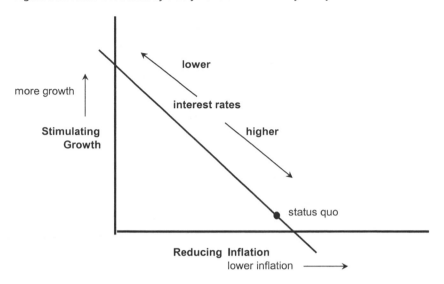

of the policy action. These attributes are confined to the estimated effects of the policy, but we can conceive of attributes that are not so closely related to general effects. Concerns about political corruption or the lack of female and minority members on the board, for example, could serve to define the policy for a time.

Figure 3.3 illustrates the trade-off.[2] The decision to raise or lower interest rates involves (1) the state of the economy at the time; (2) the estimated effects on inflation and growth of an anticipated move; and (3) the weights that policymakers give controlling inflation versus encouraging growth. These weights are important. There is no reason that attributes in a complex decision-making situation be weighted equally; indeed, in most situations they are not (B. D. Jones 1994).

We noted above that debates about the setting of interest rates were once conducted in a space of higher dimensionality. In particular, the distributional effects of rate setting were factored in as a third attribute. That clearly made the trade-off more difficult. Interest rates still have distributional effects. Debtors pay more and creditors win as rates move upward. But at present there is general political consensus to ignore distribution; that attribute is

2. The relationships between growth, inflation, and interest rates are considerably more complicated than implied in the graph—they are likely to be nonlinear, for example. Incorporating such aspects would unnecessarily complicate the exposition.

typically ignored in today's discourse and debate. This has the effect of trans-forming a three-dimensional policy space into a two-dimensional one. That is equivalent to making the weight of the "distributional dimension" equal to zero. Other dimensions that some political actors might consider relevant are probably also ignored; most policy debates are partial, as there is no possible way they could be completely inclusive.

Adding more attributes or dimensions to the characterization of a policy problem quickly complicates the debate about the policy. One reason is that people have difficulty in making trade-offs in general. It is easier just to ignore potential effects unless those cross some threshold (or perhaps unless there is some constituency to insist that this dimension be institutionalized into the debate). But the problem undeniably increases in complexity as attributes are added, making it objectively more difficult to solve. If we were to reinte-grate the distributional attribute in monetary policy, policymakers would then need to evaluate not one trade-off (between inflation and growth) but three (between inflation and growth, growth and distribution, and inflation and distribution). If we had four attributes, the number of trade-offs would be twelve.[3]

Even though any public policy is characterized by a potentially complex set of attributes, choices must always be made in a single dimension (Jones 2001: chapter 6). In the rational choice model, expected utility is the final di-mension that allows the comparison, but comparing among alternatives that are arrayed along a single dimension of "utility" is easy. Combining the vari-ous attributes that characterize the issue in terms of the payoffs that are de-rived from each dimension is the difficult part. In legislatures, such shortcuts as the party leadership's recommendations are often used to reduce the com-plex space to a single choice dimension. Most commonly in the spatial model, a simple left-to-right continuum is used to represent "ideology." While ide-ologies may not be one-dimensional (Hinich and Munger 1994), they often are depicted that way.

In any case, all of these devices represent ways in which people use heur-istics to simplify complex choices. The "correct" simplification in the rational model would be the weighted sum that yields the dimension of "expected utility." Whether ideology, or party leadership, or some other heuristic corre-sponds to "expected utility" is an open question and an empirical one that cannot be answered by analytical fancy footwork.

So we can think of politics as occurring within a policy space consisting of two components: alternatives (or policy solutions) and attributes (or policy

3. $_kC_2$, where k is the number of attributes.

interpretations, including heuristic simplifications). This space is not static; it is clear from the example of monetary policy that the policy space can change over time. We capture this dynamic through the idea of a policy characterization. A *policy characterization* is just the set of attributes and the weights used in applying those attributes.

We can depict a policy characterization spatially as a choice dimension (that is, the policy alternatives arrayed along a line) and its associated attributes, weighted by their importance in the choice. The importance or salience weights can vary over time—they are sensitive to context. Indeed, that is a primary mechanism of policy evolution.[4] For example, welfare reform was fought out over the relative weights of the attributes characterizing the policy. To the previous characterization of helping the destitute versus helping the undeserving, neoconservatives added the new dimension of work incentives to the debate. In the approach we develop here, that would move the attribute weight from zero (no impact in the policy debate) to some positive value.

The notion of policy characterization helps us understand the evolution of policy solutions. Policy proposals evolve through the process of argumentation, debate, and reformulation, a process that goes in fits and starts, with bursts of activity interspersed with long periods of incremental activity. In this process, there is no beginning or end. After a policy is created, it is subject to debate and recharacterization. A recharacterization now can be understood as simply a reweighting of the attributes that structure a policy debate. Congressional histories are full of stories of issues redefined over time, either quickly, as a crisis forces attention to a dimension that had previously been ignored, or more slowly, as evidence accumulates that a given issue or issue definition deserves more attention (C. O. Jones 1994). Paul Burstein and his colleagues have shown in a comprehensive analysis of bills directed at family and work policies that a particular characterization can drift up in importance over time (Burstein and Bricher 1997; Burstein, Bricher, and Einwohner 1995). Congressional committees entertained some twenty-five distinct problem characterizations, but they focused on a limited number of these during the period of study (1945–90). The debate was punctuated by two distinct intrusions of new characterizations during the period. One of these dimensions involved new definitions of gender equality, basically involving the entrance of women into the workforce, and the other involved the competing demands

---

4. Adding salience weights to the simple characterization of policies in space moves us from a simple Euclidean space to a weighted Euclidean space. Allowing the weights to vary across time adds a dynamic to what would otherwise be an unchanging policy space. In effect, the dynamic allows our understanding of the characterization of a policy to evolve over time.

of home and work for men and women. Interestingly, these transformations were unrelated to differences between the two parties in Congress.

As in the case of gender and the workplace, recharacterizations often promote major policy changes. Because recharacterizations are based on new information or reinterpretations of old information, they are critical components of the information-processing dynamic.

Issue Intrusion and Attribute Intrusion

Issue intrusion is the emergence of a previously unappreciated issue into a stable policymaking system. Attention is directed to some aspect of the environment that went previously unnoticed or at least unappreciated. It is captured by the implicit index model developed in the first section of this chapter. But major changes can also occur even when the list of issues on the agenda does not change. New attributes that were previously ignored can rise and gain more attention. As our attention is almost always focused on fewer issues than could be of interest, and for each issue we virtually always use a simplified heuristic focusing on only a subset of the attributes that really matter, we may periodically "rediscover" a lost issue or a lost attribute from an existing issue.

The intrusion of new attributes into a previously one-dimensional debate is a key mechanism for expanding conflict and bringing new participants into a political debate (Baumgartner and Jones 1993). When new issues present themselves for consideration, they almost always carry with them unappreciated attributes that are simultaneously debated. When old issues are refreshed by increased debate, they almost always are recharacterized with previously unappreciated attributes. In sum, both new issues and new attributes can be destabilizing.

Attribute Intrusion and the Disruption of Equilibria

The intrusion of a new attribute can disrupt previously stable policymaking systems. Stable systems are at equilibrium. A legislative body may reach equilibrium and stay there between elections if new issues and events do not intrude (Krehbiel 1998). It does so by enacting policies high on the priority list of the new majority that enters the legislative body after an election. Once this high priority list is exhausted, no further major policy moves are possible, given the existing set of preferences of policymakers, the set of institutional rules governing the policymaking process, and the information available.

A major characteristic of a legislature at equilibrium is that partisanship and ideology correspond. Over time ideology adjusts to partisan concerns, and vice versa. Issues at equilibrium are generally well understood, and the parties have adopted positions on them. These party positions help to define issues for members, and the ideological positions of members affect what positions parties take on issues.[5] More broadly, party systems tend to be stable to the degree that they offer coherent views on the most salient issues of the day (Hinich and Munger 1994).

Party coalitions can be destabilized or even destroyed by the rise of new issues. Carmines and Stimson (1989) have documented the destruction of the old party allegiances in the 1960s with the emergence of race as a new issue cleavage, and more recently Stimson (2004) offers a more general version of the theory of issue evolution.

In two-party systems, if ideology and partisanship correspond, then voting will occur along a single dimension, whether that dimension is termed partisanship or ideology. In such cases, in the absence of supermajority requirements, the successful policy proposal will be that proposal most preferred by the legislator at the median (if legislators were arrayed from most conservative to most liberal on the ideological dimension). Things are more complex in a system of separated powers with supermajority requirements, but the same analysis holds. In principle we could put the president's ideological position on the same line as those for Senate and House members.

In this situation, in effect, the choice dimension and the ideological or partisan dimension correspond. Choices for policy solutions occur in a liberal-to-conservative space. Indeed, it may be the case that equilibrium in a legislature can be defined as occurring when the choice dimension for an issue falls along ideological and partisan lines—that is, it is completely defined by partisanship and (what is close to the same thing) ideology.

But what happens when issues or attributes intrude? This means that a previously ignored element of discussion, for whatever reason, receives intense attention. The adjustment process may be simple. If the issue is just redefined on the primary ideological or partisan dimension, then it will be business as usual. But it is possible that the issue opens up a new dimension of conflict—that is, the salience weight of a characterizing attribute moves from null to positive. If it does so, it can destabilize the existing equilibrium. In

5. A major debate in the legislative politics literature concerns whether "party" or "ideology" organizes legislative conflict. In our view, party influences ideology and vice versa in a dynamic adjustment process, but they are analytically distinct.

effect, politics is now operating in a multidimensional space, and such spaces are characterized by far more instability than are single-dimension spaces. Since new information can flow into the system independent of elections, there is no reason to expect that major policy changes will be confined to election mandates. These are clearly important, but they are not the whole story.

In later chapters we develop a stochastic process approach that allows us to test our model of policy change systematically, across the entire system, and to show that the recharacterization of issues is a general property of the American political system. Here we focus on a single issue to illustrate how this process works. As an exemplary case study we look at the rise of the issue of corporate governance early in the George W. Bush administration. It is useful to quickly review related issues of the decline of regulation of business and finance in the 1990s. This makes clear that the new corporate governance issue was a punctuation from the previous policy but also shows how policies beget the possibilities of new issue intrusions by their own inherent incompleteness.

Corporate Corruption: An Incident of Issue Intrusion Resulting in Reinterpretation

Since the 1930s, securities and financial regulation has been a policy subsystem of the classic variety. Established following the financial collapses of the Great Depression, it had developed strong links to banks, securities firms, and accounting agencies. Unlike the subsystems that we examined earlier (Baumgartner and Jones 1993), it had never suffered major collapse, even though its banking regulatory policies had been seriously challenged in the 1950s and it suffered a major crisis in the 1980s with the manipulation and collapse of the savings and loan industry (Hall 1997; Worsham 1997). It developed a strong, positive policy image over time as memories of the Great Depression and collapse of American financial institutions faded.

During the 1990s, the subsystem became even more independent. Not only did congressional oversight of business regulation decline precipitously, but regulatory agencies aggressively pursued the general deregulatory plan. Fueled by the economic boom of that decade, the move toward deregulation by the federal government, already accomplished in transportation and elsewhere, was extended to banking, finance, and securities. Some idea of the precipitous decline in congressional interest in business regulation may be gleaned from figure 3.4. There we have combined several subtopics from the Policy Agendas Project hearings dataset that reflect business regulation and

Figure 3.4. The Rise and Decline of Interest in Business Regulation by Congress

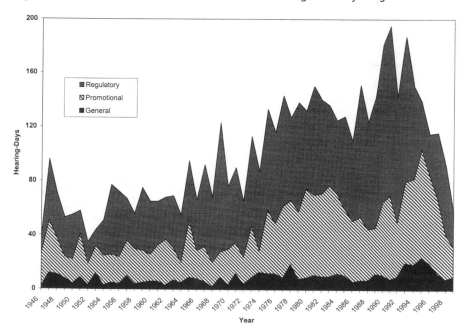

The subtopics for Policy Agendas topic 15, banking and financial regulation, were combined to generate the categories. Business promotion includes small business issues, disaster relief, and patents and copyrights. Business regulation includes antitrust, financial and banking regulation, consumer finance regulation, and consumer safety.

business promotion. The measure is the number of days of hearings devoted to the topic during the period of study. Generally, business regulation and promotion increased from the early 1950s until about 1990. Of course, without further study we can't say if the hearings concerning business regulation involved proposals for more regulation or less. But we can say that the whole matter pretty well dropped precipitously off the agenda during the 1990s. There was a very low level of monitoring business activity in general during that period.

With the urging of Federal Reserve chairman Alan Greenspan, several acts were passed relaxing rules on bank activities, including the depression-era prohibition on selling stocks and bonds. The Federal Reserve, responsible for bank regulation, itself relaxed regulations. The Securities and Exchange Commission (SEC), responsible for regulating the issuance and sale of securities and corporate governance and auditing practices, had similarly engaged for years in deregulatory activities, but by the mid-1990s had found some accounting and auditing problems among some corporations. As a consequence, with the support of President Clinton, the agency had written bills that would have tightened some auditing procedures. Congress rejected the package, with the opposition led by congressmen with large campaign donations from major accounting firms.

With little general interest in the arcane matters of corporate governance, financial and accounting regulation was supervised by a classic policy subsystem. While there were few calls for major overhaul, to the extent that the parties differed on the issue Republicans were more sympathetic to further deregulation, Democrats more sympathetic to tighter regulation. But many Democrats, including Senator Charles Schumer of New York, a recipient of major donations from accounting firms, resisted increased regulations.

In 2001, President George W. Bush appointed Harvey Pitt to head the SEC. Pitt, a securities lawyer whose clients had included major accounting firms, immediately promised "an accountant-friendly agency." The SEC would promote self-regulation by the accounting industry. An already "captured" regulatory subsystem was rapidly moving toward even more independence from general legislative oversight, and even more friendly attitudes toward the regulated.

The comfortable system of lax regulation and powerful positive policy image was destroyed by the corporate corruption scandals of 2001–2. The Houston-based energy company Enron declared bankruptcy in early November of 2001, at the time the largest bankruptcy in the history of the United States. Enron, under the leadership of Kenneth Lay, had transformed itself from a stodgy pipeline company into a market maker for energy contracts, using modern Internet technology to invent a more efficient way of trading and delivering energy. Unfortunately, the trading strategies were overextended and abused, with the company using questionable accounting practices to generate enormous profits while its auditor, the Chicago-based accounting giant Arthur Anderson, certified the result. The company's actions at Enron were to cause it to go out of business after losing a lawsuit. Investors lost billions of dollars, and "corporate governance," "corporate accountability," and "accounting scandals" were suddenly on the public agenda.

Initially, the Enron issue did not receive heavy press attention outside of the business pages. That all changed in December of 2001, when the extent of the scandal became clear. The share price of Enron had collapsed from over $80 in early 2001 to under $0.20 by early December; many workers' retirement accounts were destroyed. At the same time, California and other western states were accusing Enron of illegal manipulative actions during the energy

Figure 3.5. Coverage of the Enron Collapse in the *Washington Post,* December 2001–January 2002

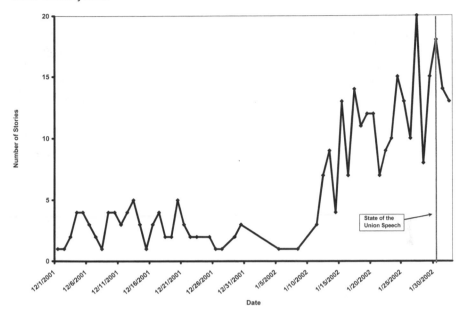

crisis of the summer. Figure 3.5 graphs the *Washington Post* coverage of the Enron collapse. Although the issue had been brewing all autumn, it gained the serious attention of policymakers and the media in mid-December—a month after the declaration of bankruptcy by the company. Just why the issue gained such traction exactly when it did is somewhat of a mystery, but it likely had much to do with the metaphorical dimensions of the issue: it "stood for" exploitation of consumers (with the company's manipulative energy policies), exploitation of workers by selfish management, and political corruption.

The Enron scandal had two results. First, serious corporate reform legislation was introduced by Sen. Paul Sarbanes of Maryland, chair of the Senate Committee on Banking, Housing, and Urban Affairs. Republican senators resisted that legislation. A far weaker bill was introduced in the House by Rep. Michael Oxley of Ohio, chair of the House Financial Services Committee, in mid-February of 2002. The Republican leadership in both houses of Congress remained firmly against major corporate reform legislation, as did President Bush, but the Enron fiasco moved the issue to the fore of the policy agenda.

Second, the scandal gave new momentum to the attempts by Senators Russell Feingold and John McCain and Representatives Christopher Shays and Michael Meehan to institute new campaign finance regulations, directed at the so-called soft-money donations. These donations, regulated in the original campaign finance legislation passed in the wake of Nixon's Watergate scandals, were intended to fund activities by the political parties to build organizations directed at turning out voters, but by the late 1990s they were being used in thinly veiled "issue ads"—essentially attack advertisements against the other party's candidates.

The effort had languished until the Enron scandal. While there was no inkling that campaign contributions to party organizations had anything at all to do with the emerging corporate corruption scandal, the McCain-Feingold bill (and the similar Shays-Meehan bill in the House) were readily available solutions. They could be used in anticipation of interpretations of the Enron scandal that could emerge. In effect, the availability of a policy solution helped to define the nature of the problem. McCain introduced his bill on January 22. It was considered by the Committee on Rules and Administration and referred to the Senate. In the House, the leadership had continued to resist the reform, but on January 24 a discharge petition was filed with the needed 218 votes (a majority) to remove the Shays-Meehan bill from committee. The bill passed 240–189 on February 14 and was sent to the Senate.

Campaign finance reform had always enjoyed likely majority support in the Senate, but chamber rules basically required a 60 percent vote to overcome a potential filibuster. During mid-March, campaign finance filled the chamber calendar for days. The Senate debated first "cloture," a tactic to break potential filibusters, which it passed 68–32, with several senators voting for debate when it became clear that the reform coalition had the majority necessary to invoke cloture. Campaign finance reform passed in final form on April 2 on a 60–40 vote. President Bush signed the bill on March 27.

The first impact of the corporate governance scandal was on campaign finance reform, an issue only tangentially related to the emerging scandal. An earlier financial scandal, the savings and loan debacle of the late 1980s, which had required a multibillion-dollar federal bailout, had implicated several legislators, including John McCain of Arizona. The scandal was a result of deregulatory legislation for savings and loan companies, essentially highly regulated limited-purpose banks. The so-called Keating Five had taken campaign contributions from corrupt savings-and-loan executives and intervened with regulators for them. The corporate governance scandal had no such story line, but clearly legislators wanted to try to blunt any such charge.

From Corporate Scandal to Corporate Governance

Major corporate governance reform faced opposition by Republicans in the House and in the Senate. But the issue was on the agenda, and on February 14 Representative Oxley introduced a bill dealing only with corporate disclosures. The Senate's Sarbanes bill included not only disclosure measures, but major regulatory reform concerning audits. Oxley's bill was debated before the chamber on April 24. Democrats attempted but failed on a party-line vote of 205–222 to recommit the Oxley bill to the Financial Services Committee with instructions to report out a stronger bill. The original Oxley bill then passed 334–90 and was sent to the Senate.

In June of 2002, the telecommunications giant WorldCom declared bankruptcy, eclipsing Enron as the largest bankruptcy ever. The corporation was accused of fraudulently manipulating its balance sheet. In late June and early July, the already shrunken stock market swooned, dropping day after day. The corporate corruption scandal just would not go away, and now pundits were drawing connections between the stock market decline and what was appearing to be rampant dishonesty among corporate leaders. President Bush, after ignoring the issue for months, gave a highly publicized speech on July 9 supporting corporate governance reform.

Legislative action quickly ensued. Rather than considering the weak Oxley bill, the Senate brought up the Sarbanes bill, invoked cloture 91–2 on July 12, and passed the bill on July 15 by a vote of 97–0. Phil Gramm of Texas, the ranking minority member of the Committee on Banking, Housing, and Urban Affairs, was highly critical of the bill. Gramm regularly invoked his status as an economist to justify deregulation, and did so again in making his deep reservations public in the debate over the Sarbanes bill. Even though he was not running for reelection, he did not vote against the bill. No senator would stand against corporate reform.

The Senate (Sarbanes) and House (Oxley) bills went to conference committee in late July, with the Senate version essentially prevailing. The House considered the conference committee report on July 25, voting to accept, 423–3. The Senate's vote of 99–0 on the same day was pro forma, since its position had prevailed in conference. On July 30, the president signed the Sarbanes-Oxley Act.

The politics of issue intrusion present a major conundrum for existing approaches to the study of American politics. Quick legislative action is clearly possible in the American system. How is one to explain the complete reversal of votes of the House Republican majority? If the House had stuck by its original position, supporting the Oxley bill while simultaneously rejecting a motion to craft stronger legislation, we would doubtless focus on the stability of ideological positions fostered by the overwhelming number of safe House districts. What sense can we make of a legislative party composed of members mostly elected from safe districts completely capitulating to a position rejected just weeks before? Why would a senator planning to retire change his position on an issue, as Gramm did?

Events break gridlock, as do elections. When issues intrude on a previously stable policymaking system, it is not unusual for any resulting legislation to be supported by overwhelming majorities. Yet major approaches stress interelection stability in the policy preferences of legislators (Krehbiel 1998) or the external role of public opinion, which in general is highly stable (Page and Shapiro 1992; Stimson 1999). An information-processing perspective, based on the limited attention spans of policymaking institutions, makes the disjoint and episodic nature of American policymaking understandable.

Neither simple partisanship nor electoral replacement can account for this dramatic policy shift. Of course, partisanship is important; the parties shaped the particular law passed. But both parties moved in response to the issue intrusion process. Second, elections cannot have generated the shift, because it occurred between elections. Finally, these were not the only cases of bankruptcy and corporate greed after the SEC was established in 1935. There were many others; yet the WorldCom scandal was the one that generated major reform. The emergence of issues can be as unpredictable as it is destabilizing.

The Geometry of Issue Intrusion

There were many signs of trouble in the nation's system of financial regulation long before Enron. The business pages carried stories about corporate excesses, and the SEC had detected problems and proposed ameliorative action. A proportionate adjustment process would have detected these problems and addressed them much earlier in the process, perhaps avoiding the corporate bankruptcies and associated upheavals of the early twenty-first century. But signals were ignored or dismissed. When these indicators were made vivid and more salient, they were incorporated into decision making, but by then "alarmed discovery" had set in. This is the classic kind of disjoint updating predicted by the implicit index model described earlier.

Issue intrusion often implies attribute intrusion—the reinterpretation of issues. We now turn to some spatial geometry to illustrate how this process works to disrupt the ideological equilibrium in a legislative body. At the top of figure 3.6 is an idealized version of Congress at equilibrium in late 2001.

Figure 3.6. The Intrusion of a New Issue Can Shift the Voting Balance in Congress

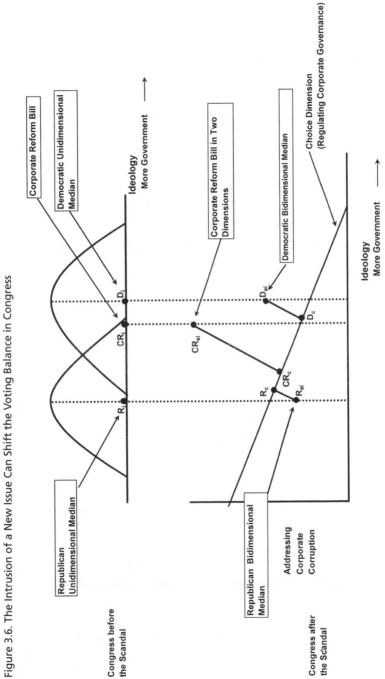
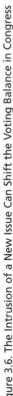

Decisions are made ideologically along a single line. Republican and Democratic medians are shown, with an indication of the spread along the dimension of individual legislators. As is the case in the modern Congress, the medians of the two parties are ideologically distinct, with little overlap between party members. Republicans are to the left and Democrats to the right, with more government intrusion to the right, and less to the left. Toward the Democratic side of the continuum is the estimated position of the Sarbanes corporate reform bill. Because of supermajority requirements, the bill, even though it is ideologically close to the position of the median legislator of the Congress (in between the two party medians) would not pass if brought up for consideration.

The effect of the intrusion of the accounting scandal was to give momentum to corporate reform legislation. The intrusion of this new attribute moves the decision space from a one-dimensional determinative system to a two-dimensional one. The bottom part of figure 3.6 shows the issue in two dimensions: the traditional ideological dimension and the new "corporate corruption" issue. Two dimensions now characterize the corporate reform bill: the older ideology dimension (in which Democrats would be more favorable toward regulation), and the new "corporate corruption" issue. Legislators do not get to vote directly on "addressing corporate corruption"; the real choice presented by the Sarbanes is rather "regulating corporate governance." Corporate corruption could be addressed in many other ways; the dimension or attribute is much broader than the actual choice dimension. The choice dimension no longer corresponds to ideology alone, since it now must incorporate both issues. Note that the corporate reform bill is high on the emergent issue, but is moderate on the ideology dimension; one can conceive of far more stringent regulations of corporate governance (and far less).

The choice dimension in effect weights the two attributes (ideology and the new corporate corruption issue) in determining the positions of the two parties and the now reinterpreted corporate reform bill. As a consequence, each of the three points in two-dimensional space (the bill and each party's median voter) is projected on this choice dimension. It can be seen that the Republican choice position is shifted much closer to the reform bill. The Democratic median is actually further away; they would prefer more effort be made to reform corporate governance. Now the reform bill passes with room to spare.

The major lesson here is that the intrusion of a new issue can destabilize the existing decision-making equilibrium. The institutional "gridlock"— which simply reflected the prevailing partisan balance and the set of institutional rules—has been broken by the intrusion of a new issue. That new issue, in this case, was a result of external events—the Enron and WorldCom collapses—but the particular interpretations that gained ascendancy centered on corporate governance.

Political gridlock does not always wait to be broken by new elections. When political gridlock is broken between elections, it is always broken by the dynamics of issue intrusion. As Krehbiel (1998) has argued, elections shift the prevailing balances of power, and these shifts in preferences, subject to the operation of institutions, should quickly establish a new policy equilibrium based on the preferences of the new legislators. Any change between elections must be a consequence of the intrusion of new issues or new attributes.

Welfare Reform and Issue Intrusion

Sometimes old issues get reinterpreted in the course of the political debate even in the absence of appreciable change in information. A case in point is the emergence of welfare reform in the late 1980s. While social welfare policies span the gamut from aid to the elderly to aid to the disabled, the term *welfare* invariably connotes aid to disadvantaged families. Government programs to aid disadvantaged families began as a measure to assist widows and orphans of Civil War veterans (Skocpol 1992), but the modern program was developed in the Great Depression as the Aid to Dependent Children program.

Throughout the late 1960s and most of the 1970s, welfare was a regular topic of discussion in Washington. President Nixon's ideas for reform centered on integrating the working poor into the system through the idea of a guaranteed national income or "negative income tax." A major argument in favor of that program was the elimination of the so-called notch effect for current welfare recipients. Because many other benefits, such as health care and housing, were keyed to the receipt of aid, many welfare parents (mostly mothers) faced a major problem in getting off welfare. If they got a job and earned as much as they did on welfare, they lost their ancillary benefits, making them worse off than if they had stayed on welfare and never gotten a job; the system had a disincentive to work, in other words. Nixon's program would have phased out payments as income rose, allowing people to keep welfare benefits while earning wages. The program was passed by the House, but defeated in Senate committee. Subsequently, under the leadership of House Ways and Means chairman Wilbur Mills, Congress passed the "earned income tax credit," which in effect paid the working poor and established, quite quietly, a negative income tax program.

Figure 3.7. Hearings on Aid to Disadvantaged Families and Hearings on Social Welfare Generally

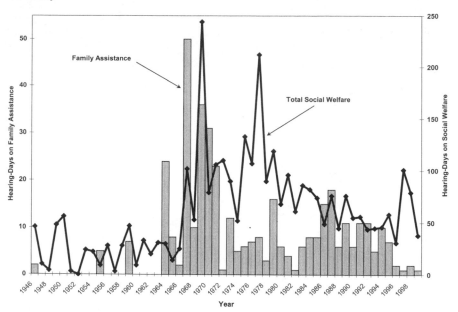

During the 1970s, congressional attention to welfare issues continued to address welfare reform, but also focused on financial difficulties of particular groups—elderly poor, rural poor, children in poverty, and so forth. After 1978, the issue dropped precipitously as a matter of national attention. Figure 3.7 diagrams the number of days congressional committees devoted to social welfare since the Second World War from the Policy Agendas Project. The figure also depicts the number of these hearings devoted solely to aid to low-income families.

Hearings on assistance for low-income families, however, trace a somewhat different path. Nixon's guaranteed national income generated considerable attention to the plan's effects on these families, but the topic dropped off the agenda in the mid-1970s, even while welfare as a more general topic was a central concern. In the late 1980s, however, family assistance returned to the legislative agenda even as welfare more generally continued to be a low-priority item. This time the impetus was the "neoconservative" welfare reform movement.

A closer look at this renewed legislative interest in poverty assistance is presented in figure 3.8. There we plot hearings focusing on targeted low-income family assistance and hearings on general social welfare, many of

Figure 3.8. Hearing-Days on General Welfare and Family Assistance

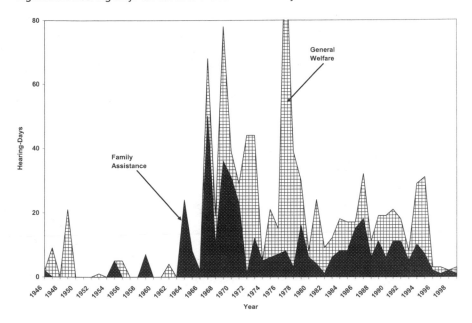

which concerned welfare reform and the administration of poverty assistance programs.[6] The renewed vitality of low-income assistance in the late 1980s and early 1990s is clear. In the 1970s, Congress and the executive branch focused on rationalizing and streamlining the diverse and confusing welfare programs, with an emphasis on cash grants to low-income individuals regardless of their working status. As is often the case in America, the reform movement failed and succeeded. It failed to eliminate the patchwork of welfare programs with particular targets—the infirm, the unemployed, children, the destitute elderly, the working poor—that had existed since the last century. It succeeded in putting in place a major nationalization of welfare programs with the earned income tax credit and the Supplemental Security Income Program.

The renewed interest in the 1980s focused again on particularistic welfare programs—and a relatively inexpensive one at that, Aid to Families with Dependent Children (AFDC). The heightened attention was a direct result of the reinterpretation of the incentive structure of poverty assistance programs—or, more accurately, the revitalization of an old argument. There is little doubt

6. We combined Policy Agendas topic codes 1300 and 1399 for the "general" category; topic code 1302 codes low-income assistance programs.

that this reinterpretation "had legs," as is said in Washington. Reinhard and Rojas (2002), in a phrase-by-phrase analysis of welfare reform hearings, detail the character of the arguments for and against reform. They show that the welfare reform movement had little relationship to any changes in information. The arguments pursued by proponents of the existing system centered on children in poverty and the numerous studies showing little variation in behavior of welfare recipients under different incentive systems. The neoconservative reformers hammered away at the logical flaws in the incentive systems, ignoring the potential effects on children and the factual studies. In addition, unlike during the welfare rights movement in the early 1970s, there had been no dramatic surge in the number of welfare recipients in the period immediately preceding the debate.

The neoconservative welfare reform movement of the late 1980s and early 1990s was based solely in logical analysis of incentive structures facing the poor. There had been no changes in the governing coalition (indeed, with the Democrats retaking the Senate in 1986, one would think that the defenders of the status quo would have been aided). There had been no change in the nature of the problem. Welfare rolls were falling. The arguments used by neoconservatives were not new; they had been used by the Nixon administration in its analysis of the welfare "notch effect" to support its arguments on behalf of a guaranteed national income. There was no "new information" in either the character of the problem or in the novelty of the arguments. Political coalitions had not shifted.

Yet the movement had serious legislative consequences. President Clinton promised to "end welfare as we know it" and signed the Personal Responsibility and Work Opportunity Reconciliation Act of 1996 doing exactly that. This act repealed AFDC and replaced it with Temporary Assistance for Needy Families (TANF), a work-oriented program with time limits. The new policy orientation is even more remarkable against the backdrop of declining legislative interest in social welfare matters more generally. Against a backdrop of declining statutory activity during the 1980s and 1990s was a surge of laws relating to poverty assistance. Indeed, family assistance policy dominated all welfare lawmaking activity during this period.

Finally we examine the role of public opinion in welfare reform attempts. Figure 3.9 traces the Most Important Problem responses by the public from the Gallup polling organization and the number of hearings on family assistance and general welfare reform. Public attention to welfare issues peaked twice: once in the 1970s, when Nixon's great reforms were a central topic of political conversation, and again, much more forcefully, in the 1980s and

Figure 3.9. "Most Important Problem" Responses Centering on Welfare and
Hearing-Days on General Welfare and Family Assistance

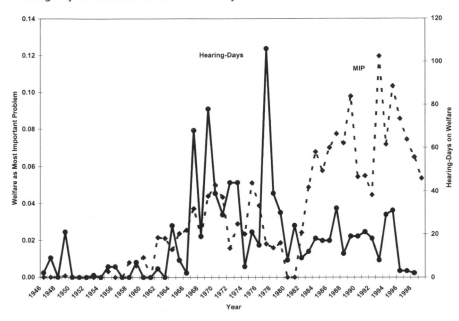

1990s. In neither case does welfare dominate the public agenda; the high point
of public concern was in 1993, with but 12 percent. Nevertheless, against the
backdrop of the past, this is impressive; prior to the increase beginning in
the mid-1980s, the peak was 5 percent, in 1975. This surge in public attention
probably was an important part of the successful neoconservative attack on
the particularistic AFDC program.

    The dynamics of issue intrusion and attribute intrusion show clearly
that as new elements arise, they can destabilize old policymaking equilibria. This can occur even in the absence of compelling or previously unknown information. Rather, mobilization cascades, lobbying campaigns, and
the search for new and potentially popular new issues make such dynamics
a permanent feature of the American policy process. They do not affect most
policies most of the time, but they are constantly in motion and always a possibility. While the Enron case clearly demonstrated the potential destabilizing
effects of a major and highly visible economic crisis, the welfare reform case
shows that new issues can be pushed successfully even in the absence of urgency. All it may take is the power of an idea that gains acceptance by many
others.

Breaking Gridlock: A Comparison between
Electoral Change and Issue Intrusion

Finally we turn from our two case studies of issue intrusion to a more general reflection on the relative roles of issue redefinition and the emergence of new political majorities as explanations of policy change. A policy equilibrium in Congress may be broken in two ways. The first is when the party balance is altered by an election. This brings in new legislators with preferences that may differ from that prevailing in the previous congressional session. Because Washington actors can come to believe that electoral change implies a policy mandate, policy change can occur on top of the electorally driven replacement changes (Peterson et al. 2003). The second mechanism is the issue-intrusion dynamic described in this chapter.

It is possible to compare, albeit roughly, the importance of these two equilibrium-breaking dynamics. Each two-year Congress is composed of two one-year sessions. If new coalitions are brought in via elections, we would expect that major legislation be passed in the first session of the Congress following the election. This does not apply to legislation generally, because much legislative activity is directed at noncontroversial matters. But for important legislation, we expect new legislation to be enacted in the first session, just after a major change in the policy preferences of participants. In terminology developed by Krehbiel (1998), the "gridlock interval" can be shifted by an election, and the resulting policy equilibrium would quickly adjust by moving right or left to match what is possible given the new majority and the set of institutional rules governing the policy process. Any electoral mandate augmentation should make first-year policy change even more impressive, because mandate effects are exclusively a first-year phenomenon. Issue intrusion can occur any time, but if major legislation is passed in the second session, the likely explanation is issue intrusion rather than elections.

We identified the 576 most significant laws passed between 1948 and 1998 (out of over 12,000 laws passed; for more detail see Jones and Baumgartner 2004). If we simply divide this important legislation into whether it passed in the first or second session of a Congress, we find that 280 passed during the first session, while 296 passed during the second. There is scant difference in the tendency of Congress to pass major legislation in the first or second session; what little difference there is favors the second session. Some congressional scholars have noted that first sessions typically are taken up with more information gathering and oversight, while second sessions see the looming next election as a clear deadline for action, so it does make some sense that lawmaking tasks might occur in the second session. But our findings are limited to "important legislation," and there is reason to expect that newly elected majorities would want to make their mark in such matters sooner rather than later. In any case, there is no relation between timing and the passage of major legislation. This fits better into an issue-intrusion model than into an elections-based explanation (though we believe that both are important causes of these changes).

While we would be able to assess the reasons for passage of these bills only through detailed case studies, the prima facie evidence is persuasive. The passage of major legislation cannot be explained by elections-induced shifts in the preferences of legislators. Indeed, the three major pieces of legislation we have examined in this chapter—the Sarbanes-Oxley Act of 2002, the Campaign Finance Reform Act of 2002, and the Personal Responsibility and Work Opportunity Act of 1996—were all passed in the second session of a Congress. We need a theory of political information processing to understand the passage of major legislation; a theory of election changes alone will not do.

Conclusions

Information has the power to shock, disrupt, and destabilize. Because people and organizations incompletely monitor the world, updating must be disruptive. The implicit index model illustrates how diverse sources of information must be weighted by a decision maker, but in the real world these weights are often incomplete. When reality impinges, implicit indexes must be updated episodically. A similar process applies to characterizations of issues. This incompleteness is not merely due to cognitive errors; the number of *potentially* relevant dimensions for any given issue is much too large to consider simultaneously. As we simplify decisions in order to make them, we make not only possible but also *inevitable* that from time to time a previously ignored attribute will leap to prominence. When previously ignored attributes and issues intrude, policy equilibria can be disrupted.

We have illustrated the shock value of information in the policy process in this chapter. In the next section of the book, we turn to more systematic tests of these ideas. These tests make use of the massive data resources of the Policy Agendas Project. The next section begins our systematic treatment of these ideas with evidence.

PART II

INFORMATION PROCESSING
AND POLICY PUNCTUATIONS

How does government prioritize problems? By what mechanisms do political leaders detect, interpret, prioritize, and respond to signals in the environment? In the previous section, we detailed a theory of how this happens. The *behavioral theory of policy choice* derives from some fundamental aspects of the cognitive architectures of human decision makers and insists that any theory of policy choice be based on a scientifically defensible model of human and organizational decision-making behavior. This theory extends those fundamentals to organizations, including public bureaucracies, legislatures, interest groups, and political parties. It emphasizes those aspects of the cognitive constitutions of humans and organizations that lead in general to an overreliance on the existing path of decision choice but which occasionally result in spasms of overreaction to information. The whole theory might be seen as an elaboration of mathematician Benoit Mandelbrot's dictum that "man tends to react by overestimation or neglect." Republican lobbyist Tom Korologos provided the organizational extension of Mandelbrot's insight when he quipped, "The things Congress does best are nothing and overreacting" (Dole 2000). This is an apt description of government more generally.

To this point we have said nothing about how the many organizations and political decision makers interact in the complex system of federalism and separation of powers that defines the American political system. After all, no single organization produces public policy in America. It takes considerable cooperation across organizational boundaries to produce policy outputs. In the most straightforward case, the supermajority requirements of American federal government require cooperation of a majority in the House of Representatives, a supermajority in the Senate, and the acquiescence of the president and, over the long run, the courts, to produce law. There are other nonconstitutional but no less formal requirements for cooperation, including internal procedures of Congress and the executive branch that must be fulfilled in pursuance of public policy actions, as well as myriad informal arrangements that also matter in how states, localities, or street-level bureaucrats may implement federal laws. And of course outside forces such as social movements, interest groups, and professional communities can pressure for change if they disagree with the policy.

This requirement of cooperation adds considerable friction to the process of making public policy. This friction, which generally operates to reinforce the status quo even beyond that predicted by the behavioral theory of policy choice, has often been described as "gridlock." Gridlock implies stasis. Scientific models of friction, however, imply dynamism. The pattern resulting from true models of friction is stable most of the time but with disjoint change occasionally—when the forces overcoming the friction are strong enough. Gridlock is stuck, locked, frozen; friction implies not being stuck, but having some level of resistance that, with sufficient force, can be overcome. Models emphasizing gridlock get the story partly right. But when that friction is overcome, the mirror image of gridlock occurs: dramatic bursts of policy change when the forces of politics are properly aligned. Friction, in other words, is not an absolute barrier to action, but rather a major hindrance. As it operates, pressures can mount, making change, when it does occur, more profound.

It is not enough to describe the formal arrangements for the production of public policy as friction or gridlock; that just is not a complete story. There has to be some understanding of the forces that overcome this friction. Changes that stem from shifts in attention come from the traditional policymaking mechanisms of political parties, interest groups, social movements, and the actions of individual policy entrepreneurs who are willing to devote time and energy to public life far beyond the rewards that would come from the expected return on the investment. Mostly these efforts are subject to the laws of negative feedback—they dampen out over time, making little difference. Once in a while, however, these efforts generate positive feedback, with more and more people becoming involved. This can break the friction that normally characterizes the American governing system. In chapter 3 we analyzed the dynamics that can produce such effects—the politics of issue intrusion. In fact, our model of collective choice shows that dramatic changes are inevitable, as the implicit index approach makes clear. Ironically, the dramatic changes are inevitable for the same reasons that the status quo bias can be quite strong. So friction is part of the story, a fundamental part, in fact. However, with friction comes lurching, once forces are sufficient to overcome the friction. So we see a combination of underreaction and overreaction to changes in the environment. This is why we agree with Tom Korologos that Congress, like government, does two things best: nothing and overreacting!

In the chapters that make up this section of the book, we analyze the complex interaction between the forces of friction and the sporadic, generally weaker, forces of political change. Our approach will be unfamiliar to many, because we drop any pretense of tracing the path of a particular policy issue. Chapter 4 explores in some detail the futility of pursuing this option. Paradoxically, this approach can be very successful for exploring the dynamics of a single policy, but it fails when one attempts to generalize beyond the particular case. (So we can *think* we know how the system works by studying a given case, but when we take that model and apply it to the next case, it typically fails, as we will show.) Instead we turn to the more global methods of stochastic processes, which put together many policies in the same analysis to examine overall patterns. These methods have the advantage of not locking us into an overly simplistic notion of policy causality; they incorporate the critical role of uncertainty and ambiguity in policy choice; and they allow the systematic testing of the policy friction notions sketched above. They also help us avoid the trap of ad hoc theorizing, or developing a different theory for each case we study. Further and perhaps most important, the stochastic approach permits some strong deductive tests of the *general punctuation hypothesis*, which states that institutions affect policy punctuations by adding decision costs, and hence friction, to the translation of inputs into outputs. Chapter 4 gets us as far as demonstrating the futility of the one-case-at-a-time approach to a general theory and shows a critical finding: when we consider all policy changes (as measured by spending) across fifty years, we see a distinctive "shape of change" that cannot be explained by any model focusing on inputs; rather, it corresponds to our friction model, and it shows both a tremendous tendency to "do nothing" as well as a great deal of overreaction, just as Korologos said. Chapters 5 and 6 develop the theory of cognitive and institutional friction, while chapter 7 demonstrates its validity with further tests.

4

"Understandable Complexity" in Policy Choice

Political systems process information disproportionately. What are the implications of that for policy change? Disproportionate response to signals implies substantial difficulty in relating policy outputs to informational inputs.
Decision makers are faced with many, often competing, indicators of problems, each of which is measured with substantial error. Each problem has
many possible solutions that are each somewhat uncertain and able to be
combined with various weights. How these many indicators, problems, and
solutions are weighted and combined is a major determinant of policy action.

The weighting of policy problems is dynamic. The connection between
signals and policy response is filtered through public debate about the priority of problems. This debate involves the standard suspects in democratic
political systems—political parties, interest groups, individual policy entrepreneurs, the media. Much debate concerns the relevance of policy instruments for addressing problems, but perhaps even more is directed at assessing and prioritizing these problems. Because different factors may come into
play at different times, there may not be any simple relationship between
indicators and policy action. The threshold for action even within a single
policy area may change over time as the nature of the problem and the desirability of government action are debated.

As a consequence, uncertainty, ambiguity, and contingency all play persistent and unavoidable roles in policy studies. The uncertainty we face is
not the simple, definable "expected utility" variety that a gambler faces at a
roulette wheel. Thinking back to our model of decision making in figure 2.1,
uncertainty and ambiguity affect each stage of the process, not only the final
linkage between the choices made and the likelihood that these policies will
achieve their goals. They include knowing what the most important issues

are, how these issues should be understood or defined, which solutions are available and appropriate, and how likely these are to work.

Unlike the game of roulette, with its relatively simple brand of uncertainty, the game of policy development never starts again; we can never rewind to the beginning. If we could, surely we would observe a somewhat different time trace of policy action. This historical contingency makes the world of policy development full of conditional probabilities—with the occurrence of one event changing the probabilities of future events—and probabilistic interaction effects, in which one event changes the probability of a second event being important in causing a third event. These interactions among events and variables compound so rapidly that one quickly loses the trail of causality. Or, more accurately, one comes to recognize the contingent and interactive nature of causality.

This historical contingency is fundamental to politics. It will not go away with calls for more general theory or more precise models. Yet, left unexamined, historical contingency becomes "thick description," undermining more general understanding. It must be incorporated as a fundamental part of our analysis of policy change. This is not impossible; evolutionary biology came out of a tradition of thick description of species but later developed into a fully causal theory. New developments in general theories of complex systems offer methods for grappling with open information-processing systems that evolve—like biological organisms, ecosystems, economies, and, yes, polities. In these next chapters, we use some of the tools developed in the study of complex systems to study policy development.

Before we embark on this task, we first set the stage by examining several cases that illustrate just how difficult the study of policy change can be. No one simple causal theory can explain policy change across all areas. This difficulty in generalization is one reason that policy studies has relied so heavily on case analysis. The clear and present danger of case studies is that a different causal theory will have to be deployed for each policy area, with no mechanism for resolving the contradictions among these various theories. This state of affairs has certainly characterized policy studies and has made it seem unripe for major theoretical advance; we believe this may be ready to change, but only with a different orientation toward what kind of theory we hope to advance, and what kind of evidence we look for.

Policies are commitments in the pursuit of achieving collective goals. These commitments can be laws or court decisions or executive orders or budgetary allocations, but they can also be investments of attention in a problem. In this chapter, we will focus on only one of these possible commitments—budgetary allocations to policy objectives in the form of U.S. congressional budget authority.[1] We trace the allocation of budget authority to several different policy areas since the Second World War. While the cases we discuss in this chapter are selected purposefully, they are by no means "cooked." They represent some of the most important arenas of federal government action in the postwar period (and, in later chapters, we will address all policy areas in a single analysis). We will show that each case is quite explicable, and we could argue for a particular causal path that dictated the outcomes we actually observe. Each case can be "explained" by reference to historical particulars, and the story will strike most as reasonable and satisfactory. But they are essentially ad hoc reconstructions with little theoretical value, in the sense that we cannot generalize the story to any kind of theory about policymaking. The "theory" that works for energy does not apply to crime; the one that works for defense does not apply to Social Security. What is a theory that cannot be generalized?

Why a "Theory of Budgeting" Cannot Be Produced

Spending money is central to politics. Budgets are key indicators of public commitments to the size of the public sector and to particular objectives when government gets involved. Given the importance of government budgets, it may seem surprising that political scientists have never produced a systematic theory of budgeting—a point noted as early as 1940 by V. O. Key Jr. The most ambitious attempt, by the 1960s' "bounded rationality budget school" led by Richard Fenno, Aaron Wildavsky, and colleagues, produced an unsustainable "incremental" viewpoint that was subsequently discredited.

A theory of budgeting has not been produced because it *cannot* be produced. The reason is simple: budgeting is part and parcel of the broader policy process, and without a theory of the policy process one cannot have a theory of budgeting. Once this is recognized it becomes clear that the incremental approach was (and still is) on target and that it missed only because of its failure to be integrated with a theory of agenda setting, attention allocation, and information processing. Surely the early students of budgeting may be forgiven for this omission; while the bounded-rationality budget studies flourished in the early 1960s, the systematic study of policy agendas was

1. Congressional budget authority is a commitment to an objective authorized by Congress. It differs from budget outlays, which occur when the money is spent. The Policy Agendas Project tabulates congressional budget authority for the Office of Management and Budget's subfunctions in a consistent and reliable manner from 1946 through 2003.

firmly established by Roger Cobb and Charles Elder only in 1972 (and the linkage between budgeting and agenda setting was not apparent at the time). There is, however, no excuse today for continuing debates about the "rights and wrongs" of incrementalism, or budget theories that are based in rational responses to events, or the selfish maximizing behavior of bureaucrats. Each of these debates is misplaced because it fails to grasp the central role of budgeting in any theory of policy change, and hence the impossibility of explaining budgeting outside of the framework of a general theory of policy change.

So far, we have shown how information processing is central to policymaking and hence cannot be explained by the traditional political forces— parties, interest groups, etc.—alone. Because of the bottleneck of attention and its system-level analogue, agenda setting, along with other facets of human and organizational cognitive capacities, information processing in the policy process is disproportionate. Surely, then, budgeting must be similarly disproportionate. This, in a nutshell, is what the incrementalists missed. They got the internal dynamics of budgeting right, but they did not appreciate the ramifications for budgets of agenda setting and disproportionate information-processing.

Whatever we say about public budgets we must be able to say about policymaking more generally. By examining first the difficulties in producing any generalizations about the process of public budgeting, we will be able to see the barriers to a more general theory of policymaking.

Macropunctuations: Looking at Overall Budget Commitments across Time

Before we examine particular policy areas, it is worthwhile to look briefly at the overall pattern of budgetary commitments since the Second World War. Figure 4.1 does this as a percentage area graph—that is, it ignores changes in the overall size of the budget, focusing only on the percentage of the total that each area consumes, for inflation-adjusted congressional budget authority. The categories are the U.S. Office of Management and Budget's major functions. The graph clearly indicates the long-term declining proportion of the budget that defense and related matters (veterans' benefits and international aid) consume. The focus on defense has been replaced with numerous different policy commitments as the public agenda has expanded. Note, however, that in the case of budgets, it is often difficult to pinpoint just when a policy begins. There are clear exceptions, such as Medicare, but most policies come from some minor commitment in the past. Income security, transportation,

Figure 4.1. Changes in Budget Authority, FY 1947–FY 2003

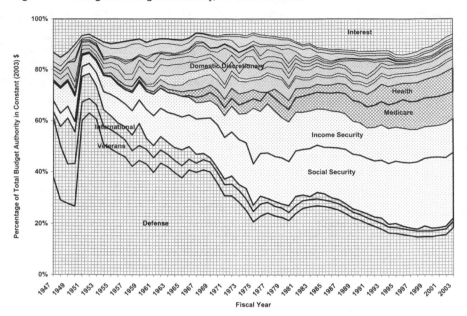

The figure shows the percentage of each annual budget by OMB major function.

health, housing, education, and most other policies had a presence in the
past—in the New Deal or before.

Often these commitments were paltry by today's standards or even by
yesterday's standards. Many programs began small and grew. But many
failed to grow, and some, even at the function level, have all but ceased to
exist. Energy is a case in point. After exploding onto the agenda in the 1970s
in response to the OPEC oil embargoes, funding commitment faded, dropping over the years to a mere fraction of the initial commitment. Government
commitments have dropped precipitously in real dollars, or have stabilized
at a level below an earlier strong commitment, in housing and community
development, transportation, science, and even agriculture as well. The surge
and decline of many domestic programs belies the argument that once established, interest groups generate pressure that causes those programs to
grow without end. This is clearly not true, and that pushes the problem of explanation to a different plane.

We cannot explain systematically just why a "warm spot" in a policy
commitment becomes "hot" and grows dramatically, any more than meteorologists can explain why any particular warm spot in the Atlantic Ocean
grows to become a hurricane (Zebrowski 1997). Most do not, of course, but a

few grow exponentially and produce great damage. So it would be nice to predict which "warm spots" will grow. So far the best meteorologists can do is to track the developing storms and understand the general highly interactive processes. They can't say with much certainty how those rapidly interacting variables will develop over short periods of time, even though they understand the process that explains their growth or decline.

Similarly, we cannot typically explain many of the differences between policies when we look at many of them; the differences always appear to be ad hoc and thus unrelated to a broad causal theory. But we can have a theory at a different level, as we will show in this book. That theory can explain the general patterns, even if it will still require close case analysis to see how it applies in each individual policy area. This is not unlike many areas of science that deal with highly interactive systems.

One explanation for observed patterns of budgetary commitment comes from changes in the general culture of government spending. Webber and Wildavsky, in their monumental *A History of Taxation and Expenditure in the Western World* (1986), note that political regimes and budgetary cultures underlie changes in budgetary commitments. Following up on this insight, in earlier work we used actual U.S. budgetary commitments to isolate dramatic shifts in "spending regimes" (Jones, Baumgartner and True 1998). Instead of examining overall budgetary commitments, we studied year-to-year percentage changes in commitments. We took the average real (that is, inflation-adjusted) percentage change for the Office of Management and Budget's (OMB) subfunctions, using the median to prevent the results from being too affected by outliers. Then we graphed the percentage change of the median subfunction across time, using time series methods to make sure the results were statistically stable.

In our study, we isolated three incidences of U.S. budgetary "macro-punctuations." These are shifts in overall spending behavior that reverberated throughout most programs funded by government. These are diagrammed in figure 4.2. The first of these occurred in fiscal year 1956 and represented a sizable upward shift in commitment to the typical government program. This upward shift, during the supposedly conservative Eisenhower administration and before the recession of 1958 brought a large and ambitious cohort of Democrats to Congress, may be surprising, but Eisenhower and Congress collaborated to build new initiatives in defense and education and science, and highways and housing and urban renewal, all of which together remade the infrastructure of postwar America. The second, an equally important downward shift, occurred in fiscal year 1976 with the "budget wars" between President Nixon and the Democratic Congress. The temporary shift was a result of

Figure 4.2. Macropunctuations in the U.S. Budget: Median Annual Percentage Change in OMB Subfunctions for U.S. Budget Authority, Actual and Predicted

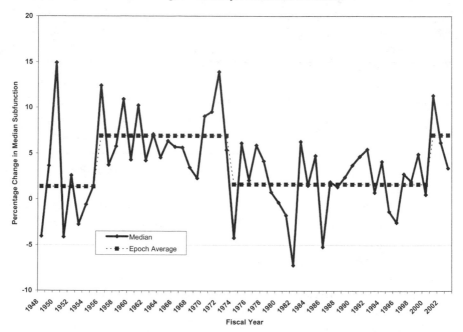

Nixon's impoundments, but the long-run drop in the growth in spending was likely a result of the Budget Control and Impoundment Act, which gave Congress a mechanism for monitoring and enforcing its budgetary commitments. This was followed up by a period in which Congress enacted a set of rules to ensure fiscal responsibility.

Recent research by James True (2004) demonstrates conclusively the existence of a third macropunctuation—occurring in 2001, following the election of George W. Bush. While one might think that the increased spending centered on defense and homeland security following the terrorist attacks of September 11, that is not the case. Spending rushed ahead in virtually every category; this was a clear and unmistakable shift from a regime of fiscal limits to a regime of rapid government growth. Particularly notable were huge new commitments in agriculture, education, and health care (with the addition of drug benefits to Medicare).

So one explanation of budgetary change is that it stems from macropolitical shifts that transmit signals downward to programs throughout government. Of course, we probably wouldn't have predicted that the major increases in budgetary commitment would occur in Republican administrations (Eisenhower and George W. Bush) or that the final upward macro-punctuation would occur during a period when Republicans controlled all branches of the national government. So by no means would we be out of the contingency problem even if everything could be explained though macro-level forces. It turns out, however, that macropolitics is an incomplete de-scription of what is going on in any case. An examination of particular pro-gram areas indicates that there are sufficient local forces affecting particular programs that a top-down model alone of budgetary change will not suffice. Let us have a look at some of these patterns.

Looking at Particular Policy Commitments across Time

If we follow the time path of a single policy, we find changes in expenditure patterns that are often associated with changes in the characterizations of the policy in public debate. New attributes emerge, and, as we detailed in the previous chapter, this can shift the focus of the debate in a manner that em-powers one side or the other. Sometimes these changes in characterizations are easily associated with external events, but many times they are not. We'll examine several traces across time of important budget categories to see this happening in policy outcome measures.

First we examine science policy. Figure 4.3 diagrams the OMB subfunc-tion "Science, Space, and Technology" for congressional budget authority in real dollars, both for totals and for annual percentage change. This is a classic policy punctuation with persistence (that is, spending ratchets up, then stays permanently at a high level). It is dominated by the response to the Soviet launching of the satellite Sputnik and by the strong commitment to a space program. This commitment led to a rapid ratcheting up of spending in the late 1950s, a decline as the symbolic goal of the manned moon walk was accomplished, followed by a leveling off at a high level of commitment. In perspective, we understand the space and science buildup as generated by a particular set of events, including Sputnik, the Korean War spend-down, and the Eisenhower administration's commitments to the development of the domestic infrastructure.

A broadly similar pattern characterizes a very different program area—income security, depicted in figure 4.4. The adoption of Supplemental Se-curity Income and the redesigning of welfare programs during the Nixon ad-ministration led to another example of a classic pattern of punctuation with persistence. Once the program was established, the government commitment to it continued. This is an explicable but essentially unpredictable outcome of

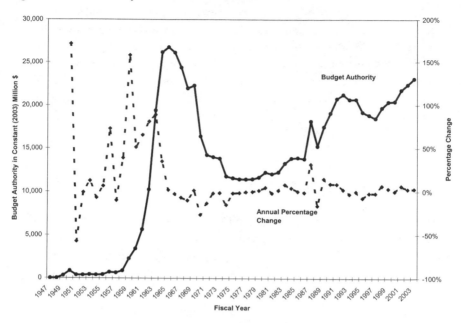

Figure 4.3. Science Policy Punctuates with Persistence

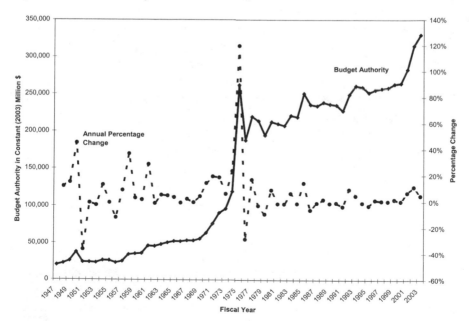

Figure 4.4. Income Security Punctuates with Persistence

a complex dialogue concerning the reform of welfare, put on the agenda by President Nixon. It is a case of clever policy entrepreneurs and public officials gaining a major policy innovation by "hijacking" existing welfare concepts to, in essence, enact the framework for a guaranteed national income.

While these two very different programs display similar patterns, they occur at very different times (the only constant is that both occurred under Republican presidents facing Democratic Congresses). The science and space buildup occurs, basically, during the first budget macropunctuation, but the increased commitment to the income security of the less well-off happened at the very end of a long period of government growth. The timings of these two punctuations are, of course, explicable by anyone with a basic knowledge of the policy history of the United States. But could one honestly say that each of these two events could have been precisely predicted? More importantly, if so, would that prediction also apply to other areas?

Figure 4.5 depicts change in budgetary commitment to education by the federal government. This pattern is in essence explicable by the overall pattern of macropunctuations. Spending ratchets up in the late 1950s, increases at a brisk rate until the late 1970s, falls back in the late Carter and early Reagan years, but resumes more modest growth in the late Reagan period. The

Figure 4.5. Education Funding Ratchets Up in Several Large Steps, Then Levels Off

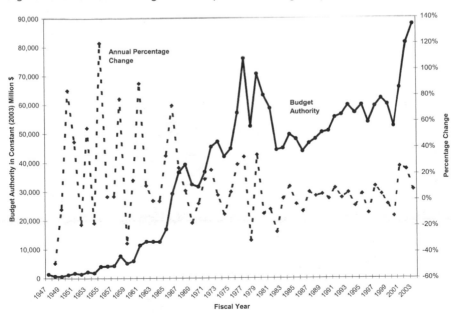

story is plausibly general: the federal government assumes a role during a period of expansion of federal powers; that role grows during a period of faith in government; economic difficulties and a declining faith in government cause a sharp retrenchment, but conservatives are unable to eliminate the federal presence. Then George W. Bush's No Child Left Behind Act pushes spending skyward.

Unfortunately, many areas, including crime, do not follow that script. The federal role in crime policy is driven by two dramatic periods of increase (fig. 4.6). The first, in the late 1960s, follows policy commitments to local governments after the civil disorders of that period. That commitment levels off during the 1970s; unlike education, which benefited from the general period of increases in government spending that characterized the United States from the late 1950s to the late 1970s, crime and justice languished. This period of inaction was interrupted in the mid-1980s with an even more dramatic increase in the federal role in crime policy, with large increases in spending from 1983 right through the end of the presidency of Bill Clinton. There was nothing "conservative" about this large-scale expansion of federal power in the very sensitive area of law enforcement.

Figure 4.6. Crime and Justice: Rapid Increase, Leveling Off, and Explosion

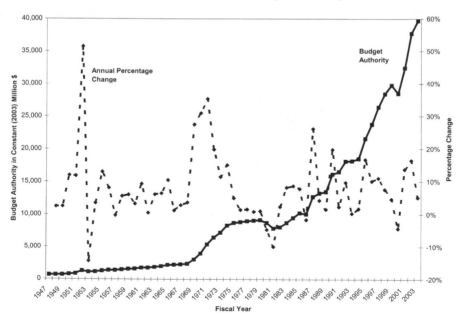

Even more problematic, while one might see the budget buildup following the Omnibus Crime Control and Safe Streets Act of 1968 as a response to events, what drove the second, more dramatic spend-up in the 1980s and 1990s? Crime statistics cannot account for the change; crime increased through the 1970s, when spending was constant, and was decreasing during the 1980s and 1990s, when spending grew. Drug use, at least as measured by surveys, declined during that period. Perhaps the public's distaste for crime and drug use was "mobilized" during a "window of opportunity" by "policy entrepreneurs." This is doubtless correct, but when are we to use the "window" explanation, and when are we to use the "increased faith in government" explanation? Even within one area we are sorely tempted to draw down on multiple theories to explain the patterns.

This by no means ends the confusing complexity in patterns of spending. Figures 4.7 and 4.8 focus on changes in expenditures rather than on total expenditures. Figure 4.7 shows that commitments to both education and the environment were boosted over a fairly short period of time and then leveled out, but that these fresh federal commitments occurred at different times. Of course, a rudimentary knowledge of history suggests why: education came

Figure 4.7. Education and Natural Resources Experience Different Periodicities

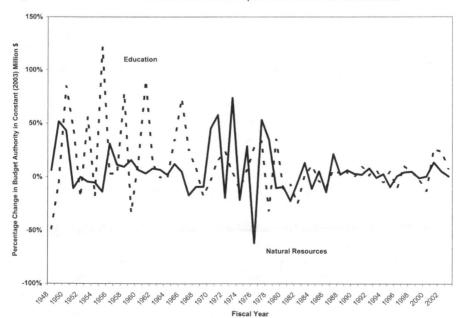

Figure 4.8. Social Security and Medicare Display Different Periods but Similar Amplitudes

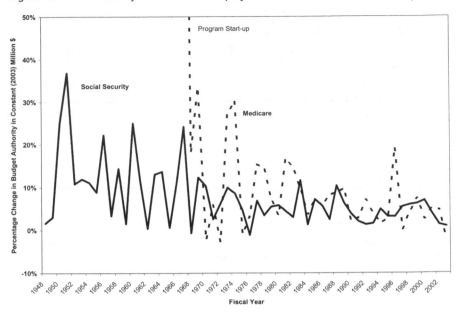

on line in the 1950s, and the environment in the 1970s, when the "times" were distinctly different. But where is the underlying explanatory frame? While one might note that environmentalism was driven by a "social movement," education quite clearly was not—at least until the more modern privatization/home schooling/charter school push. While new elements certainly entered the equation—the GI Bill after the Second World War, the Eisenhower science initiatives in the 1950s, and the commitment to the cities and the poor during President Johnson's Great Society—the explanation must include established interest groups and government employees. When would one use a "social movement" to explain change, and when would one not? And in any case, where did the social movement come from?

Figure 4.8 compares the two major national entitlement programs: Social Security and Medicare. Both display a tendency to "settle down" over time—that is, percentage changes decline across time. Earlier in a program's development there seems to be a tendency to increase it, probably in response to its popularity among beneficiaries. As cost estimates increase, the program is reined in. But Medicare tends to be more volatile than Social Security, as a consequence of its relationship to the health-care costs that are beyond the direct control of policymakers. Changes in Medicare are explained by funda-

Figure 4.9. Agriculture and Education Experience Different Periodicities and Amplitude

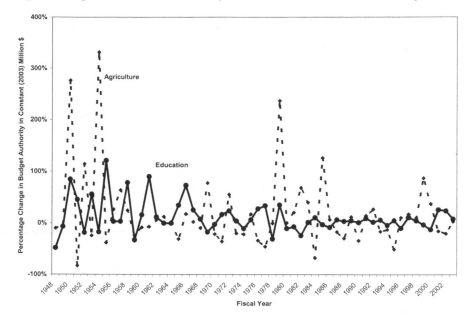

mentally unpredictable forces in the economy, whereas changes in Social Security are a function of the choices made by policymakers and can be traced through fairly straightforward actuarial methods. Any theory of budgeting must incorporate more than the preferences of policymakers; it must take account of changing circumstances that affect program development—that is, it must incorporate information flows.

Finally, figure 4.9 shows that education and agriculture are characterized not only by different periods of growth, but also by differing amplitudes during the buildup. As dramatic as the increases in education seem in figure 4.7, they are dwarfed by the bursts of commitment by the federal government to agriculture. Agriculture is complicated by the fact that farm payments are affected both by legislation and by the state of the farm economy. Legislation can be written (and is in the case of farm policy and some other areas) in a manner that holds budgets hostage to the details of the legislation: That is, the legislature can write itself into a "nondiscretionary" or "mandatory spending" commitment—in this case, to make up the difference between some target price of commodities and the world market price. Budget writers need not honor this legislation—there are many areas in which they simply ignore statutory commitments to budget levels—but they do not in the case of agri-

culture. Why? Because of the "strength of the farm lobby"? Would we measure lobby strength by the ability to lock in budgetary commitments? Congress did not have to pass this as a mandatory program in the first place, and
in any case, undoing a "mandatory" program involves only another legislative vote.

The Fascinating Case of Defense

If there is one area in which external events simply and directly drive budgetary commitments, surely it is defense policy. Wars affect defense budgets.
In figure 4.10 we depict defense budget authority. Our use of congressional
budget authority rather than budget outlays is an improvement on earlier
studies, because budget authority is tabulated at the time a commitment is
made. For example, for the acquisition of a new weapons system over a ten-
year period, BA is recorded at the time the commitment is made; outlays
would be tabulated over the entire ten years as the Department of Defense
paid for the system. In the figure, the Korean War spend-down is clearly in
evidence, as is the three-year spend-up for Vietnam and the just as rapid re-

Figure 4.10. Defense Budgeting Is Responsive to War and Politics

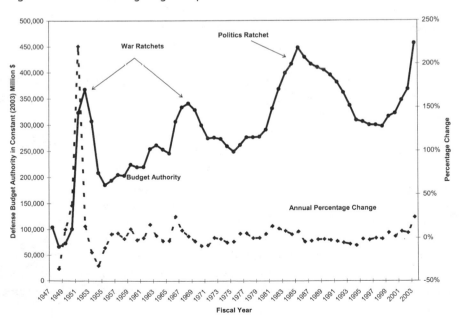

turn to normalcy during 1970–72. The war ratchet works. What dominates the graph, however, is the Reagan mobilization. Neither war nor a change in threat capabilities but political attention to a perceived opportunity drove a vast and sustained defense mobilization between 1980 and 1985. The Reagan buildup actually began in the last years of the Carter administration. Following the 1979 Soviet invasion of Afghanistan and the failed U.S. effort to rescue embassy hostages in Iran, the last Carter budget submission called for substantial increases for defense. That was augmented by a Reagan supplemental budget request in 1981, with new growth in defense expenditures until 1986.

There was no evidence at the time that the Soviet threat had increased. Indeed it is clear now (and was known with high probability then) that the Soviet Union was so crippled internally that any threat to the United States would be driven by a breakdown of the "balance of terror" that had characterized the relationship between the two superpowers since the mid-1950s. President Reagan argued that the "evil empire" could be defeated, not contained, and set about on a military program that could not be matched by the Soviets. This was both good policy and good politics, as it turned out, but the deliberate destabilization of the quarter-century of stable relationships carried substantial risks of an attack by a dying giant.

In any case, by no stretch of the imagination could the Reagan defense buildup be characterized as a response to external threat. It was, pure and simple, driven by politics. No better picture of how exogenous and endogenous factors combine to yield public policy can be drawn than this picture of defense spending. War mobilizations since the Second World War yielded less pronounced increases in military spending than the 1980s Reagan "politics" buildup in real dollar terms.

It is not possible to see the Reagan defense increase as somehow stimulated by an "external shock." The war ratchet cannot account for *all* defense buildups since the Second World War; it is a sufficient condition but not a necessary one. We do not argue that this response was somehow detached from the external threat. But we do claim that understanding this incredible increase requires an eye both to external events and to how these events are defined and communicated internally. In the terminology of chapter 2, the characterization of defense policy underwent a change in the Reagan administration. While we might be willing to view great budget increases as a consequence of the outbreak of wars as "exogenous," are we willing to so treat an outbreak of politics?

We can go even further. Over the years, as James True (2002) has shown, the bases and justifications for military policy have changed; the weighting of the attributes underlying our understanding of defense shifted as the public debate and the wishes of the military establishment changed. These changes are often vigorously debated within and at times outside of policymaking circles. With alterations in the political understanding of the use of defense power come changes in deployment and expense. Money follows politics.

Cynics may argue that this is all about the care and feeding of the "military industrial complex"—the network of uniformed military, congressional defense and appropriations committees, industrial suppliers, and local interests seeking to preserve and enhance jobs and economic growth. So any excuse to build up the complex will do. If so, then how do we explain the spend-downs? By the late 1990s, in real dollars, defense spending was only marginally above what it was in 1963—$280 billion versus $251 billion in 1996 constant dollars. In 1963, the defense budget consumed 60 percent of federal spending. In 2000 it was down to 20 percent. This would seem to be a very poor performance for an all-powerful steamroller.

Our budget analyses in this chapter stop with fiscal year 2003. The United States continues to be in the throes of a massive military buildup under the administration of President George W. Bush. In real dollars, fiscal year 2004 registered the largest percentage change for defense since the Vietnam War. From 1965, the first year of the Vietnam buildup, through 1968, the defense budget grew 39 percent. With only the first Iraq supplemental included, the inflation-adjusted defense budget swelled by one-third from 2001 through 2004. The comparable Reagan defense buildup, from 1981 through 1984, was 25 percent. But politics, rather than straightforward external threat, has again driven the defense budget. The Bush doctrine of "preemptive war" justified the attack on Iraq and has led to massive expenditures.

A Cross-Sectional Look at the Budget

The story we can tell through the time traces of budget changes might be characterized as "understandable complexity." The patterns are complex and confusing, but, on examination, are entirely understandable. That is, they can be reconstructed with a plausible story line. Each time trace of budgetary commitments to a governmental objective is comprehensible from a simple knowledge of American political history. Certainly, policy experts think they understand each of these particular cases. Education experts understand the education story, defense specialists will not learn from us about the defense story, and so on. Yet a description of the overall pattern of change is elusive.

Figure 4.11. Percentage Change in Real Budget Authority by Subfunction,
FY 1955–56

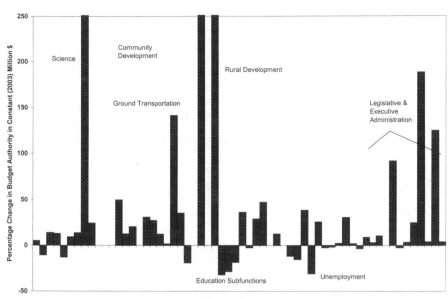

OMB Budget Subfunction

The same conclusion emerges if we cut the budget a different way. Instead of looking at a subfunction across time, we look at all subfunctions during a single year. We tabulate the percentage change in noninflated money commitment to all objectives from one year, say 1955, to another, 1956. Indeed, this comparison is an interesting one, because 1956 was the "Eisenhower growth budget," setting off a period of vigorous government growth in domestic programs that continued for two decades. Figure 4.11 is a bar graph of percentage changes in subfunctions that occurred between fiscal year 1955 and fiscal year 1956.

The powerful growth forces are clearly in evidence. Major expansions occurred in science and technology (belying the notion that the postwar investment in the scientific infrastructure was driven by the Soviet space successes; Sputnik was launched on October 4, 1957); community development and urban renewal, disaster relief, health care, highways and mass transit, and a host of other initiatives. Even during this year of budgetary plenty, however, several important governmental functions suffered large curtailments. Education, in particular, was affected, with funds going to higher education, elementary education, and research each cut by more than 25 percent. Energy

Figure 4.12. Percentage Change in Real Budget Authority by Subfunction, FY 1981–82

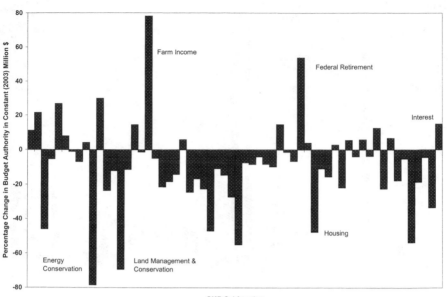

and unemployment spending were cut heavily, as was foreign aid. In the case of the postwar budget explosion, the rising tide did not lift all boats.

Let us have a look at a second budget cross section. Figure 4.12 depicts the changes in budget authority that occurred in fiscal year 1982, the year following the Reagan-initiated budget reconciliation cuts of 1981. Figure 4.12 shows how draconian the cuts implemented in that year were, at least for domestic subfunctions. Many of the Reagan cuts did not prove to be permanent (several bounced back in FY 1983), but the general trend is accurately reflected in the figure; compared to figure 4.11, figure 4.12 shows more long lines in the negative territory than in the positive area. Reagan cut the budget substantially in many important areas.

Land conservation, energy conservation, employment training, and housing sustained large cuts in 1982. Also hit hard were air transportation (President Reagan terminated federal air controllers who went on strike in defiance of federal law) and several urban development programs. At the same time as these areas were cut, however, several programs did well, including defense, nuclear defense programs (Reagan promoted and funded the nuclear missile defense shield), and farm income stabilization (which soared 77 per-

Figure 4.13. Percentage Change in Real Budget Authority by Subfunction, FY 1990–91

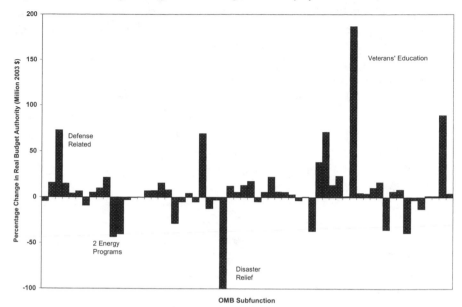

cent). Reagan and Congress were also unable to prevent a large rise in interest payments, driven by large deficits and by increases in federal retirement payments. So even in this year of many cuts there were many substantial increases as well. Incrementalism is certainly not the entire story. But neither is fiscal conservatism.

Finally, we examine in figure 4.13 fiscal year 1991. That year was the high point of the post-Reagan growth in liberal public mood, yet it is located well within the "era of limits" inaugurated in 1976. Growth occurred, but it occurred very selectively. Several defense programs benefited from the Gulf War, as did veterans' education programs, which soared 180 percent. Selected transportation programs received increases, as did health, housing (70 percent real increase), and unemployment insurance. Disaster relief expenses dropped, as did certain business promotion and energy programs. This pattern looks very much like what might be expected from a government addressing problems issue by issue rather than sticking to a predetermined limit or getting caught up in a cascade of new government programs. If there were a typical "incremental year" in government, FY 1991 is what it would look like.

"Understandable complexity" just as surely characterizes a year-by-year approach to budget behavior as it does a time-series program-by-program look. We need to know a great deal to understand budgets. We need to know the general era of growth or retrenchment; we need to know the particulars of programs; and we need to know the political dynamics of specific years. If large changes in particular programs were always associated with shifts in overall levels of government activity, then we could neglect program and annual variability and just concentrate on a general model of budget behavior. Unfortunately this "top-down" model does not invariably hold. Rather, major program punctuations can occur at any time, and *these punctuations change the budget landscape for a very long period of time.* In policy studies, the past is prologue.

All Together Now

It makes sense to try to combine all aspects of budget change into a single picture. We do this by making a frequency distribution of budget changes. In essence, we combine the program-by-program and the year-by-year analyses we went through above. That is, we simply combine into a single analysis all annual percent changes in spending from year to year, for each of about sixty categories of spending as tabulated by OMB since 1946. The result is a budget change frequency distribution, depicted in figure 4.14.

The bars on the figure represent the number of real-dollar annual percentage changes in subfunctions that were in a particular range. The center of the diagram is at the modal year-to-year change. This is not quite zero because the typical (modal) government subfunction moved upward at over 4 percent a year over the period. Lots of these changes were fairly small— many, many of them were between a 4 percent real cut and a 12 percent real increase. But lots of them were very big—seventy-five grew at an annual rate greater than 160 percent.

The figure also depicts several of the program changes that we have focused on in this chapter. In 1951 and 1952 the Social Security reforms of 1950 began to hit the budget, and they did so in a dramatic fashion. In FY 1956 the impact of the massive Federal-Aid Highway Act of 1956 began, but it is clear that Congress had lots of money to spend from the Highway Trust Fund as Americans turned en masse to the automobile. (The Highway Trust Fund is funded by the federal gasoline tax; the more miles driven, the higher the tax revenues. This money does not go into general funds and cannot be spent in

Figure 4.14. Budget Change Frequency Distribution

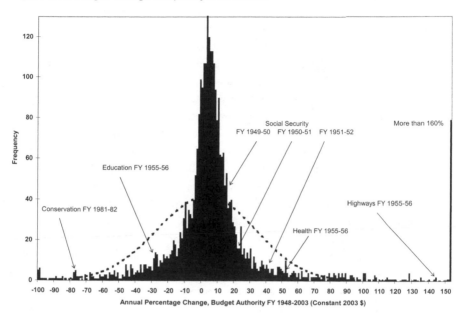

other areas.) In at least some areas, money can drive statutes. Conservation took a heavy hit in the early years of the Reagan budget revolution, as did education in 1956. Clearly, ideology and politics matter in other areas.

More programs grew than shrank during the postwar period, and by a substantial margin. Not only did the modal program grow, but there are more cases in the positive tail of the figure than in the negative one. Nevertheless many programs were cut, some substantially. A 25 percent cut in a government program is not that unusual.

More important is the overall shape of the distribution. First, it is *skewed* toward the positive side. This just indicates that more programs grew than shrank. Second, and more importantly, it has a combination of fat tails and a slender central peak. Statisticians refer to "peakedness" of a distribution as *kurtosis,* and this particular distribution is *leptokurtic:* compared to the normal curve, it has a higher than expected central peak, weaker "shoulders," or numbers of moderate changes, and a great many more outliers than would be present in a normal curve of similar variance.

For students of policy change, this distribution has a very important meaning. Many, many programs grew or were cut very modestly—that is, incrementalism was the order of the day for most programs most of the time. *Hyperincrementalism* might be a more accurate term for what happened in the vast majority of the cases. But sometimes programs received huge boosts, propelling them to double or triple their original sizes or more. Sometimes, but less often, programs lost half or more of their funding. Moderate increases or decreases were rather unusual, on the other hand.

It is not at all hard to understand why this pattern occurs. Once new programs and agencies to implement them are created, a set of budget rules and operating procedures are established. The agencies attract interest groups and are monitored by individual supportive congressmen and oversight committees in Congress. Inertia sets in. Only a major mobilization or a major problem or scandal is likely to disrupt the prevailing pattern of conducting business. That mobilization can be part of a general turn toward government, but it can also be a specific response to a particular problem. For example, disaster relief funding is very volatile, as are farm programs; these programs are very sensitive to changes in external events. Other programs may take major political mobilizations to change—such as was the case with the Reagan attacks on housing and urban programs in the early 1980s. It is, however, not unusual for programs to experience dramatic growth later in their development. Social Security was expanded in such a fashion in the early 1950s, and highway transportation jumped in the mid-1950s.

Figure 4.14 should end the debate about incremental budgeting once and for all.[2] Incrementalism and punctuated budget change coexist within a single framework. The slender peaks of the figure mean that the vast bulk of year-to-year budget changes are indeed incremental. They are minor tweaks on past appropriations. But the fat tails of the distribution mean that a sizable number of changes are abrupt and distinctly nonincremental. As we have seen, these abrupt changes are not always associated with program start-ups. Rather, they appear to be a constant part of the process; there is always the chance that a given area of policy will become the object of renewed attention and fundamental rethinking. Sometimes these come from external shocks, but at other times from complex social and political mobilizations. So the process combines an extreme status quo orientation with the possibility of dramatic change, and the dramatic change is not related only to external shocks

2. The finding is not specific to the U.S. national government. Research in a variety of different settings has confirmed the basic finding of leptokurtic distributions of budgetary change. Jordan (2003) finds the pattern for U.S. local expenditures, John and Margetts (2003) for the national budget for Great Britain, Mortensen (2003) for Danish local budgets, Robinson (2004) for Texas school districts, and Breunig (2004) for Germany. It is a general characteristic of public budgeting.

but also to internal issue redefinitions. Note also that these dramatic changes can be on the high side, but they can also be and often are on the low side. Programs are drastically cut as money is reallocated to other purposes. Attention shifts have great consequence.

Conclusions: "There Are a Million Stories in the Budget"

We have now come full circle in our examination of budgeting in the United States. We argued pages ago that political scientists had not developed a theory of budgeting because the task could not be accomplished. It cannot be accomplished because budget outcomes cannot be tied to budget behavior. Bounded rationalists thought that budget behavior operated within a set of norms that stabilize expectations. Comprehensive rationalists thought that agency chiefs maximized their budgets subject to constraints. Neither model is satisfactory, because broader policymaking forces tied to the flow of events and ongoing policy debates can intervene to upset the "normal" behavior of bureau personnel.

Early studies of budgeting emphasized the incremental nature of budget rules and basically swept major changes under the table. The next generation of budget scholars "threw the baby out with the bathwater" when they found many programs were not incremental at all. A better approach is to integrate the incremental theory, which holds quite well for times in which major attention is not directed at a program, with a theory that appreciates the role of policy punctuations as well.

This is fine as far as it goes, and certainly an improvement on either the first or second generation of budget studies. Things would be simplified if major changes in programs occurred only when public opinion shifted, or when party control changed, but that is not the case. It is the case that major budget changes that do not correspond to political changes are easily explicable, at least with the benefit of hindsight. We are dealing with an "understandable complexity," not a bewildering randomness.

Understanding "understandable complexity" requires, if not a "million stories," at least a story line for every budget observation.[3] Otherwise, the elusive goal of "prediction at a point" can never be attained. Unfortunately, telling a convincing story about each budget observation means that no generalization is possible. Creating a budget frequency distribution with clear

3. "There are a million stories in the budget" is a comment by Jim True about efforts to impose order on "understandable complexity."

characteristics of punctuation and incrementalism gives us a starting point for a more systematic investigation of policy change. It is the distribution we want to understand, not the historically contingent particulars. This approach, known as a stochastic process approach, will not, in the end, allow us to make "point predictions" about just when major punctuations will occur. But it will allow us to discuss the stages of public policy in a whole new light, one far more amenable to systematic thinking than are current approaches. And it allows us to test our theories of disproportionate response. We turn to this task in earnest in the next several chapters.

5

Incrementalism, Disproportionate
Information-Processing, and Outcomes

We closed chapter 4 with a picture of a frequency distribution of year-to-year changes in U.S. budget authority since the Second World War. Summing across a diversity of different causal processes—the "understandable complexity" of that chapter—yields a distribution of outcomes that is generally very stable but is interrupted by occasional strong shifts: the large changes, positive and negative, of the tails of that distribution.

Chapter 4 summarizes our ignorance about the causal processes underlying budget change. By summing our ignorance, however, we have learned something very valuable. The overall pattern of budget change is characterized by large-scale disruptions, even if the vast majority of changes from year to year are very small. Moreover, it seems futile to try to describe policy change in overly simple terms. The obvious historical contingency apparent when analyzing any one of the policies that we followed in that chapter shows that any general model, no matter how complex, is unlikely to predict policy change very well, or even to describe policy change in more than one policy arena.

We can nevertheless move well beyond description. We will do so by harnessing a methodology that addresses directly the stochastic processes underlying policy change. In stochastic process approaches, randomness and uncertainty are fundamental to the process. Regression studies, popular in political science, policy studies, and social science more generally, are based on a model that would exactly predict particular outcomes, except for an "error term." This error term summarizes uncertainty, so that uncertainty is an "add-on" to the model, not fundamental to it. And of course, the error is assumed to be unbiased, with an average value of zero, and to be normally distributed.

Stochastic process models try to ascertain what kinds of probability distributions could have accounted for an observed distribution of outcomes, and therefore what kind of process could have produced it. They are most useful when the exact specification of a model is not possible, either because of essential complexity and uncertainty or because of the current state of scientific knowledge. While political scientists have tended to gravitate more to point prediction models and regression studies, stochastic process approaches have become increasingly popular in the natural and biological sciences, especially in those areas where analysts are dealing with multiple interacting variables—complex environments, in other words. A major reason is the recognition of the key importance of extreme values in the determination of the time paths of complex systems (Sornette 2000). Like the enormous meteorite that brought about the demise of the dinosaurs, extreme values can shift the very nature of a system. The more traditional regression studies relegate these critical values to the error structure of "unexplained variance." Such an approach is warranted when the model is well understood and the errors are normally distributed, but in the process we describe the processes are not well understood nor are the underlying distributions statistically normal. When there are many extreme values, not just an occasional outlier, the assumptions underlying traditional regression studies break down. So we need to look for more appropriate models.

In this chapter we use this stochastic process approach to examine the connections between the standard incremental model of policy change and the information processing model we develop in this book. First we discuss policy change, the incremental model, and its stochastic implications. Incremental decision making implies a normal distribution of policy changes. Then we return to the information-processing approach, showing that proportionate information processing—making decisions proportional to the strength of environmental signals—is consistent with incremental decision making. It also predicts a normal distribution of policy changes. Disproportionate information-processing, however, requires major modifications of the incremental model. It predicts a particular type of distributions of outcomes that can be distinguished from the normal with simple statistical tests. As a consequence, we can be certain that any non-normal distribution of policy change is sufficient to reject the incremental model. Non-normality, moreover, signals disproportionate information-processing. So we demonstrate that our model of disproportionate information-processing is expected to produce a particular non-normal statistical distribution of policy changes over time. In later chapters we will show that the observed distributions, such as that in figure 4.14, are consistent with the information-processing approach but not with an incremental approach or any proportionate-response model of the policy process. For now, however, we focus on showing how our model of policy change relates to different possible patterns of outcomes.

Policy Change

Patterns of change can be described as time series or as change distributions. A *time series* simply follows a variable of interest (like a category of expenditure) through time, as we did in the previous chapter (see figs. 4.3 through 4.10). A *change distribution* takes the period-to-period change (year-to-year change in expenditures, for example) and studies them without respect to when they occurred, as we did in figure 4.14. How many big changes, how many small changes, were there? How volatile or stable was the distribution? Was it normally shaped, bimodal, uniform, or did it have a different shape? If we look at a picture of a time series, we are inevitably drawn to the study of particular changes, and we tend think about what caused the changes at particular times when we see that something dramatic occurred. If we look at a picture of a change distribution, our attention is drawn to the pattern of changes rather than to the particulars of individual changes over time. The two approaches are useful for different purposes. Of course, the time series approach is much more familiar to all of us.

A policy change is an alteration in the commitment of a government to an objective. This may involve a budgetary commitment, as we analyzed in the last chapter, but it may also be a commitment of the legitimacy of government through a statutory enactment, or the commitment of organizational capacity in implementing a policy. It can also be a commitment of attention. Attention is a scarce good, and its allocation to a policy objective is an important indicator of governmental commitment. So there are many lenses through which we can study government commitments: attention, capacity, legitimacy, and spending. To be sure, attention can be purely symbolic, with neither legislation nor money following suit, but as will see in later chapters, all these measures of commitment share important properties, all involve significant costs, and all involve a commitment of resources. We lump them together for the purpose of this analysis; each can mean different things, and for other purposes we have studied them separately.

Two distributions of policy commitment are important. We already described what a policy change distribution is: the annual changes in commitment to a policy. This can be studied with respect to all the kinds of commitments we just described. Much more common than studying policy changes are those studies that focus on what we can call *policy outcome distributions.* An outcome distribution is simply the frequency distribution of the levels of effort expended across different policy arenas. For example, it could be the budgetary amount allocated to all different policy arenas, for one year (as one might see in a pie chart showing the proportion of the federal budget going to defense, interest, Social Security, etc.). The outcome distribution is a static representation of the state of policy commitments at a given time. Far too many studies of comparative public policy rely on the outcome distribution, postulating all sorts of causal mechanisms to account for a static outcome distribution in one nation versus another. The most common mistake is to compare levels of spending on, say, general welfare programs in Western Europe and the United States, note large differences, and refer to "American exceptionalism." But such static comparisons give no clue to why such differences have emerged. A few studies, notably that by Peter Hall (1985), focus on policy changes in response to similar inputs from the environment; this approach is far more successful.

One more detail is essential before we start our analysis: Policy change distributions can be calculated by *first differences* (the value in one year minus the value in the year before), or they can be calculated as *annual percentage changes* (the percent of the total in one year minus the percent of the total in the year before). Using percentages is especially useful when aggregating change processes across policy arenas, since budget categories can be of dramatically different scales. Focusing on first differences in such circumstances will lead to overweighting the large-budget categories. (Naturally, if defense spending is measured in the tens of billions each year, even small percentage changes are going to be large in absolute terms when compared to spending on, say, federal parks.) For the most part, in the analysis that follows, we use percent differences (as were reported in figure 4.14).[1] Now that we have clarified these various details, let's move on to the analysis.

Incrementalism

We turn now to an examination of the precise linkage between outcome change distributions and models of decision making. Chapter 4 provided the

---

1. In the most important aspect, the overall shape of the distributions that result, our findings are robust. That is, the general shapes remain largely leptokurtic whether we use raw differences or percentage change figures. Percentage change figures are more appropriate for theoretical reasons, but our broad findings do not hinge on this.

intuitive basis for this more systematic examination; Figure 4.14 would seem to rule out at least a naive form of incrementalism. But just how does this work? And what is to replace incrementalism (Jones and Baumgartner 2005)?

The notion that decision makers make incremental course corrections from the status quo has dominated thinking about policy change since the late 1950s. While the concept is general, it has been applied with particular success in the study of public budgets. Scholars drawing on Lindblom (1959), Wildavsky (1964), and others have argued that annual budget results tend to drift rather than to shift abruptly. Budgets were powerfully affected by the concepts of "base" and "fair share," which assume that each year's budget should be based on the previous allocation and that any increment should be shared relatively equally across categories and agencies.

The incrementalists based their approach to budget behavior on models of decision making featuring "considerations of limited rationality in the face of complexity and uncertainty" (Davis, Dempster, and Wildavsky 1974:421). In that framework, outputs are governed by standard operating procedures, and these SOPs are incremental. Participants were expected to use incremental decision rules for three reasons. The first involves the relative ease of reversing mistakes if they are only incremental changes rather than dramatic ones. The second concerns the desire of participants to establish stable expectations in a complex and uncertain environment. The third concerns the nature of overlapping, conflicting, and interacting institutions in American politics, which push participants toward compromise (Lindblom 1959; Wildavsky 1964; Fenno 1966; Davis, Dempster, and Wildavsky 1966, 1974).

Incremental Change and Policy Distributions

Considerable debate, much of it based on misunderstandings, has characterized the notion of incrementalism. Much of the debate has centered on "how large" a policy change would need to be to qualify as "nonincremental." Any particular policy change in the eye of one beholder can be trivial; in the eye of another, huge. In the absence of an agreed-upon standard, the question of policy change versus continued policy stability is unanswerable.

That argument is needless in the distributional perspective, where any change is judged relative to the overall pattern. The distributional perspective leads automatically to a model for incremental policymaking that can be compared to actual policy outcomes. If many small factors impinge on the course of public policy, the result will be an incremental pattern of change often characterized by policy scholars as "policy drift." This is the typical situation when Congress assigns policy responsibility to the executive bureaucracy and its own oversight committees. Interest groups are attracted to the new center of policymaking authority. As the law is implemented within the general confines of the statutory requirement, interest groups reach an equilibrium (Redford 1969), even if some interests are benefited at the expense of others in the initial statute. As a consequence, subsystem politics is incremental politics, with minor adjustments and successive limited comparisons to the status quo.

Equation 5.1a is the traditional equation for incrementalism. Political forces are balanced, and the broader public is inattentive. Policy today, P_t, is policy last year, P_{t-1}, plus an adjustment component, ε_t.

$$P_t = P_{t-1} + \varepsilon_t \tag{5.1a}$$

The adjustment component, ε_t, is important. If we assume that the adjustment to last year's policy is made up of lots of more or less independent factors, then the term will be normally distributed. Intuitively, some factors may lead to increases in the policy, others to decreases, and most of them just to cancel each other out.[2] The Central Limit Theorem tells us that the sum of many independent factors will itself be normally distributed; the key is that many unrelated factors, not just one or two, determine the outcome. If so, we can be confident that the result will be bell-shaped. If government were made of up 100 relatively autonomous subsystems, each reacting to a wide variety of input factors, with consistent but relatively distant oversight from central authority, then we would observe a normal distribution of outcomes; some would go up substantially (when factors happened to combine in their favor), some would decline precipitously, and most would be in the middle, with a large number of modest changes: a bell curve.

Because of the assumptions about the adjustment factor, ε_t, equation 5.1a describes a *random walk* over time. A random walk is a time series in which the next value is completely random, given the previous value as a base.[3] If we subtract the policy at time 1 from the policy at time 2 (this is known as the

---

2. The precise assumption is that $\varepsilon_t \sim \text{IID}(0, \sigma^2)$. This just means that the adjustment, or "error," terms are drawn from similar distributions with 0 mean (there are no systematic factors affecting policy change) and similar variance. If many factors influence each error term, then the Central Limit Theorem proves that, in the limit, the distribution would be normal.

3. In the sense of being drawn from a probability distribution of mean 0 and finite variance. The classic illustration is the case of counting the number of heads in a number of tosses of a fair coin. Will the next coin be heads? Taking the number of heads that occurred previously each time we toss a coin is a random walk through time.

first difference), we get a random number, as shown in the equation. If we were to form a frequency distribution of first differences like that of figure 4.14, with which we finished the last chapter, the result will approximate a normal, bell-shaped curve.

$$(P_t - P_{t-1}) = \varepsilon_t \tag{5.1b}$$

Equation 5.1b shows that the year-to-year change in budgets in the incremental perspective is equal to a random variable. If we subtract last year's value from this year's value—that is, if we take the first differences—we get an expected value of zero. There is no expected direction of change. (We can adjust for inflation or drift, of course, and we do this below.) Now, if we were to make a frequency distribution of all these first differences across all policy areas, like figure 4.14, we would observe a normal distribution. Incremental policymaking generates a normal distribution of first differences; this is an unavoidable consequence of the model (Padgett 1980).

Normal curves can have different standard deviations, of course, so the curve may have more or fewer cases "near" the central peak. But the incrementalists never went so far as to define what would be an incremental shift and what would be a nonincremental one, or whether the magnitude of the standard deviation might be involved in the definition. As we show shortly, this is not necessary, because disproportionate information-processing, which predicts punctuated equilibria, predicts an entirely different shape for the policy change distribution. We don't predict a normal curve at all. (And of course figure 4.14 is not normal, statistically speaking.) The main point here is simply that an incremental process will generate a bell-shaped curve; exactly what the standard deviation of that curve is does not matter.

Incrementalism and Upward Drift

An important modification of the incremental model might be called "incrementalism with upward drift." Government budgets in most developed democracies have moved upward since the Second World War, a payoff of successful economic management. In such an environment, incrementalist politics of mutual partisan adjustment and successive limited comparisons (Lindblom 1960) is played out within a growing pie. Moreover, many programs are funded by formulas that include the size of the target population, as for example in the Social Security system; with no change in policy the budget will have to grow because of demographic changes in the population producing more people eligible for the payments. These aspects of program funding can result in growth of budgets as the economy grows or as demographic trends continue.

This suggests that the year-to-year upward drift is proportional to last year's budget. Economists have faced a somewhat similar problem, the growth of firms over time. If the factors influencing growth were similar for large and small firms, as they would be if a growing economy lifts all boats, then the growth of firms over time would be proportional to the size of the firm. This assumption is enshrined in economics as the Gibrat thesis (Cefis, Ciccarelli, and Orsenigo 2001), but empirically it has been challenged (Ijiri and Simon 1977).

Incrementalism with upward drift would imply a similar thesis with regard to government budgets. The economy would lift all programs, leading to a proportional growth increment rather than the additive growth increment postulated in the pure incremental model of equation 5.1a. If this stronger form of upward drift, the Gibrat thesis, were applied to government budgets, it would imply that the annual percentage change (rather than the annual dollar change) would be constant—up to the random component. In this formulation the annual percentage change in budgetary commitments would follow a random walk, and the annual proportional (or percentage) difference would follow a normal distribution.

Equation 5.2a says that the policy at time t equals the policy at the earlier time period $t - 1$ plus a component that is proportional to the policy at the earlier time period and a random component:

$$P_t - P_{t-1} + kP_{t-1} + \varepsilon_t \tag{5.2a}$$
(sometimes written as $P_t = (1 + k)P_{t-1} + \varepsilon_t$)

Which we can express as

$$P_t - P_{t-1} = kP_{t-1} + \varepsilon_t$$

and

$$\frac{P_t - P_{t-1}}{P_{t-1}} = k + \omega_t \quad \text{where} \quad \omega_t = \frac{\varepsilon_t}{P_{t-1}} \tag{5.2b}$$

This shows that the proportional change—the change in policy positions between time 1 and time 2 divided by the policy position at time 1 is a constant. That is, the proportional change (or percentage change, if we just multiply by 100) is a constant, k. This proportional growth increment is constant across time.

The pure incremental model predicts a normal distribution for first differences; the Gibrat model applied to government budgets implies that the percentage change distribution will be normal. The constant, k, just augments each value of the frequency distribution and hence will not affect the shape of the distribution. What we would observe is a location of the center of the distribution at some positive number, rather than the zero predicted by the pure incremental model. Punctuated change can coexist with upward drift, as is indicated by figure 4.14. The typical program grew at 4 percent or so. The Gibrat form of the incremental model, however, predicts that the 4 percent growth is the whole story, and that all the other changes would just fall in a normal distribution around this value.

So, whether we have upward drift or not does not really matter. The key point to understand is that an incremental process will lead invariably to a normal outcome change distribution. And vice versa: *Any normal distribution of policy changes must have been generated by an incremental process.* Any time we observe a non-normal distribution of policy change, we must conclude that incrementalism cannot have caused it; some other process must have created it. So distributional analyses can be used to study processes; indeed, they should become central to future tests of policy processes since they allow clear distinctions among competing hypotheses, and clear generalizations beyond one policy area at a time, which is not the case in traditional time-series approaches.

Information Processing and the Incremental Model

The incremental theory of budgeting had been thoroughly routed by its detractors long before we produced the distributional analysis of figure 4.14.[4] Critics noted problems in the particular models used by the incrementalists (Gist 1982; Natchez and Bupp 1973); in the measures used (Wanat 1974); in the conceptual clarity of terms (Berry 1990; Hayes 1992); and in the nature of the underlying decision-making model (Padgett 1980). Others have complained of problems in capturing the complexities with simple theories of budgeting, particularly the incremental model (Kiel and Elliott 1992; Rubin 1988; Schick 1988). We argue, quite to the contrary, that the theory is completely serviceable, at least when integrated with a sensible theory of infor-

4. Introduced in True, Jones, and Baumgartner 1999.

mation processing. We don't want to throw the baby out with the bathwater. But we have to know the limits of incrementalism; in fact, it gets the story only partly right.

The incremental approach was very nearly correct at the outset. But it was incomplete, and for this it was heavily criticized. It lacked an analysis of how a move from the status quo was accomplished. We know from studies in psychology and decision making that updating a prior choice is anything but smooth and seamless; as a consequence, it is not always "incremental." Most importantly, as we detailed in chapters 2 and 3, choice in politics is attention-driven, and attention shifting leads to disproportionate updating. In essence, the incremental model postulates proportionate updating, but that has not been widely recognized. Because incrementalism has served such yeoman duty in policy studies, and because incorporating a more realistic model of information processing into it makes it serviceable again, we will develop this connection in some detail here.

From Information to Information Processing

Information processing hinges on responsiveness of a system to signals in its environment. All models, including the earlier budget studies, have incorporated such responsiveness in one form or another, but this incorporation has generally not been connected to the internal dynamics of the responding system. Information processing requires an appreciation of both the nature of the signals and the capacity of the system to detect, analyze, and act on these signals. As a consequence, focusing on political information processing implies a focus on the interactions between external signals and internal system dynamics.

The information-processing model and the associated punctuated-equilibrium model are not alone in predicting abrupt change. Many different models of the policy process predict abrupt change, but they generally assume that exogenous events stimulate the response of the system. Some event external to the political system occurs, and the system responds in a straightforward manner to the event. This is the most common version of what we have called "proportionate information processing"—responses of political systems are proportionate to the signals from the environment. Strong events in the environment produce strong responses from the political system. Weak signals produce weak policy responses. After all, maybe the distribution of outcomes we showed in figure 4.14 occurred simply because the government faced a series of events that were similarly distributed; why assume the inputs would be normal in the first place? It is crucial to determine whether our findings there (and more to be presented in subsequent chapters) stem from some transparent, proportionate response by government to a strange distribution of inputs, or whether they come from a transformation that takes place within government itself. We provide evidence that the input series is essentially normal, but that the responses are laden with friction, and that this friction is associated with the disproportionate-response model we have presented. The leptokurtic changes that we demonstrate in figure 4.14 stem not from the inputs to government, but from the process of decision making within government—both human cognitive and organizational facets on the one hand, and the formal nature of institutional rules on the other. This chapter and the next lay out the reasons why this is the case, and in chapter 7 we provide a wide range of evidence from many different government institutions.

There is ample precedent in the empirical and theoretical literature on public budgeting to expect budget punctuations, beginning with Davis, Dempster, and Wildavsky (1974). Their studies focused on decision makers' use of budget decision rules. These rules, understood by participants and offering a stable organizational environment for decision making, were grounded in the concepts of base and fair share, which led to incrementalism in both process and output. But they also wrote that "although it is basically incremental, the budget process does respond to the needs of the economy and society, but only after sufficient pressure has built up to cause *abrupt changes precipitated by these events*" (Davis, Dempster, and Wildavsky 1974: 421, italics added). That is, the budget process is punctuated by periods of abrupt change; the periods of stability were termed "epochs."

So the characterization of the early bounded rationalists in budget studies as supportive of incrementalism is not entirely true. Davis, Dempster, and Wildavsky (1966, 1974) detailed the operation of boundedly rational budgetary procedures, but those were embedded within budgetary epochs. These epochs shifted the parameters of the incremental model (to larger or smaller coefficients during different periods), implying a nonincremental step between epochs. The epochs, however, were driven entirely exogenously.[5]

Models of exogenously forced policy change not only are found in the budget literature, but also are suggested in the work of comparativists (Krasner 1984), students of American institutions (Dodd 1991; Kelly 1994),

---

5. Davis and his colleagues estimated a statistical model in which exogenous variables that presumably governed epoch shifts were allowed to influence the parameters that described the incremental budgeting procedures observed within the periods.

and students of the process of representation. In the case of representation, changes in public policy are exogenously driven by changes in public opinion (Stimson, MacKuen, and Erikson 1995) or both respond to opinion and cause changes in opinion through a thermostat-like device (Wlezien 1995). Punctuations should occur in such models *only if there are changes in macrolevel forces.*

Other authors have allowed for endogenous and exogenous changes. Kiel and Elliott (1992) have suggested that budgeting be approached from a perspective of nonlinear dynamics. They write of nonlinearities in the budgeting process in which "exogenous and endogenous forces simply have varying impacts on budget outlays over time" (Kiel and Elliott 1992:143). Thurmaier (1995) reports the results of experiments in budget scenarios in which decision makers shift from economic to political rationalities after the introduction of new information about political calculations. These kinds of processes can lead to punctuations even without exogenous shocks.

Internal Dynamics in Response to External Signals

In a theoretical breakthrough a quarter of a century ago, John Padgett (1980) provided a model of budget decision making that does not rely on the artificial distinction between exogenous punctuations and more typical and incremental decision making. Padgett's (1980:366) serial-judgment model implies "the occasional occurrence of very radical changes." Decision makers move from a status quo point by serially processing the next closest option until a satisfactory one is found. External changes can shift the attention of policymakers to new political realities, changing the internal dynamics of decision. Like our model, Padgett's did not rely on external shocks to produce the punctuations; they can happen, of course, but they are not required.

Our information-processing model of policy change is in many respects a generalization of Padgett's basic work. Both Padgett's serial-judgment model and our information-processing approach allow for endogenous mobilizations as well as exogenous shocks, whereas Davis, Dempster, and Wildavsky suggest only exogenous shocks. All three models suggest punctuations in the budget process.

The information-processing model implies that punctuations ought to occur at all levels of policymaking, and not simply be driven by external (exogenous) factors. This is a consequence of two factors. First, policymaking is rooted in human decision-making processes that are hostage to the dynamics of selective attention to underlying attributes structuring a political situation, and these should more or less continually affect the policy process. Second, the model of punctuated policy equilibrium is based in part on a "bottom-up" process in which policy change may occur in isolated subsystems, or may spill over into other, related subsystems, or may be affected by exogenous shocks (Baumgartner and Jones 1993).

The information-processing approach to policy change emphasizes the interaction between factors internal to the policymaking process and exogenous events in the political and economic environment. The mistake of the incrementalists was to ignore the reverberations of external events on the organizational processes upon which policy choice rests. The mistake of those focusing on exogenous forces is to ignore the role of internal dynamics in responding to external change.

Simulating a Proportionate Information-Processing Model

Our information-processing perspective suggests that external information is important in policy debates but is not determinative. Responses to new information are disproportionate, which means that sometimes the system does not respond at all. So we cannot assume that observed changes in outcomes stem from changes in the information coming into the system, since sometimes the system does not react, and sometimes it overreacts. In sum, we need to know more about the process than we need to know about the inputs. In order to explain these ideas most clearly, let us start with a model of what would happen if decision making were proportionate to the severity of problems in the environment. Then we will compare this proportionate model with what we observe empirically. The deviations between the proportionate model and empirical distributions can only be attributed to the disproportionate model laid out in chapters 2 and 3.

If all policy changes were keyed to changes in the external environment, then the budget change distribution would look approximately normal, or bell-shaped, rather than like the leptokurtic distribution we observe. This may be a surprising claim to some readers, so it is worthwhile to examine it in a little detail. Recall that the normal curve describes many phenomena, such as heights, intelligence, and grades. The reason that bell-shaped distributions emerge from, for example, heights, is that numerous random factors add up to determine how tall a person is. Many of these "cancel out" or come close to canceling out, but once in a while these factors cumulate to produce a very tall or very short person. The overall distribution has an average and some deviation around that average; empirically, this distribution is bell-shaped. The normal curve also describes repeated measurements of any quantity, because sometimes we make small mistakes, a few times we make moderate mistakes, but we almost never make really large mistakes. So unlike the budget distribution, the "curve of errors," like the curve of heights, has very few cases in the tails. So long as our errors are uncorrelated—that is, so long as an error on the high side is not typically followed by another error on the high side— then the error distribution of measurements will be normally distributed with a mean, or average, at the true quantity. (Better measurement instruments produce a smaller standard deviation, but the shape remains the same.)

This process is also characteristic of proportionate information processing. Proportionate information processing in the face of uncertainty in the external world and fallibility in the indicators we use to monitor change in that world implies the need to combine various sources of information in making a choice. Our standard model for proportionate information processing is the implicit index model of figure 3.1. That diagram shows how various sources of information were combined to make a decision. A decision maker might in theory combine the various indicators into an index and make decisions based on that index. We might term this process "rational adaptation," because the political system would produce policy changes in direct proportion to the intensity of the sum of a set of fallible indicators of problems. If we were to observe this process over a long enough period of time, we would observe a normal distribution of values, even if the underlying indicators were badly skewed—so long as the indicators were not highly correlated (that is, didn't just measure the same thing over and over again). The Central Limit Theorem (CLT) of statistics proves why this is the case.

It is often the case, however, that decision makers "lock onto" a single indicator and overweight it in the index. Overweighting a single measure also violates the assumptions of the CLT, so if this occurs, then a normal distribution of choices will not be foreordained. There are lots of reasons for this "lock-on" phenomenon. One is heuristic decision making, the tendency of people to take shortcuts in processing information. This directly implies the use of a subset of indicators—overweighting.[6] A second is the garbage-can "solutions searching problems" phenomenon, which will cause a bias toward examining only indicators favorable to the cause. This overweighting is a major source of disproportionate information processing, because measurement

6. An unfortunate tendency among some political scientists has been to assume that heuristics lead to rational, or at least adaptive, decision making. This is just not true, as the example of "indicator lock-on" illustrates.

error will ensure mistakes, mistakes that can become magnified over time. We might term this disproportionate updating "boundedly rational adaptation." The policymaking result is the issue-intrusion process described in chapter 3.

The diagram presented in figure 3.1 applies to a single decision based on information from numerous sources. But governments make thousands of decisions every year. Earlier we made the distinction between decision making on a single topic, in which a decision maker juggles several indicators of the severity of the problem, and juggling the various topics that compete for attention. The distinction is analytical, in the sense that both are actually going on simultaneously within government. At the same time that policymakers are debating the priorities of the problems they face, they are also attending to (or ignoring) the various indicators of each problem's severity. Our analysis of disproportionate information-processing applies equally well to either level of decision making. If indicators are combined in a rationally adaptive way, the result is a normal distribution of outcomes. If they are not combined this way, such as will happen with indicator "lock," a normal distribution will not result. In fact, since abrupt shifts occur at each stage of the process laid out in figure 2.1 (which problem to attend to, which dimensions to consider, which solutions to choose from?), the multiplication of these factors makes the process we describe wildly different from normal, rather than only marginally different, as it might be if these processes were occurring only once.

Simulating the Stochastic Processes of Index Construction

It is no stretch to think of the problems facing government as more or less random. We may face a natural disaster this year, or an economic decline that generates unemployment, or a very wet year that destroys crops, or a challenge to national security. But we are unlikely to face all of these at once. As a consequence, in a hypothetical policymaking system that responds efficiently and proportionately to changes from the environment, budget changes would be distributed normally. But our case is even stronger, since the individual series do not have to be normally distributed, each separately. We know that a variety of series will combine into a single, normally distributed index, so long as the component series are not themselves highly correlated; this is true because of the Central Limit Theorem. Strictly speaking, the CLT holds only when there are very many ("infinite") external causes of government programs. Indeed, there are very many causes, considering the great range of different issues that affect government, as we showed in chapter 4. Of course, some series are correlated with each other (crop disasters and hurricanes, for example). But luckily for us, we live in a large country, and when hurricanes destroy the citrus crop in one part of the country, there may be fine crops and pleasant weather thousands of miles away.

It turns out that the Central Limit Theorem is very robust with respect to the number of variables that must be combined into an "index" in order to yield a normal distribution. We may show this by using a simple simulation. We have drawn a sample of 10,000 random digits for five different variables. These will serve as the indicators of problems facing government. We may think of these as various indicators of an underlying problem. To take one example, we can think of intelligence analysis of the potential threat from a potential enemy abroad. These indicators must be combined in order to make judgments about the necessity of government action.

Some of these indicators may be subject to severe threshold effects—for example, an indicator of the threat from North Korea could increase non-linearly if a serious attempt at acquiring nuclear arms is discovered. In order to model these effects, we apply five different nonlinear transformations to the five simulated random variables. That is, to make our test more difficult, we do not use the random variables; rather we transform them so that each individual series has a deliberate non-normal shape.[7] Then we sum the five variables, constructing an index. Figure 5.1 presents the frequency distribution of this index, similar in format to the budget-change data we presented in figure 4.14.

It is evident that the distribution approximates the normal distribution, and statistical tests indicate that it does not differ significantly from the normal. This is in many ways an astounding result, because of the limited number of variables we included and the very non-normal shapes of each of the underlying indicators.[8] Rational adaptation, in the sense of combining several indicators, each of which may itself be fallible and skewed, will lead over time to a normal distribution of responses to the problems that government faces. In general, if government makes policy according to the diagram of figure 3.1, then the outcomes would be normally distributed. This is an important

7. The random variables were drawn from a uniform distribution with mean of 0 and standard deviation of 1. The transformations were powers of 3, 5, and 7, the log of the absolute value, and the exponential of the variable minus the mean.

8. This result will not "astound" the statistically knowledgeable. Early software packages by IBM actually used six uniform distributions to generate what was called a normal distribution but what should really have been called "pseudo-normal." In any case, such a procedure does generate a close approximation of the normal distribution. We thank Jim Stimson for pointing this out.

Figure 5.1. Frequency Distribution of the Sum of Five Non-normally Distributed Random Variables

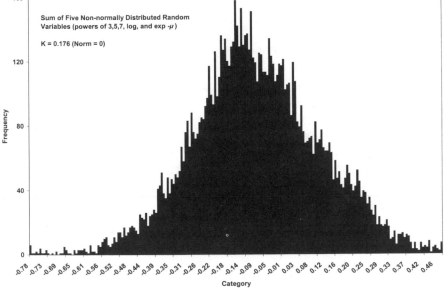

standard against which to measure our observed frequency distribution of figure 4.14.

The fact that U.S. budget authority is not normally distributed tells us something very important. It must mean that adjustments in budgets (that is, changes in budget allocations) are not simple sums of external challenges. That is, policymakers don't just study the various sources of information that they have available to them, combine them in some sort of index, and produce policy keyed to the index, as many a frustrated policy analyst will attest. If they did that, budget outcomes would be normally distributed. Figure 5.1 shows that this would be the case even if they were facing a great range of different inputs, each being generated by a very different process. As long as there were many inputs, the combination of many different ones would lead to a normal distribution of outputs.

We can extend this argument in an interesting way. One might argue that the reason distributions are not normal is that decision makers are beholden to constituencies that make demands that, in effect, cause deviations from the index. But so long as there is a diversity of constituencies, then the set of demands from these constituencies will also be subject to the strictures of the

Central Limit Theorem. As Madison recognized in *Federalist* No. 10, a large republic would yield more moderate policy responses than smaller governmental units under the sway of the "fires of passion."

Proportionate Information-Processing as Updating in the Incremental Model

The reader may wonder at this point how all of this is related to incremental decision making. It seems that we now have two models—the incremental model and the proportionate information-processing model, each of which implies a normal distribution of outputs. In fact we have only one model. The reason is that decision makers never respond to signals of emergent problems without reference to the ongoing policy directed at the problem. Sometimes there is no policy, but most often there is something relevant to the issue going on in government. As a consequence, policy responses to the implicit index model, representative of proportionate decision-making, may be seen as updating from the previous policy.

If decision makers update the status quo proportional to changes in social and economic inputs facing government, then the resulting policy change distribution will be normal. This can be seen as an elaboration of the incremental decision-making model when the responses of decision makers are proportionate to the incoming information. It matters not a whit if the incoming information is non-normally distributed; a sum of even a few indicators will yield a normal outcome distribution. We may infer an important result: *Incremental decision making updated by proportional responses to incoming signals will result in a normal distribution of policy changes.* Incremental decision making updated through proportionate information processing is rational adaptation.

Disproportionate Information-Processing in Policymaking

If policymakers were to monitor as few as five indicators, sum them into an index, and produce policy proportional to the magnitude of the index, the results would be a normal distribution of policies. (This holds, as we noted, even if the individual input series are not normally distributed; they must only not all be related to one another.) If the index is used to update from the policy status quo, the resulting *change* distribution will be normally distributed. Now we ask what happens if policymakers rely too heavily on a single indicator within the index (or, Madison might note, if government comes under the disproportionate sway of a single faction advocating a single policymaking point of view).

Examples of overreliance on single indicators (or, similarly, the "alarmed discovery" of something that could have been clear to systematic observers for a long time) can be drawn almost every day from a reading of the newspaper. In May 2004, graphic pictures of abuse by U.S. military police at Abu Ghraib prison in Iraq were aired by CBS News. It had been clear for months that there were serious problems in the U.S. approach to gaining information from captives. Already available from standard news sources were reports on the use of extraordinary means to obtain information from the "illegal combatants" in Guantanamo Bay, Cuba; a Red Cross study, published in the autumn of 2003, on U.S. abuses of Iraqi detainees in several prisons; several reports from soldiers that should, in hindsight, have alerted the U.S. military command hierarchy; and letters from relatives of the military policemen to members of Congress expressing concern. Each of these "indicators" was discounted, until the graphic visual images suddenly focused attention on this one indicator of the problem. The response was intense, virtually dominating policy discussions in Congress and in the news media to the exclusion of much else for many days. Clearly, we can see a disproportionate response, both in the lack of attention to the issue before the scandal and in the level of attention to one prison rather than to a general policy afterward.

In the waning hours of 2004, Congress passed and the president signed massive changes to the structure of U.S. intelligence gathering. Not only did the intelligence failures of 9/11 bring attention to this problem, but they simultaneously demonstrated that previous ways of defining the issue and solving it were not working. So, as we describe here in general terms, we see a simultaneous surge in attention and a destabilization of previously accepted wisdom about how to define the issue, about which solutions are best suited to solve the problems; each of the stages in figure 2.1 is apparently in play at the same time.

If this sort of response is fairly common in politics—with inattention to indicators alternating with intense interest in others over time—what would be the resulting distribution of policy outcomes? We may simulate this disproportionate-response process in a manner similar to our simulation of proportionate information-processing. We again generated 10,000 random numbers each for five separate variables and transformed the results as we did before. This time, instead of weighting each one equally, we gave one in-

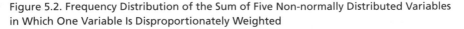
Figure 5.2. Frequency Distribution of the Sum of Five Non-normally Distributed Variables
in Which One Variable Is Disproportionately Weighted

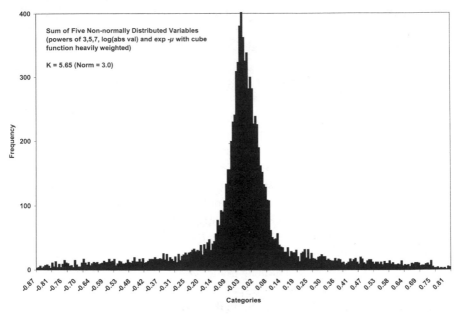

dicator a weight of 0.8, and the rest were weighted at 0.05.[9] Then we summed
the weighted indicators and plotted the results as shown in figure 5.2.

The distribution is not at all normal. It is leptokurtic, with a kurtosis of
5.65 (where kurtosis for the normal equals 3.00). This distribution cannot
have resulted from the non-normality of indicators; it can only have been
generated by the weights. If the heavily weighted indicator had been normally distributed, then the weighted series would be closer to normal. But
a decision maker relying on a single indicator whose distribution was normal
would be "lucky," because there is no statistical reason (or empirical reason
that we can discern) for assuming an arbitrarily chosen input stream would
be normal. If a few indicators are simultaneously monitored, however, the
result will inevitably be a normal distribution. Where only one or two indicators are focused upon, no expectation about the distribution of outputs can
be asserted based on the happenstance that an arbitrarily chosen input distribution will be normal.

9. The overweighted indicator was the cube. Overweighting any of the other indicators
yields similar results, although the extent of the leptokurtosis changes.

Grasping this is important. Even if each component part of informational input is non-normally distributed, the full input distribution will be, so long as decision makers monitor a "basket" of indicators. If they produce policy responses that are proportional to the basket of indicators, they will produce normally distributed outputs. If they "panic" in response to one indicator, then the outputs will not be normal. They will be leptokurtic. *Leptokurtic distributions in policy choice are prime indicators of disproportionality in the choice process.* Political systems often panic. As we noted in the introduction to this section, government often responds to things by doing nothing or by over-reacting. This is what we mean by disproportionate response.

The key difference between what we showed in figure 5.1 and in figure 5.2 was not in the inputs; these were the same. Rather, the difference that we created there was simply that in one case a relatively broad "basket" of indicators was monitored, and in the other case, the decision maker placed excessive weight on just one of many indicators that were available. Disproportionate response, then, can simply be created by a model of attention shifting. Sudden appreciation of the importance of some previously ignored condition is sufficient to explain the difference between relatively rational updating to changing conditions as posited in the incremental model and the surging, lurching, friction-laden, overreacting and underreacting processes that we in fact observe in government.

Conclusions

Decision makers are bombarded with information from many sources, and they may seek out other sources to inform themselves. How do they prioritize the information from these many sources, and how do they combine them in making decisions? As we indicated, the best way would be to weight the information streams by importance and add them to make an index. If participants in an institution receive information from independent diverse streams and weight and sum these diverse streams in an index, then the resulting distribution would be normal by the Central Limit Theorem, at least in the limit.

Let us now turn to less-than-perfect human systems. If individual decision makers rely on a limited set of indicators to monitor their environments, and update them or include newly salient aspects of the environment in the decision-making calculus episodically, the result will be a flow of "news" (that is, the information flow that the decision maker attends to) that is not normal (Jones 2001: chap. 7). If decision makers act on the "news," rather than a basket of indicators, they will produce a distribution of outcomes that is not normal.

As we shall see in later chapters, actual policy-change distributions drawn from observations of government activities are virtually never characterized by a normal distribution. Because of this, a simple model of incremental decision making can be quickly ruled out. We do not, however, want to stop with a simple up-down decision about the utility of incrementalism as a model for public-policy decision making. If we study lots of policy-change distributions, we find a particular pattern of non-normality; leptokurtosis characterizes virtually all of them, to a greater or lesser degree. That is to say that actual outcome distributions from observing what government does over the past fifty years show that, in comparison to the normal, there is simultaneously too much dramatic change (the fat tails represent a great number of large changes in a policy-change distribution) and too little change (the strong central peaks indicate what we might call "hyper-incrementalism"— extreme allegiance to the status quo). What is absent in such distributions is moderate change. This discredits incrementalism as a full model, but the strong central peaks indicate that most of the time policy making is indeed incremental (in the easily understood sense of the term, meaning changing little from previous policies). It is the extreme tails that disrupt the pattern. Look at that central peak, and you appreciate the importance of the incremental model of politics. Look at the tails, and you find dramatic evidence of disjoint change. Figure 4.14 and our analyses in subsequent chapters should reinvigorate the study of incrementalism, because we find most policies most of the time to be exceedingly incremental, or status-quo-oriented. But they should also convince readers that this is only part of the story. There are far more dramatic changes than could possibly be expected from rational response to changing inputs. Rather, alarmed discovery and overreaction are also fundamental parts of the process; these generate the surges, the lurches, and the punctuations that are fundamental to the process as well.

6

Cognitive Architectures, Institutional Costs, and Fat-Tailed Distributions

Focusing on whole distributions of changes in policy commitments leads us to examine the causal processes that can generate such distributions. Simple additive processes such as those captured in the incremental model are precluded, since they generate normal distributions. Simple interventionist models in which an external event generates uniform responses from all policy process distributions are unlikely. As we noted in chapter 4, each policy arena seems to need a separate causal explanation because of the complexities inherent in political choice. A distributional approach pushes us to a level of analysis that transcends these particulars, but of course at the loss of important detail.

In this chapter we take a step back and review the underlying processes that can generate leptokurtic distributions (we return to an empirical focus in chapter 7). In linear models, one causal explanation suffices, but in our case it is clear that there are two "regimes"—our attention-shifting model operates differently during periods when attention is routinely focused on a given issue and a given way of thinking about that issue than it does during those periods when attention shifts. Clearly, we need to focus on the mechanisms responsible for both stability and radical change. It is all to the good if the processes are integrated into one theory, but even here the processes within the theory are likely to be distinct, as we shall see.

We present a general model that integrates the effects of both disproportionate information-processing and the formal institutional structures of American politics on decision-making distributions. We do so by developing a generalized approach to decision-making costs. Such costs have effects much like those of friction in the physical world. Further, both the "cognitive costs" of disproportionate information-processing and "institutional costs" of American Madisonian democracy have similar effects on outcome distributions. Finally, we present some simulations of the process we are describing. These simulations strongly support our argument that cognitive and institutional costs combine to generate leptokurtic policy outputs.

Generating Stability *and* Change:
Cascades, Sieves, and Friction

Students of the policy process understand stability better than they understand change. Indeed, it is not farfetched to suggest that we have serious theories to explain stability and modest change, but we have mostly anecdotes and ad hoc theorizing to understand radical change. Incremental models, standard operating procedures, policy learning, and the blocking effects of American political institutions all imply stability. Major theories of government seem to focus on explaining the causes of stability and treat large changes, innovation, as flukes. But the system produces both. We need a theory of both, not a theory of just one or the other.

Because of the focus on the processes generating the extreme values of a distribution, a branch of statistical analysis called "extreme value theory" has emerged, focusing on the study of the "fat" (sometimes called "heavy") tails of the distribution (Kotz and Nadarajah 2000; Sornette 2000). All fat-tailed distributions are generated by some process that causes interdependency among the observed cases. That process acts to propagate change throughout the system. This is quite a different starting point than in the typical social science study, which assumes "independence of observations." Independence of cases is a requirement for the typical regression study but is also enshrined in the assumption of "methodological individualism" from classical economics.

Modern approaches to complexity emphasize this interconnectedness. As Greg Brunk (2000:6) puts it, "complexity is a measure of the sensitivity of particles, people, organizations, or nations to each other's behavior." The modern view of complexity differs greatly from classical views of social science, which emphasized what Herbert Simon (1996: chap. 8) termed "near decomposability," pointing to the independence of the component parts of a system. Near decomposability is the idea that each part of a system can be analyzed in isolation from the rest, ignoring complex interactions among parts. In the face of interdependency, analyzing parts of a complex organization as if they were decomposable leads to the "understandable complexity" problem of chapter 4—it renders it impossible to put the parts back together in a general story.

So fat-tailed distributions are indicators of interdependency among the component parts. If events were independent of one another, then the Central Limit Theorem would apply, and many of them would cancel out, leading to a normal distribution of outcomes. Where cases are in fact interrelated, a high score on one can lead to an even higher score on the next, and so on; such a process violates important assumptions of classical regression, vitiates the CLT, and occurs more often than many analysts appear to realize. Such self-reinforcing processes are sufficient to create distributions like the ones we observe; compared to the normal, they have many cases in the extremes and more in the central peak (Sornette 2000).

We see three particular types of self-reinforcing processes as being especially important for our study: cascades, sieves, and friction.[1] Cascades are processes in which positive feedback dominates—each change begets another even larger change. Sieve processes come about when decision makers apply ever greater constraints to a decision-making process. Adding constraints rules out options, causing greater changes from the status quo when adjustments finally do occur. Institutional friction occurs when institutions retard change, but result in a large-scale "jump" when the built-in friction is overcome. All three processes can generate leptokurtic policy-change distributions.

These three processes may or may not all operate simultaneously. It may turn out, for example, that cascades are the key to understanding how friction is overcome in policy systems. However, they are clearly not sufficient—as with fads, the pressures generated may just fade away. Decisional sieves may be decision-making reflections of cascades—but they may not. We just don't know. But the isolation of these three stochastic mechanisms has the decided advantage of specifying complexity. Rather than claiming that everything is contingent, contextual, and complex, we can begin to try to reason through just what mechanisms are responsible for the observed complexity in any given case of policy change.

Here we discuss briefly the roles of cascades and sieves in policy choices, and then we develop in considerable detail the friction model. It is critical because it has the potential of unifying static institutional analyses with the dynamics of public policy studies.

---

1. Thanks to John Padgett and John Brehm for highlighting this distinction in the Organizational Theory and State Building Workshop at the University of Chicago.

Cascades

Cascades explain the extreme values in a policy change distribution by a process in which one action begets other actions, independent of the nature of the external event stimulating the initial action. Cascades result from positive feedback effects (Baumgartner and Jones 2002). Positive feedback effects may be contrasted with more typical negative feedbacks, which occur when a process causes a dampening effect on itself. For example, in a well-behaved market, scarcity of a good causes the price to rise. This encourages producers to make more of the good available, which then causes the price to fall. As prices fall, producers earn less per unit and shift some productive capacity somewhere else. As production falls, the price may rise again. Negative feedback processes reach an equilibrium and explain a mechanism by which any deviations from that equilibrium are "reined back in" by forces reacting to the change in the previous stage of the process, keeping the equilibrium relatively intact, just as a thermostat keeps the temperature of a house relatively constant.

Positive feedback occurs in markets when a price rise causes a further price rise. In financial markets, bubbles can occur in this circumstance. Crashes occur when a price drop causes further price drops—the self-correcting feature of negative feedback has been replaced by positive feedback. In properly functioning markets, this does not happen. But in real life it does occasionally occur: certain goods become popular, fads sweep through a market, or real estate prices rise based on an expectation that other buyers will be willing to pay ever higher prices. Whenever buyers are basing their behaviors on the expected future behaviors of others (rather than each independently basing them on their own preferences), then the assumptions regarding independence of statistical observations have been breached, and in economics a bubble is a strong possibility. Both positive and feedback processes are in evidence in politics as well. In previous work we explained some of the most prominent examples of positive-feedback processes in politics—bandwagons in elections, for example, and the destruction of policy subsystems in the face of social mobilization (Baumgartner and Jones 1993). Negative feedback damps down. Positive feedback produces explosions.

In social science, a major source of cascades is the process of monitoring and mimicking. In many situations, people may observe carefully not the real world directly, but how others around them are responding to the real world. Then they take action based not on real-world indicators but on their observations of the responses of others. This process results in chain-reaction dynamics, in which major changes can occur rapidly. Social cascades have been used to study elections and policy change in political science (Bartels 1988; Baumgartner and Jones 2002), fads in sociology (Bikhchandani, Hirshleifer, and Welch 1992), peculiarities in pricing in economics (Becker 1991), residential segregation (Schelling 1972) bubbles and crashes in economics (Shiller 2000; Sornette 2003), revolutions and collective action (Chong 1991; Granovetter 1975; Kuran 1989), and a variety of other topics (Kirman 1993), all with considerable success. There are many cases where individuals' behaviors are driven more by what they expect or see others around them doing than by their own preferences. Gary Becker's classic example is when people choose restaurants based on how difficult it is to get in (1991). If this happens, then initial success begets future success; a positive feedback process. This can lead to a "restaurant of the moment" phenomenon, leading to dramatic success for some time, but potentially also to catastrophic failure at others—as epitomized by Yogi Berra's comment, "Nobody goes [to that restaurant] any more. It's too crowded." Cascades are by nature unstable and explosive, and they can end abruptly.

These cascades cause punctuated behavior, because (in a pure situation) either there is no change in behavior or everybody changes. In many situations, there can be different groups engaged in monitoring and mimicking, but they are not tightly connected to one another. For example, Democrats in Congress organize separately from Republicans and may be sensitive to different informational cues. This deconcentrated organizational structure limits the size of the cascade—one of the arguments that in effect the constitutional framers made on behalf of the proposed system of divided and separated powers.

While some have modeled cascades as fully rational informational shortcuts in decision making (Hirshleifer 1995), these attempts are unpersuasive (Jones 2001). In the case of financial markets, mimicking can result in severe and unpredictable explosions and crashes, resulting in a risk structure that should deter decision makers capable of rational expectations from engaging in mimicking. Most people studying these processes base them on bounded rationality, in that people caught up in cascades are goal-oriented but make systematic mistakes, compared to a rational expectations model, where people properly discuss the strategies of others (Shiller 2000).

Imitation and herding are the bases of a class of models of financial markets that are designed to explain bubbles and crashes. Let us say that rather than monitor the state of the world independently, you come to trust the analysis of someone else, perhaps because they have been very successful in the past. You imitate their behavior rather than decide independently. Of course, this again violates the assumption of the independence of observations. More important, if many actors within a system do this, it renders the system liable to dramatic rises and crashes rather than smoothly operating equilibria. Computer simulations of these processes have demonstrated how imitation by investors can lead to market crashes. Interestingly, the heart of the problem is in communication. In these models, if investors do not communicate with one another, then mimicking cannot occur, and crashes will not occur. More correctly, any crash will be a proportionate function of an external event, so that only major calamities could cause crashes.

But if investors in these models communicate, then crashes can occur, and the more widespread the communication, the more likely the crash. In such circumstances, we may observe a crash that seems not to be connected with external events. Some seemingly trivial happening can cause a massive sell-off, because the system has moved into a very fragile state. Summarizing this line of research, Didier Sornette (2003:159) writes that the risk of a crash "increases dramatically when the interactions between traders become strong enough that the network of interactions between traders self-organizes into a hierarchy containing a few large, spontaneously formed groups acting collectively."

Actual financial data have also been studied using Markov switching models. These models simply treat financial time series, such as stock market returns, as being generated by one of two "regimes"—a normal regime, when things work according to standard market theory, and a "bubble" regime, when positive feedbacks are in effect (Schaller and Van Norden 1997; Sornette 2003:167–68). Similarly, political scientists have noted the "critical periods" in which attention toward a policy matter causes a shift from the typical negative-feedback processes characteristic of policy subsystems to the intense period of positive feedback associated with major reforms (Baumgartner and Jones 1993, 2002). Conceiving of a kind of Markov on-off switch for positive feedback systems has the potential of adding substantially to the theory and analysis of complex systems.

Sieves

A second way to explain extremes occurs when policymakers try to solve problems presented by external challenges and must sequentially search for alternatives rather than examine all comprehensively (Padgett 1980, 1981). In complex and uncertain circumstances, decision makers will winnow the realistic alternatives until they find one that will satisfy the conditions imposed by the external challenge. First they decide in which direction to move from the initial status quo point. Should a budget be cut or increased? Should there be more or less regulation of an industry? Then they cycle through the available options until one option satisfies the constraints of the situation. If the alternatives are ordered, as they are when deciding how much to increase or cut a budget, then as constraints get more difficult to satisfy, a decision maker will have to move further away from the status quo. Simple constraints lead to simple adjustments, with few alternatives in the vicinity of the status quo rejected. But difficult constraints imply large movements from the status quo.

In Padgett's serial choice model, constraints are generated from two considerations: whether program increases (or decreases) are justified "on the merits" and whether the increase (or decrease) is justified under "the current fiscal climate" (1980:364). The second consideration in effect brings into a decision-making situation external and contextual considerations. Indeed, the mechanism for propagating change throughout the system (and hence enforcing the interdependencies that generate fat tails in a budget change distribution) are general fiscal targets or constraints (Padgett 1981). The targets or constraints are top-down propagators of interdependencies. So the serial-choice model can be seen as a particular mechanism of disproportionate information-processing. *Both* the conditions of merit and fiscal/political climate must be satisfied.

It cannot be the case, however, that top-down processes of the type that Padgett postulates are the whole budget story. As we showed in chapter 4, hierarchical models of budget change—the macropunctuations—are not enough to account for observed patterns in U.S. budget data. Selective attention and disproportionate information-processing are necessary to understand these patterns. How do policymakers decide to prioritize programs for cuts or expansions? What is the "political climate" that sets the terms of the cuts or increases? These are policymaking issues, and Padgett's model is a decision-making model. To explain fully outputs, we need a theory of policymaking; a theory of budgeting alone will not suffice.

This does not detract at all from Padgett's accomplishment—it remains the only decision-making model that predicts correct (that is, fat-tailed) distributions of outputs. So it is worthwhile to have a brief look at its internal dynamics. Padgett's model is nonlinear, as are all models of disproportionate processing. If the probability of deciding that the program deserves a specific budgetary increase is p_i, and the probability of deciding that the same alternative is acceptable under the current political climate is k, then the probability of accepting the particular alternative is $P(\text{accept}) = p_i \times k$. The "i" subscript indicates the program; there is no subscript for k because the political climate is presumed to be constant across programs. This may well not be the case; Republicans in Congress may support military spending while insisting on domestic program decreases. But it is a good start.

If the decision maker judges the merits of a program to be high, then the probability of an increase based on the merits would be positive. But if the fiscal climate were judged to be unfavorable, then multiplying p_i by k would yield zero (because k, the probability that the fiscal environment is favorable, is zero). No matter how meritorious the program, there will be no budget increase until the fiscal climate improves. With an improvement in the fiscal climate, meritorious programs whose budgetary increase was zero in the past suddenly receive increases.

While incremental budgeting leads to a normal distribution of policy changes, sequential search leads to strongly punctuated outcome changes. Padgett derives the particular budget change distributions that theoretically should emerge from his analysis and finds that the serial-choice model leads to a double exponential distribution. The "double" comes from the fact that budgets can be cut or raised, so there are positive and negative values for the curve. The two curves meet at the 0 point (that is, 0 percent change in the budget). The exponential distribution has fatter tails and a more slender peak in comparison to the normal—it is leptokurtic.

That is what would hold for a single program according to Padgett's model. But there are lots of programs, each of which has different characteristic parameters—different means and variances, for example. If we combine programs, as we did in figure 4.14, the result is a double Paretian distribution, which is even more fat-tailed and slender-peaked—leptokurtic—than the exponential distribution.

Padgett's serial-choice model is a model of decision making; the cascade model described above is a policy process model. Lots of decision makers interact in the cascade model—as, for example, when all members of Congress simultaneously got concerned about corporate governance in early 2002. Clearly these interactions can be transmitted down into bureaucratic decision making as part of the political climate—modeling in effect the notion of "political feasibility." No securities regulatory body could conceive of decreasing regulation in the face of the corporate scandal. The "political climate" constraint leads to a probability of zero for decreases in regulations, even though regulators may well have thought that desirable (indeed, the head of the SEC, responsible for regulating financial accounting, had spoken of bringing a more "accountant-friendly" environment to the agency in 2001). We can see some linkages between the general insights from the sieve and the cascade models.

The cascade and sieve models give little attention to institutional structure. It may be fairly easy to get members of Congress to focus on a problem and hold a hearing. But it may be very difficult to get a statute passed. Clearly, different institutional structures operate differently, creating different constraints on those acting within them. How can we build this into a model that retains the merits of the other two approaches in helping us understand both stability and change? A friction model can be helpful here; different institutions may have different levels of friction.[2]

Friction

The final way leptokurtic policy change distributions may emerge is through friction. If there is resistance to change—and this resistance can be political, institutional, or cognitive—change may not occur until some level of friction is overcome, at which point a "jump" in a policy commitment may occur. Institutional friction is the most familiar process to political scientists, but it has tended to be thought of as static and often has been critiqued as "gridlock." What is characterized as gridlock may be better characterized as institutional friction: hard to overcome, but major shifts in policy may occur when it is.

Let us turn to a real-world policy example. On August 28, 1950, President Truman enthusiastically signed Social Security reforms he had urged for years, reforms that expanded Old Age and Survivors Insurance (OASI) benefits by 77 percent, expanded the covered population dramatically, and decreased the required contributions in the system. The result was a transformation in the program from a small system covering only 6 percent of the elderly in 1940 into a program "firmly established as part of American public policy" (Sparrow 1996:34).

The 1950 legislation radically transformed the small program established in major amendments to the Social Security Act in 1939. The 1950 statutory changes caused an explosion in Social Security expenditures. From FY 1949 to FY 1950, real expenditures grew 3 percent. From FY 1950 to FY 1951, they grew 25 percent, and the next fiscal year they grew an additional 37 percent—the largest two-year percentage increase in the history of the program—even though most payments would come much later as the newly covered pensioners retired. By 1952, expenditures had increased by an astounding 71 per-

---

2. This section draws from Bryan D. Jones, Tracy Sulkin, and Heather Larson, Policy Punctuations in American Political Institutions, *American Political Science Review* 97 (2003): 151–72.

cent, and expenditures increased 10 percent a year or more for the next three fiscal years (True 1999).

Between these two landmarks, Congress enacted only two very minor adjustments to the program. This almost complete absence of legislative output was not for lack of trying. Presidents Roosevelt and Truman urged change; major advisory commission reports indicated the desirability of reform; many bills were introduced, and both House and Senate committees held hearings and reported legislation. Sporadic, but vocal and persistent, calls for reform emerged immediately after the 1939 enactments and continued until 1950, but there was no reform.

Moreover, there were good objective reasons for action. Sparrow (1996: 39) calls the failure to enact reform "puzzling" and points out that "a further expansion in the Social Security system would have guaranteed a large net increase in federal revenues, since most of the government's obligations would not be incurred until contributors retired. In the meantime, the government would receive desperately needed funds and would ease inflationary pressures by limiting consumer spending." In other words, a "window of opportunity" existed; the issue occupied the national agenda before, after, and during the war; great effort was expended in proposals, bill writing, and hearings; yet Congress failed to pass legislation. When Congress finally acted, the result was not incremental adjustment but major policy reform.

In democracies at least, it is easier to talk about an issue than to get serious action on it. In the United States, executive support or even support of legislative leaders may not ensure passage of a popular act; the system requires concurrent majority support in both houses of the legislature in addition to the president's acquiescence. In the case of Social Security, Republicans posed important counterarguments to Social Security expansion based on wartime revenue need—a kind of "lockbox" argument mimicked sixty years later. Airing of arguments takes time; opposition to change can be entrenched; even extraordinarily good ideas can be thwarted for a long time.

We can take the Social Security story one step further. Figure 6.1 diagrams the percentage change in real budget authority and major Social Security amendments since the Second World War.[3] Major statutory enactments are associated with major changes in budget commitments, even though changes in Social Security commitments affect future retirees far more intensely than current ones. Even a policy area that is thought of as quite stable and consistent is rent with periods of punctuations (True 1999). Not all budgetary punc-

---

3. These are the Social Security laws that were rated as among the most important statutes enacted by a weighting system that we devised. See appendix 3 for details.

Figure 6.1. Percentage Change in Real Social Security Budget Authority and Major Social Security Enactments

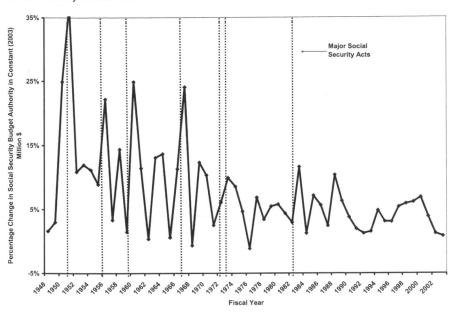

tuations are associated with major statutory reforms—there are in fact more budgetary punctuations than major statutes. The story in Social Security is not major reform followed by incremental adjustments, but major reform, incremental adjustment, *and* substantial policy reform.

The general lesson is that policymaking institutions are "sticky"—they do not respond simply or directly to demands or needs. Social, economic, and political changes are not automatically registered in public policies in democratic systems. Moreover, agenda access itself may also exhibit "stickiness," albeit on a less dramatic scale. The agenda space is severely limited, and many issues can compete for the attention of policymakers. In the case of Social Security, during the "missing decade" (Sparrow's term) of the 1940s many bills were introduced in some years (fifty-four in 1941), while very few were introduced in others (seventeen in 1943) (Sparrow 1996:60). Executive and legislative attentiveness shifted from intense to absent during the long period of policy inactivity as other matters clamored for governmental attention.

Political institutions impose costs on policy action in direct proportion to how far a policy proposal has proceeded in the lawmaking process. It is easier to get an issue discussed than it is to get serious attention for a specific line of policy action; it is easier to get a hearing on a bill than to schedule it for a vote; it is easier to get one house of Congress to pass a bill than it is to get it enacted. These institutional costs act in a particular way. They keep the course of public policy steady and unvarying in the face of lots of changes; that is, they do not allow for continuous adjustment to the environment. Early decision theorists termed this pattern "incremental." But these costs also cause major policy changes when dynamics are favorable—a "window of opportunity" opens, in the language of Kingdon (1995).

Our review of three types of constraints on policymaking—friction, cascades, and sieves—has revealed quite different dynamics and causal structures. They are not mutually inconsistent; indeed, they almost certainly all operate together to produce the extraordinarily complex patterns we observe in American policymaking. All three processes are similar in their implications; they all help explain the unusual shape of change we observed in figure 4.14. We now turn to a more intensive examination of the friction model, because it has the potential of integrating the dynamics of policy process studies with the equilibrium statics of institutional analysis.

Earthquakes and Sandpiles

To get some insight into how friction models might operate in policymaking, we take a brief detour into the natural sciences. It turns out that leptokurtic distributions have an important role to play where some form of friction is involved. One such place is in geophysics. The earth's crust is divided into major segments, or plates, that slide against one another. This phenomenon— plate tectonics—explains continental drift; it also accounts for earthquakes.

If we order observed earthquakes from the smallest to the largest, we will observe many very small earthquakes (the incremental), and a number of very large ones (the punctuations), but very few moderate quakes proportionately. The earth's surface plates slide against one another, driven by powerful forces in the earth's core (the "inputs"). Even in the face of steady pressure from inside the earth, however, most of the time friction holds the plates together, allowing small-magnitude quakes to release some (but not all) of the pressure. But as time progresses, and the pressure builds, at some point a potentially disastrous "jump" must occur. Exactly when and where this may occur is, of course, a difficult thing to predict. But geologists understand the general process. The "inputs" of plate pressure are not directly translated into "outputs" of earthquakes. Geologists and seismologists have found that, in fact, the distribution of earthquakes by size is leptokurtic: The friction of the earth's crust keeps moderate quakes from occurring. This means a greater than normal proportion of very small quakes occur, fewer moderate ones, but then a greater-than-expected proportion of very great ones, once the underlying forces of change are strong enough to overcome the friction imposed by the earth's crust. This is a pattern that should now sound familiar. In geophysics it is known as the Guttenberg-Richter law (Rundle, Turcotte, and Klein 1996; Sornette 2000). To make things even more maddening, because the earth's crust is so complex, sometimes ruptures in the plates propagate across the surface, and sometimes they are constrained by local conditions. This kind of indeterminacy is characteristic of complex systems and is the reason that earthquakes, like policy changes, are so hard to predict.

A second model, Per Bak's sandpile model, received much interest for its simplicity and power in generating insights about the behavior of complex systems (Bak 1997). If we have a pile of sand on a flat surface, such as a plate in the laboratory, and steadily drop grains of sand on the pile, one grain at a time, and measure how many grains fall off the plate in reaction to each grain that is added to the pile, we find that the constant input is not at all reflected in constant outputs. Rather, landslides occur. Usually, when one grain is added to the pile, nothing happens; none falls off. But eventually the additional grain of sand disrupts the system, and a landslide occurs. The observed landslides are of all different scales. Most are very small—minor output adjustments to an incremental process. But others are very large, sweeping down large portions of the pile. Very few, however, are moderate. The distribution, like that of earthquakes, is leptokurtic.

Even though Bak was able to measure the input perfectly, indeed to control completely the input series by steadily dropping one grain of sand at a time, the output was neither steady, nor incremental, nor proportionate to the input, nor normally distributed. Output was "lumpy," with some drops of sand generating no or only very small changes, and others generating large landslides. The resulting frequency distribution of changes is leptokurtic, like figure 4.14. When Bak related the frequency of the categories (the y-axis) to the size of the landslide (the x-axis), he found that they followed a Paretian or power function. The frequency of earthquakes also has a Paretian distribution, as do at least some public budgets. (We will show this in chapter 7.)

We can think of Bak's sandpile as a system adjusting to input—the steady, uniform drops of sand onto the pile. If the system processed inputs proportionally, the outputs would be linearly related to the inputs, which clearly is not the case. Similarly, with earthquakes, geologists believe that the pressures pushing one tectonic plate against another are constant, though the responses as measured at the earth's surface are leptokurtic. In sandpiles and earthquakes, incremental adjustment is an incomplete description of the process. It is the friction supplied by the pile—the internal structure of the system—that accounts for the disproportionate and nonlinear relationship between inputs and outputs. Now, if Bak had used a hypothetical material that had no friction, then he might have observed steady outputs in proportion to the steady input streams. But the friction associated with the grains of sand held them together in the face of small pressures. After sufficient pressures built up, however, the friction was overcome; landslides resulted. Further, like earthquakes, sandpile landslides are unpredictable due to the complex surfaces of the grains of sand.

Policy change where institutional friction operates parallels this general description of sandpiles and plate tectonics. One might think of the drip-drip of sand on Bak's sandpiles as informational input, and of the landslides as policy outputs. It is not generally the case, however, that inputs are so well behaved in the case of policy change, but the general picture is apt. Even if inputs were well behaved, outputs would not be. In the particular case of Social Security, the 1940s witnessed demands that resulted in minor adjustments to the 1939 basic statutory structure—minor incremental adjustments.[4] When reform came in 1950, it came in monumental fashion. No moderate adjustments occurred anytime during the period.

Unlike Bak in his laboratory, geophysicists can observe neither the friction of the earth's tectonic plates nor the inputs from the earth's core that push the plates directly (although they can now assess the pressures associated with fissures in the crust). Instead, they measure the outputs from the process (the earthquakes) and study their frequency distribution. We are in a similar position, but with one important advantage. It is relatively easy to order political institutions according to the extent to which they impose decision costs on policymaking activity. To the extent that a political institution adds decision costs to collective action, the outputs from that institution will exhibit periods of stability ("gridlock") interspersed with periods of rapid change. The higher the decision costs that must be overcome to achieve a collective goal, the more punctuated the outputs are likely to be. And there are clear statistical tests we can use to determine just how punctuated, or leptokurtic, any distribution of outputs is.

---

4. Seamen affiliated with the War Shipping Administration were added to the system in 1943, and survivors of veterans killed in the war were added as beneficiaries in 1946 (Sparrow 1996:36).

Disproportionate Information-Processing
in the Policy Process

We have concentrated thus far on human factors in decision making that generally lead to disproportionate information-processing. Even without the friction of formal institutional arrangements, policy would be produced disproportionately. Add institutions into the mix, and the disproportionality can be magnified. One advantage of the stochastic approach we employ here is that we can examine theoretically these two sources of disproportionality even though we have no idea of the particular combinations that might emerge in any particular situation (such as any of the policies we briefly examined in chapter 4).

Costs in Political Institutions

We need to be somewhat more precise about the idea that decision-making costs lead to institutional friction. The payoff will be a very general framework for studying political, economic, and social change where interactions among actors are structured by institutions. An *institution* may be defined as a set of individuals acting according to common rules resulting in collective outcomes. Institutional rules are not neutral, in the sense that different rules often lead to different outcomes (Jackson 1990:2). These aggregations of individuals interacting according to rules react to information from the environment and come to a collective response (even if the collective response is simply the sum of individual actions, as it is for markets and elections and roll-call voting in legislatures).

Decision-making systems impose four kinds of costs in making decisions in response to a changing environment: decision costs, transaction costs, information costs, and cognitive costs. *Decision costs* are costs that actors trying to come to agreement incur. They include bargaining costs and institutionally imposed costs, such as those built into a separation-of-powers governing arrangement (Bish 1973; Buchanan and Tullock 1962). *Transaction costs* are costs that parties incur after they come to agreement (North 1990). In market transactions, these involve such items as the cost of ensuring compliance to contractual agreements, and other payments to third parties to complete the transaction. It ought to be clear that in advanced democracies decision costs in the policymaking process heavily outweigh transaction costs. Bringing relevant parties to agreement in a system of separated powers (decision costs) generally outweighs the costs of holding hearings, enacting statutes, or changing budgetary allocations once agreement has been reached (transaction costs). In any case, we combine these costs in our analysis, terming them together "decision costs."

Information costs are search costs—costs of obtaining information relevant to making a decision. These are costs that exist when a person (or an organization) *wants* to make a decision. *Cognitive costs* are costs associated with the limited processing capacity of any social institution composed of human beings. These are costs that occur because people *don't know* they need to make a decision. If one is not attending to a key component of the environment, then he or she cannot decide to incur search or information costs. Information and cognitive costs will be imposed in any decision-making system, but decision and transaction costs are highly sensitive to the particular rules and procedures of institutions. These are pure institutional costs. Institutional costs in politics may approximate the manner in which friction operates in physical models.

Information Processing in Institutions

How can we assess the level of friction that is present in a decision-making institution? We now turn to a straightforward extension of the analysis presented in chapter 5. In essence, we will treat the cognitive architectures of decision makers, simply modeled by the implicit index model, as part of a general "cost structure" that affects the processing of information. That will allow us conceptually to integrate the formal institutional costs with the cognitive costs of boundedly rational decision makers.

The manner in which a policymaking system responds to information is critical in assessing policy change. As we have seen, the major problem with the initial incremental model of policy change is that it did not incorporate the flow of information from outside the system. No matter what the external challenge, the system responded incrementally. That is quite unrealistic and led to models that are easily rejected. If we can understand how decision-making systems respond to information in the absence of any institutionally imposed costs, then that idealized model can serve as a basis of comparison for systems that impose such costs.

A hypothetical fully efficient decision-making institution that imposed no costs would respond seamlessly to the world around it. That is, it would incorporate all relevant aspects of the information it encountered and would "use up" all the information in its decision-making process. The outputs of such a system would perfectly reflect the information flows coming from its environment (Simon 1996). If there were big changes in the environment, the system would respond with big changes. Similarly, small changes would generate only small changes. The major example of such a cost-free system is the classical model of a competitive economy.

In such a pure system,

$$R = \beta S \tag{6.1}$$

Where:
R = response = ΔO = change in output
S = information (signal)
β = benefits derived from the information flow (< 1).

The system reacts directly to the input flow by changing its output. What happens in real institutions in which decision-making costs are imposed? If costs are assumed to act linearly on the system, then

$$R = \beta S - C \tag{6.2}$$

Where C = costs.

Our hypothetical system continues to respond directly to the input flow. Now, however, it will not act until it recovers the costs that must be invested in reacting to the flow of information. Where costs are low, signals of low power get reflected into public policy. Where costs are high, only the strongest signals are translated into public policy. But the addition of set decision costs would have no great impact on the classical model; it simply generates a constant subtraction from the reaction of the system to the inputs— the reaction remains proportionate. In any case, set costs are not realistic.

In politics costs are imposed only when actors take the trouble to use the system to block action. For minimal changes, actors that would normally be opposed might not take the trouble. For major changes, they can mobilize and make use of the system to try to block changes, but they can also get on a bandwagon and push for even greater action than the signal might indicate. Costs might be proportionately high for signals of low strength (making the response less than the signal); but they might decline if the signal got stronger (making the response potentially more powerful than the signal). This leads to a model in which costs go down as the strength of the signal increases. While we cannot know exactly the form of the equation translating inputs into outputs, we do know that it is multiplicative rather than additive as in equation 6.2. The signal and institutional costs interact with each other to magnify the effects of the signal. This severely complicates matters and generally leads to leptokurtic output distributions.

$$R = \beta S \times C \qquad\qquad\qquad (6.3)$$

In this model, costs interact with the signal. We explain more below.

Distributions

What would the different types of costs we just described generate in terms of distributions of outputs, when dealing with the same series of inputs? Figure 6.2 depicts idealized response functions to input flows for a frictionless, cost-free policy system, a system with fixed institutional costs, and an interactive system. The frictionless system is highly sensitive to incoming information. For a hypothetical one-unit change in relevant information, the system responds with a proportional level of outputs. (If $\beta = 1$, then the inputs and the reactions are equal, if $\beta > 1$, outputs are stronger than inputs; if $\beta < 1$, then outputs are less than the inputs. But in any case the reactions are directly proportionate to the size of the input; this is reflected in the straight line going up from the origin along the 45 degree angle; it reflects a hypothetical β of 1.)

Figure 6.2. Information-Processing Policy Systems with Institutional Costs

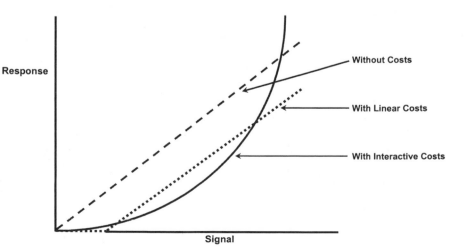

Figure 6.2 shows three curves: the frictionless one just described, one with fixed costs (also a straight line, but to the right of the first one); and one with interactive costs (showing responses being very low but curving sharply upward as the size of the signal grows). The system with fixed institutional costs ignores signals of low intensity, then responds proportionally to the strength of the signal after some threshold in signal strength is reached. Like the first one, this model reacts proportionately, but systematically at a lower level of response than if there were no decision costs. But let us consider the third line in some detail. This is the one where costs interact with the strength of the signal. In fact, the way we have modeled it here, costs reduce action up to some threshold, then gradually shift so that they amplify rather than reduce the reaction of the system to larger inputs. Such a model will produce virtually no response when signals are low, but massive reactions to strong signals; leptokurtosis results from its disproportionality.

As we argued in chapter 5, the cognitive architecture of the decision maker imposes a selective bias on the flow of information. Of course, decision makers in politics will not cling forever to bad information, but they undoubtedly believe it far beyond its utility. When the information is exposed as faulty, the decision maker must shift to a new understanding of the situation. In effect, the decision maker locks choice into a set of facts based in the past and must update in a punctuated manner in the face of change that cannot be ignored. The "news"—that part of the information stream a decision maker attends to and interprets—is leptokurtic. (This is a different way of saying that the system may substantially underrespond to changes in inputs— if policymakers ignore them—only then to overrespond to inputs after these reach some level of intensity. In effect, it corresponds to the attention-shifting model of chs. 2 and 3.)

Complexity in Information Processing

The preceding discussion reflects the complexity of decision-making systems. We have here tried to simplify by analyzing institutional costs within a single framework. The key question is how people interacting in political institutions process and respond to signals from the environment. If institutions add friction to informational inputs, then outputs will not be directly related to inputs. But how will inputs and outputs differ in policymaking systems? We posit that whatever the input flow, the output flow will be both more stable (ignoring many important signals) and more punctuated (reacting strongly to some signals).

Much work in political science points toward an information-processing approach with political institutions playing major roles in creating the friction and disjointedness associated with this approach. Institutional analyses show that a "policy core" exists that is not responsive to changes in preferences (for example, through replacement of legislators in elections), but when preferences change enough to move the pivotal legislators' preferences outside the core, then major punctuations in policy can occur (Hammond and Miller 1987; Krehbiel 1998). Policy process scholars have argued that policy agendas change when attentiveness and mobilization are directed at particular aspects of a complex environment, raising the probability of major policy innovations based on new ideas. Again, stability (when attention is not directed at the issue) and punctuation (when it is) occur in a single process (Baumgartner and Jones 1993). Similarly, in elections, first-past-the-post voting systems and partisan identifications by voters operate together to add great stability to election patterns that are nevertheless occasionally disrupted by realignments.

Institutional decision costs will add to the kurtosis of output distributions.[5] In chapter 7 we will explore explicitly the idea that different institutions of American government impose higher or lower levels in decision costs and therefore produce outcomes characterized by different levels of kurtosis. But for now, let us finish this discussion of costs and move to a simulation of the process we describe.

Simulating Generalized Cost Structures

In chapter 5 we reported the results of some simulations for the implicit index model that indicated the effects of overweighting a single measure in an index of the severity of problems facing a political system. We return to that approach to simulate the effects of generalized interactive cost structures on the output distributions of decision-making systems. We present the results of two different simulations. The first is a static simulation, in two stages. For the static simulation we think of information processing as occurring in stages: one associated with cognitive costs, one with institutional costs. At each stage, costs are assumed to be disproportionate to the size of the input

---

5. Institutions can also simplify decisions and overcome information and cognitive costs, leading to less kurtosis in outputs (Robinson 2004). But American national institutions were designed explicitly to impede overresponding and hence should lead to more kurtosis. Federalism, however, ought to operate against kurtosis by undermining veto coalitions (Baumgartner and Jones 1993).

signal. Informational inputs are transformed first because of the cognitive costs that would be there no matter what the institutional setting. The resulting series is then transformed a second time to simulate the institutional costs that may also be present. For the sake of simplicity, both transformations are identical. This allows us to know whether a simple two-stage transformation can generate leptokurtic output distributions of the form of figure 4.14. Then we turn to a more complex but more realistic dynamic simulation and ask the same question.

Think of an input stream affecting a policymaking system. We may characterize the input stream as a distribution. Because informational signals stem from numerous diverse sources, it is a reasonable assumption that the underlying (but unobserved) input distribution is normal, as would be the case for the implicit index model. Then the system imposes nonlinear transformations on the input stream, as in figure 6.2. This simulates the case of delay in responding to input signals at low levels of intensity, then responding with increasing intensity to the signal as it increases. For our static simulations, we use a cubic transformation. The particular form of the transformation is arbitrary, but the general logic is not.

$$R = \beta S^3 \tag{6.4}$$

Before we simulate the likely situation of a normal input distribution, we present in figure 6.3 a simulation for the case of a uniform input distribution in order to get a firmer understanding of just what the transformations do. This is a kind of limiting case in which the world has some uncertainty, but it may be monitored by one indicator, and that indicator is uniform and unchanging. We generated 10,000 random numbers drawn from a uniform distribution with mean of 0 and standard deviation of 1. We cubed these numbers once and cubed the resulting numbers once again. Then we made frequency distributions for all three sets of 10,000 numbers. The input series, being uniform random, has a strongly negative kurtosis value (i.e., it is platykurtic rather than leptokurtic). The first cube law transformation yields a kurtosis of 3.70, slightly more than the normal, while the second's kurtosis is 9.73 and is leptokurtic. Even in a hypothetical uniform world, nonlinear cognitive and institutional costs will yield leptokurtic output distributions.

Now we turn to a more realistic distribution of inputs in a complex world. The Central Limit Theorem, and the associated implicit index model, dictates that the input distribution would be normal if diverse input streams are com-

Figure 6.3. Frequency Distributions of a Uniform Information Input with Two Cube Law Transformations Applied Sequentially

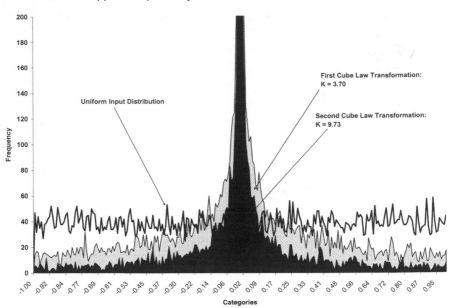

The *y*-axis is truncated to illustrate the differences between the bodies of the distributions.

bined to yield an index, or sum of the indicator values. Figure 6.4 simulates this situation, again with the two sequential cube transformations. Again the distributions are highly leptokurtic, with the first transformation producing a kurtosis of 36.30, and the second 977.44. In both of these two important cases for the distribution of information coming into a policymaking system, outputs will be leptokurtic when costs are nonlinear.

Much more important, however, is the fact that the leptokurtosis increases disproportionately as the costs move from cognitive costs alone (the first cube law transformation) to cognitive costs and institutional costs (the second transformation). This happens regardless of the input distribution— the ordering of the distribution by extensiveness of cost imposed leads to a parallel ordering of the magnitude of kurtosis. Remember that an informationally efficient institution (or, for that matter, decision maker) would translate information into policy outputs in a proportional manner. As costs are imposed, either by the cognitive "stickiness" of the decision maker or by the formal "stickiness" of the political institution, the result is increasing kurtosis in the distribution of outputs. Exactly how sticky the process is will be an em-

Figure 6.4. Frequency Distributions of a Normal Information Input with Two Cube Law Transformations Applied Sequentially

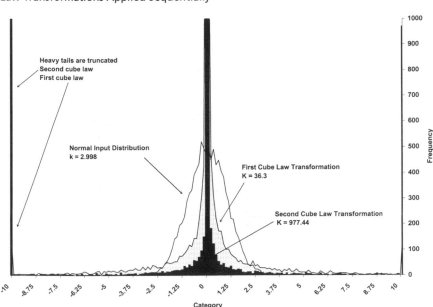

The *y*-axis is truncated to illustrate the differences between the bodies of the distributions.

pirical manner that we will investigate in detail in chapter 7; our simulations in figures 6.3 and 6.4 are intended only to show that a nonlinear transformation such as a cubic transformation would produce shifts of this type. In any case, figures 6.3 and 6.4 demonstrate that processes within institutions may transform a uniform or a normal distribution of inputs into a leptokurtic distribution of outputs.

Further Observations on the Transformations

We have reason to expect that cognitive costs will be added in a convex curve relationship like the cube law represents. Attention allocation and the general bias toward the status quo in most systems of decision making work to delay responses; but then internal dynamics can operate to respond increasingly intensely to the stimulus via positive feedback effects. The cube law and other upward-turning, convex curves model this kind of general process. It is also possible that cognitive costs act to cause immediate overreaction, and then a dampening down of response. This would be modeled by a concave curve, such as the logarithm or a power function under 1.0. But based on our understanding of the structures of American government, we are pretty sure that the institutional costs of the Madisonian variety operate to cause delays in responses. These institutional facets can be overcome, but they generally operate in a single direction: toward more delay. Therefore, we can imagine the two sets of costs in our model to operate differently; we assess that possibility below.

Table 6.1 reports the results of a few more simulations of the form described above. Here we use a variety of different assumptions about the form of cognitive costs but continue to use a cube law to model institutional costs. That is, we assume that a variety of curves might describe the disproportionality associated with cognitive costs, but only a convex curve such as the cube law can model the operation of American-style institutional decision costs. The first column in the table lists the transformations used to model cognitive costs. The second column reports the results of several transformations representing cognitive costs. All save one—the square root transformation—have kurtosis values considerably in excess of 3.0, the value for the normal distribution. The value for the square root transformation is less than 3, suggesting that cognitive costs can yield distributions that are less punctuated than the normal.

Table 6.1. Kurtosis Calculations for 10,000 Random Normal Numbers, Transformed Nonlinearly and Subjected to a Second Cube Transformation

Distribution Used for the First Transformation	First Transformation (Cognitive Costs)	Second Transformation (Institutional Costs) (Results from the First Transformation, Cubed)
Power 3 (cube)	39.304	974.441
Power 5	368.044	5,393.799
Power 7	8,880.357	9,999.961
Exponential	38.239	3,947.561
Logarithm	6.771	133.913
Square root	2.500	7.534

Note: The table shows kurtosis values of a distribution of data after transforming a normal random input series once, then a second time. The first transformation, designed to simulate possible cognitive costs, multiplies the input series by the factor described in the left-hand column. The second transformation simulates institutional costs, and this does not change; it always cubes the results from the first transformation. For example, the first row shows that when the input series is cubed, the resulting distribution has a kurtosis value of 39. When this series is again cubed in the second transformation, the value is 974. In the second example the first transformation raises the input series to the fifth power, leading to values of 368 after the first transformation and 5,394 after the second. A wide variety of transformations are used to simulate possible cognitive cost structures. All generate high kurtosis scores.

In the third column of table 6.1, a cube transformation is applied, and all values substantially exceed the normal. This will be true generally of the general class of convex transformations that model institutional decision costs—power functions of values above 1, the exponential, and other such transformations all will lead to kurtosis values above 3.0 for most if not all input distributions.

If we were to monitor a rational-adaptive decision process over time, in which diverse input streams were combined through the implicit index model, we would see a normal distribution of outputs. Proportionate information-processing implies a normal distribution and a kurtosis value of 3.0. Cognitive costs move the kurtosis value of outputs away from 3.0 in this manner: if the decision-making process generally encourages delay and over-response, the kurtosis value will be greater than 3.0; if it encourages over-response and then dampening down, the value will be less than 3.0. Because of the manner in which attention must be allocated, we expect that generally the former will be true, but there is no way to be absolutely certain. We can say with certainty, however, that decision-making costs, such as those imposed by formal American governing institutions, will work to increase kurtosis values, because they build in delay.

Figure 6.5 presents a graphical display of the effects of cognitive and institutional costs on the stages of decision making. The figure is just a reproduction of figure 3.1 with the simulated distributions displayed. As decision making proceeds, outputs at any stage become increasingly characterized by extreme stability and occasional punctuations. While the figure is suggestive only, the general form of the diagram is completely supported by the empirical analysis of American policymaking institutions, as we shall see in the next chapter.

Estimates for Particular Distributions

At this point, we introduce one more technique from the stochastic-process tool bag. While it is a little bit tricky technically, its logic is straightforward. It turns out that for a few distributions, plotting the value of the category midpoint of the frequency distribution (the x-axis for figures such as 4.14, 6.3, and 6.4) against the transformed frequencies of those categories (the y-axis) will yield a straight line whose fit can be assessed by standard regression techniques. Specifically, we can see if a particular distribution follows a Paretian distribution by taking the logarithms of both the categories and the frequencies, and we may check for the exponential distribution by taking the logarithm of the categories and plotting this against the raw values

Figure 6.5. The Effects of the Stages of Decision Making (Simulated Results)

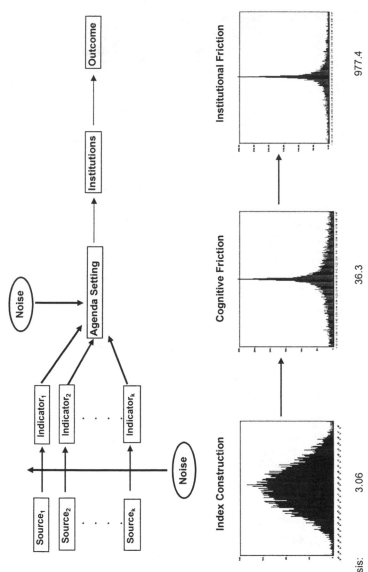

Figure 6.6. Semi-Logarithmic Plots of Category Midpoints versus Cumulative Frequencies in the Categories for Both the First and Second Cube Law Transformations

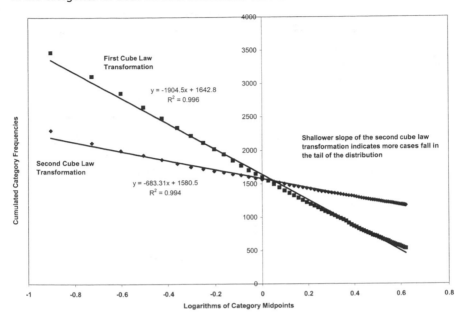

of the frequencies.[6] This is the technique Bak used to study the distribution of sandpiles, as did Richter for earthquakes.

In figure 6.6, we plot the logarithms of the categories versus category frequencies for our simulated values taken from figure 6.4 for both the first and second cube law transformations. We fit only the positive values for the frequency distribution, for ease of presentation. The data simply show the same frequency distributions as presented in figure 6.4, but with the magnitude of the changes expressed in logarithms and the number of such changes in raw numbers. Each distribution fits the exponential distribution very well, but the slope of the second cube law transformation is shallower (that is, it has a lower regression coefficient) than that of the first cube law transformation. This is as expected, because the second transformation has more cases in the tails (the extreme categories), in effect pushing up the lower end of the regression line and causing the slope to be smaller. Notice that we are able to compare directly the slopes of the two with respect to how large the tails

6. We usually use the *cumulated* distribution instead of the frequency distribution, because the small number of cases in a distribution's tail can cause sampling fluctuations.

are, and hence know the relative severity of the punctuations (they are much more in evidence in the second transformation). A major reason for this approach is the unsatisfactory behavior of standard measures of kurtosis in certain situations (particularly for the very leptokurtic distributions that we will need to compare).

The data from figures 6.4 and 6.6 fit the exponential model, as is clear from the straight line in semi-logarithmic coordinates. Other leptokurtic distributions could better fit the Paretian model, producing a straight line when both the category values and the frequencies are logged. A normal distribution would clearly not fit either transformation; it displays distinctly concave (downward-opening) curvature. So we can use these simple graphical tools to get further information about the degree to which various distributions show the characteristic leptokurtosis we have found in figure 4.14. These techniques are simple, graphically clear, and more robust than only kurtosis scores. We return to this form of analysis, using actual observations from various institutions of American government rather than simulated data, in the next chapter. But the reader can see here how these transformations affect the series, and how we can use these tools to assess the degree to which the series are wildly, or only mildly, leptokurtic.

Dynamic Stimulations of Institutional Friction

Now we turn to a dynamic simulation of institutional friction. In association with Prof. James Stimson of the University of North Carolina, we have designed a computer simulation to study the effects of institutional friction on the distribution of policy outputs.[7] Our theory is dynamic, so the model is similarly dynamic, but it is more complex than the simple transformations we discussed above. We ask the basic question of whether a simple dynamic model of institutional friction can generate leptokurtic output distributions of the form of figure 4.14. If we can confirm our static simulations with a dynamic one, we will be all the more confident that we are on the right track.

The model examines only the friction component of our theory; it does not incorporate negative or positive feedback effects that can affect the policy process. It has four fundamental components:

7. We are deeply indebted to Professor Stimson, who suggested the idea of a dynamic simulation and wrote the code. We encourage readers to try this simulation themselves. The program can be downloaded from the Policy Agendas Project Web site: www.policyagendas.org.

- A *signal* that is input into a hypothetical policymaking system
- A *friction mechanism* that sets a threshold below which the system responds only partially
- An *error accumulation* feature that builds up pressure in the environment that may produce subsequent policy action
- A *response* that is dictated by the strength of the input signal and institutional friction that has accumulated from previous periods

Basically, we draw an input signal from a normal distribution and run it through a system that adds friction. Friction is modeled by a parameter that operates as a threshold. Above the threshold, the signal generates a response equivalent to the strength of the signal—the signal has overcome the friction. Below the threshold, it generates a partial response. Friction is slowing down the response. If the "partial" response is set to zero, then below the threshold we have "gridlock"—no response whatsoever. If the partial response is positive, then the system responds to the input signal with some fraction of the signal strength. The policymaking system has added friction by attenuating the response but not entirely blocking it. The model also has an "error accumulation" feature by which partial responses allow the system to get out of adjustment with its informational environment. That part of the signal that is not responded to accumulates and can affect the policymaking process in the future.

The model has two variables, the information signal and the policy response, and it has three parameters that model the institutional friction and govern the policy response. The signal flows through the system, generating a policy output that is dependent on the operation of this simulated institutional system.[8]

We simulate the input signal at time t by a random draw from the stan-

---

8. The model may be written as follows:
The variables:
   R_t = Response
   S_t = Input signal
The parameters:
   C = friction parameter
   λ = efficiency parameter
   β = amplification parameter
$R_t = \beta S_t$ if $S_t + \Sigma S_{0<k} > C$; otherwise, $R_t = \lambda \beta S_t$
Where: $0 < \lambda > 1$; [λ may vary between 0 and 1];
   $0 < t > k$ [the time series goes from period 0 to period k]
   $S_t = N(0,1)$ [each input signal is drawn from a standard normal distribution]

dard normal distribution (that is, with mean of 0 and standard deviation of 1). One might think of this as input from an implicit index with "rational adaptation," so that the simulation will focus on institutional friction alone.

The friction parameter, C, acts as a threshold, and its level can be set by the user of the simulation. Above the value of C, the signal generates a response proportional to the strength of the signal. Below the value of C, the signal generates only a partial response. The extensiveness of the response is governed by the efficiency parameter, λ; if $\lambda = 1$, then there is essentially no threshold and no institutional friction. The signal passes through the institutional frame unhindered, generating a response proportional to its strength. If $\lambda = 0$, then there is no partial response to the signal, and friction is at its maximum. The λ parameter is also user-specified.

If the signal is hindered, that portion of the signal that does not generate a response cumulates and is added to the next period's signal strength. This simulates the buildup of pressure when problems fester and are only partially addressed. But it is possible that the whole situation will "blow over," and that happens in the model when an input signal receives a negative sign when the cumulated signal is positive (and vice versa). That is, the model allows accumulated pressures both to build up and to dissipate.

Finally β, the amplification parameter, is set by the user. β allows for the signal to be magnified or attenuated in the translation process. It is linear only, whereas positive feedback effects might be modeled in a more complex fashion. But at present we simply want to examine whether a simple dynamic friction process can generate leptokurtic outputs.

The simulation relies on repeated random draws that are run through the system. These random draws are the S_t—that is, the hypothetical time series, and t is one million. Results of our hypothetical policymaking system that has run for a million time periods are input into a frequency distribution. This allows us to study the shape of the distribution, including its kurtosis. We can then alter the friction and other parameters of the system (there are only three parameters, and each can be adjusted easily by the user) and observe the results. On a portable computer, each simulation takes just a few seconds, even with a million observations.

The primary finding from the simulation is clear and unambiguous: for appreciable friction, output distributions are invariably leptokurtic. Numerous runs of this simulation yield leptokurtic output distributions.[9] A direct

9. For $C = 1$ and greater. The friction parameter has standard deviation units, so $C = 1$ may be interpreted as a system that responds to about one-third of the signals it receives.

comparison between figure 4.14 and one of our simulations gives some indication of the extent to which we have properly modeled the friction process by our simulation. Figure 6.7 directly compares a simulation incorporating a great amount of friction with a considerable partial response.[10] A normal distribution with similar standard deviation is presented for comparative purposes. The similarities between the two are remarkable, with both having strong central peaks and very fat tails. Clearly, institutional friction is capable of producing policy output distributions consistent with what we observe empirically. Nevertheless, there are some differences; the simulated graph is not as leptokurtic as the actual data, which have both a more concentrated central peak and fatter tails. In effect, institutional friction (at least the way in which we have modeled it) cannot fully account for budget distributions. This is almost certainly due to the exclusive focus on friction in the model, with no provisions for positive feedback and cascades.

More complete results are presented in figure 6.8. There we graph the kurtosis of the resulting output series against λ, the parameter that captures partial response, for three levels of the threshold parameter. (Recall that the input series are always the same.) The system works entirely as expected. The stronger the friction, the more punctuated the policy output. Kurtosis is a function both of the threshold, C, and the extent of partial response—leakage through the threshold. As the threshold increases, kurtosis increases exponentially (note the log scale). When little leakage occurs with a high threshold, kurtosis is exceptionally large—most of the cases represent no change, but a small number of really big punctuations occur. When the leakage around the institutional friction reaches a maximum (at $\lambda = 1$), the level of the threshold is irrelevant, and kurtosis for all values of the threshold equals 3, the value for the normal input distribution. No friction, no leptokurtosis. It's that simple.

In general, the dynamic simulation supports our general argument here that the interaction of cognitive factors with institutional friction invariably leads to a pattern across time of general stability with episodic punctuations. And our simulations allow us to show that with friction set to zero or leakage set to its maximum, there is no punctuation at all. So we believe there is something important in these parameters that explains the punctuated-equilibrium patterns that we observe in the real data.

---

10. $C = 3$; $\lambda = 0.4$; $\beta = 1$.

Figure 6.7. Budget Authority (top) and Simulated Institutional Friction Model (bottom)

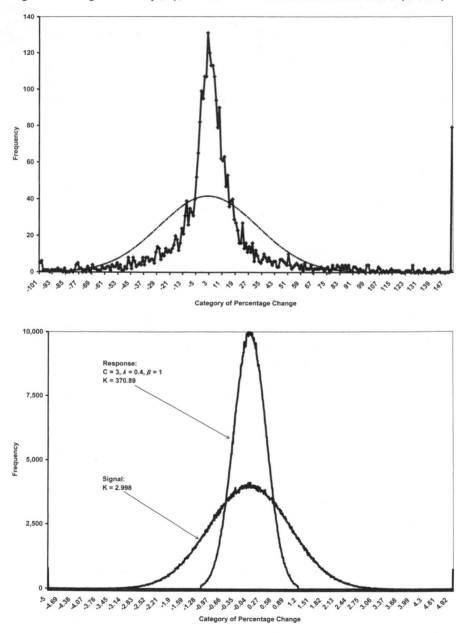

Figure 6.8. Kurtosis Values as a Function of the Extent of Institutional Friction

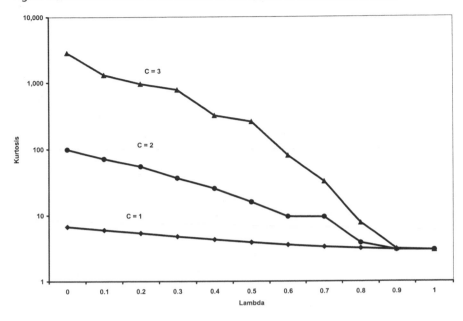

The General Punctuation Hypothesis

The American policy process follows a distinct pattern. Attention is directed at a perceived problem. The matter is raised to the formal agenda. Policy action may or may not result. If it does, serious budgetary commitment to the matter may or may not occur.

Each stage of the process requires the expenditure of considerable resources to overcome the dual frictions of the attention spans of actors and the cost structure of political institutions. Political activists work to move their favored policy into the limelight, but the attention of policymakers may be directed elsewhere. When attention shifts, bills can be introduced and hearings can be scheduled, matters with low institutional costs. But the next stages, passage of laws and major budgetary commitments, require much more effort—because of the design of American governing institutions.

The interaction of political demand and institutional costs is written in traces of policymaking activities across time. This trace is, as a consequence of this interaction, punctuated with periods of intense activity and periods of more quiescence. If we aggregate the time traces of policy change, their frequency distributions are found to be leptokurtic.

The result of our analysis of general cost structures leads to a testable hypothesis about the interaction of boundedly rational decision makers and the institutions within which they make choices. As all government institutions impose costs, we expect all outputs from them to show positive kurtosis. Further, we know that costs are added as a policy proposal moves through the policy cycle. As decision-making costs increase—that is, as it is more difficult to translate informational inputs into policy outputs—the more leptokurtic the corresponding output distributions. We term this the *general punctuation hypothesis* and provide some straightforward but rigorous empirical tests in the next chapter.

Conclusions

Fat-tailed distributions are generated by interdependencies among cases. In this chapter, we presented three models of change that have been developed to understand this signature pattern: policy cascades, decisional sieves, and institutional friction. Each alone can account for leptokurtosis in policymaking distributions. When they are combined, we have an order of complexity that defies simple case-by-case analysis. Staying focused on the distributions, however, allows us to see the patterns. Our simulations of friction models suggest that adding costs affects the kurtosis of distributions—the extent to which they are punctuated—in a straightforward manner. If we order these distributions from those from institutional arrangements that impose the least costs on collective action to those that impose the most costs, the kurtosis of the associated distributions should move from low to high. In the next chapter, we do exactly that.

7

Policy Punctuations
in American Political Institutions

In the previous chapters, we laid out a series of expectations about the nature of decision making in situations, such as government settings, where attention is allocated disproportionately and where various types of costs and inefficiencies characterize the process. We wanted to know what could explain the particular "shape of change" we noted in figure 4.14. Apparently something in the U.S. political system produces extreme allegiance to the status quo, interspersed with occasional frantic overreactions. The simulations of the previous two chapters demonstrated that disproportionate information-processing, which stems from cognitive processes and institutional arrangements interacting with signals from the policymaking environment, yields these distributions. Those were simulations; now we look at real data.

In this chapter, we examine distributions of change in a number of key American political institutions. If we can find variation in how efficient various institutions are, then the outputs produced by those institutions should have different characteristics. And, we will show, different institutions of American government can be arrayed along a continuum of efficiency in translating input signals into policy outputs. Those closest to the input stream, those focusing on monitoring and reporting relevant social indicators, are the most efficient, and those closest to the output stream, further along the policy cycle, are by nature less efficient in their response to problems. Since policies are made through a multistage process—from paying attention in the media, to holding hearings, to gaining government attention, to passing legislation or presidential orders, and finally to budget allocations—we can expect a progression from more to less efficient. This should then be reflected in the degree of leptokurtosis visible in the outputs of various institutions.

So, in this chapter we focus on many different institutions of U.S. govern-ment and politics. We study the nature of change in agenda setting (congres-sional hearings, congressional bill introductions, *New York Times* stories, and *Congressional Quarterly* coverage), lawmaking (statutes enacted and presiden-tial executive orders issued), and budgetary commitments. In addition, we study elections (presidential, congressional, and senatorial) and, for compar-ative purposes, the stock market. Some idea of the magnitude of this task is suggested by the fact that the number of observations upon which these distributions are based total more than 400,000 cases. First we lay out our ex-pectations in more detail.

Institutional Costs and Stochastic Processes

Recall that our discussion of costs in political institutions emphasized those associated with the process of decision making itself, costs that would emerge in any institutional setting. Informational and cognitive costs fall into this cat-egory. Because of the manner in which informational heuristics and the cog-nitive capacities of decision makers affect the process, no matter what the institutional setting, overreliance on the status quo and occasional cascades generated by monitoring and mimicking can affect decision making. Search processes and cognitive mechanisms both result in change distributions that are leptokurtic, because they operate to cause peakedness (in the monitoring stage) and fat tails (in the mimicking stage).

What happens when we incorporate institutions? Considerable friction would exist even if institutions of government were informationally efficient, because American political institutions are not designed to be fully respon-sive. Supermajorities in Congress, presidential vetoes, separation of powers, and federalism all combine to produce a purposeful status quo bias in our in-stitutions; the framers wanted it that way. When pressures are great enough, of course, the system responds, but it is not designed to respond easily to every whim of the population. Existing formal studies of institutions are equilibrium-based, but they clearly imply that continuous preference changes would result in discontinuous policymaking processes (Hammond and Mil-ler 1987; Krehbiel 1998). As opinion shifts gradually, it crosses a "pivot point" threshold, and the expected collective institutional response shifts disjointly. Policymaking responses by government can change quickly even if the un-derlying positions of all voters are changing gradually as a pivot point is crossed. There are other reasons for disjoint change, such as changes in leadership preferences, periodic elections, how costly and time-consuming it is to mobilize social movements, etc.

Stickiness and inefficiency are not flaws; they are characteristics designed into the system in order to create stability and for other perfectly justified reasons. By referring to them as inefficient we do not imply that they are pathological. But they do add costs, and these costs are known as decision costs (costs of coming to a decision in the face of diverse preferences) and transaction costs (costs of making a decision when all are agreed on the need for a decision). Different parts of the policy process, however, have higher or lower decision and transaction costs. For example, holding a hearing on a policy-relevant issue entails decision costs, but these are far less onerous than actually passing a law.

These considerations allow us to formulate two key testable hypotheses that relate cognitive, organizational, and institutional factors to the distribution of policy outputs. We term these together the "general punctuation hypothesis." The first hypothesis relates to the generality of leptokurtic outputs in human decision-making systems, and the second to the systematic operation of institutional friction.

H_1: *Output change distributions from human decision-making institutions dealing with complex problems will be characterized by positive kurtosis.*

If our reasoning is correct, we expect *always* to find positive kurtosis in the outputs of institutions—elections, lawmaking, budgeting, media coverage, scheduled hearings on bills, etc. Wherever institutions deal with complex issues, we expect disproportionate responses because of attention shifting. These induce output distributions with high kurtosis. (Note that we discuss institutions dealing with complex problems here, not just government. The analysis is quite general, and there is no reason to expect that what we observe would be limited to government as opposed to other complex organizations.)

Institutions can be more or less efficient, as we noted. This leads to the second hypothesis:

H_2: *The more friction that an institution imposes, the more leptokurtic its output distribution will be.*

As the framers purposefully designed certain inefficiencies into the U.S. political system, we expect to see this reflected in their outputs. These constitutionally designed inefficiencies are not the only ones operating, but in general it is straightforward to rank the various institutions of U.S. government by how efficient they are. This allows a strong series of tests of our hypotheses.

Ranking Institutions

To rank institutions we need to think through how each institutional setting would increase decision costs relative to a hypothetically fully efficient system (that is, one that translated informational inputs into institutional outputs directly and seamlessly). We have already noted that modern stock and bond markets impose low transaction costs (and no decision costs). As a consequence, in the United States at least, these asset markets closely approximate the fully efficient institutional mechanism. They are not perfectly efficient, of course, but compared to other institutions they are much closer to this ideal.

Elections are more problematic. In the past, high transaction costs have been imposed on some voters: non-property-holders, blacks, women. The 2000 presidential election as conducted in Florida indicates that transaction costs may still be imposed on some groups, even though the systematic and large-scale exclusion practiced in the past no longer exists. The long historical coverage we have for elections in our analysis makes the changing nature of the cost structure problematic. In the modern era, however, transaction costs have been relatively low, and theories of electoral choice have emphasized cognitive friction (in the form of partisan identification and, more recently, heuristic reasoning) to the virtual exclusion of institutional costs. In any case, whatever transaction costs have been imposed in the past should be imposed similarly for the three kinds of elections we study, and they should differ among themselves only in cognitive stickiness. We hypothesize that presidential, senatorial, and congressional elections should be increasingly more leptokurtic in their change distributions. The visibility at the presidential level ensures the availability of information, but less is available for Senate elections, and less still for House elections. With less new information, voters are forced to rely more on party identification, biases, cues from others around them, etc. Each of these introduces more friction; hence, we expect the more visible elections to be the most efficient and the least visible ones to be the most leptokurtic. All the election data we expect to be relatively efficient compared to those indicators that come further down the policy-making stream (but less so than economic markets).

Now we turn to the policymaking distributions. Policy process scholars find it useful to divide the policymaking process into stages such that an issue must access one stage before moving to the next. For example, an issue must access the agenda before it is enacted into law; and it must be enacted before a budgetary allocation (DeLeon 1998). The process looks roughly like this:

Systemic $\longrightarrow$ Policy $\longrightarrow$ Enactment $\longrightarrow$ Resource $\longrightarrow$ Implementation
Agenda   Agenda   Commitment

The distributions we study essentially monitor the process at the agenda-setting, enactment, and resource-commitment stages; we do not have implementation measures in our study. The existing literature indicates that institutional costs increase as a proposal moves through the policy stages. It clearly is more difficult to get a statute passed than to get a hearing scheduled on a proposal. These institutional difficulties reflect decision costs—the blocks to collective policy action on the parts of the legislative and executive branches. Policy stage theory allows us to rank these distributions by the stages they assess, under the assumption that decision and transaction costs will be higher as we move through the policy cycle.

In sum, we rank the various social processes we study in terms of institutionally imposed costs (least to most) as follows:

1. *Markets.* Pure markets have low transaction and decision costs; modern stock and bond markets come very close to this ideal. Information is freely available. (The appendix to this chapter details a smattering of the long history of the empirical study of financial markets.)
2. *Elections.* Voting in modern times has low transaction and decision costs, but elections themselves differ in the extent to which they impose information costs. In presidential elections, information is widely available (but can require cognitive resources to interpret). Less information is available in most House races. Senate races fall in between.
3. *Policy Processes.* Policy stage theory implies the following ranking, from the least to most costly.
   a. *News coverage.* We assess the systemic agenda via general news coverage. Changing from one topic of coverage to another is not cost-free (for example, journalistic beats may institutionalize coverage of one topic more than another), but it is relatively easy compared to lawmaking.

b. *Bill introductions.* Any member of each chamber of Congress may introduce bills, but many bills, such as appropriations and re-authorization measures, must regularly be scheduled for debate and voting. In general this is a low-cost process, however.

c. *Congressional hearings.* We assess the policy or governmental agenda through hearings. The topic of scrutiny must attract attention (a cognitive cost) and incur some institutional costs (the minority party cannot schedule hearings alone; only so many hearings are likely to occur at a time; it takes staff and effort to schedule the hearings). This is more costly than introducing a bill.

d. Congressional Quarterly *Coverage.* The coverage of inside-the-beltway issues likely mimics the salience of issues on the governmental agenda. The specialized press has no independent agenda-setting power; rather, it reflects the lawmaking activities of Congress.

e. *Executive Orders.* The president alone acts, but executive orders often have major policy impacts (Mayer 2001). Decision costs are high but are concentrated within a single branch of government.

f. *Statutes.* Both houses of Congress and the president must cooperate in the lawmaking process; decision costs imposed by the structure are very high.

g. *Budgets.* The literature indicates a complex interaction between cognitive and institutionally imposed costs. Institutionally, large changes are subject to the same dynamics as statutes. Cognitively, budget routines and operating procedures dominate the process, and these tend to be highly resistant to change. Final budget allocations come at the end of a long process with many veto points and areas of friction. We expect costs to be highest here.

Aspects of this ranking may be debatable, but at least it provides a starting point for comparing the outputs of diverse institutional arrangements. In any case, it is clear that political institutions impose decision and transaction costs because of their deliberate design and operation, and that this facet of political life can be examined empirically. Table 7.1 indicates the nature and sources of the data we employ.

We noted above that what we term cognitive costs interact with institutionally imposed costs, so that it is somewhat artificial to try to disentangle them. However, in cases where institutionally imposed costs are very low, leptokurtosis in output distributions very likely indicates that cognitive costs are the reason. We know that the distribution of information is normal, given

Table 7.1. Distributions Studied

Distribution	Description	Source
Asset markets (stock market average returns)	Daily percentage change in the Dow Jones Industrial Average, 1896–1996	(Dow Jones 1996)
Elections: U.S. president	Election-to-election swing in the two-party vote for president, pooled across counties, 1828–1992	Made available by Peter Nardulli (see Nardulli 1995).
Elections: U.S. House of Representatives	Election-to-election swing in the two-party vote for the House of Representatives, pooled across districts, 1898–1992	King (1997)
Elections: U.S. Senate	Election-to-election swing in the two-party vote for the U.S. Senate, pooled across seats, 1920–1998	Calculated from U.S. Senate web site
Media coverage	Annual percentage change of the number of New York Times stories on policy topics, pooled across 19 major content categories, 1946–94	Tabulated from the Policy Agendas Project
Hearings	Annual percentage change in the number of scheduled hearings, pooled across 19 major content categories, 1946–98	Tabulated from the Policy Agendas Project
Bill introductions	Annual percentage change in the number of bills introduced, pooled across 19 major content categories, 1973–98	Tabulated from the Congressional Bills Project
Specialized coverage of lawmaking	Annual percentage change in the number of stories, and (separately) in the length of those stories, in the Congressional Quarterly, pooled across 20 content categories, 1946–94	Tabulated from the Policy Agendas Project
U.S. lawmaking	Annual percentage change in the number of enacted laws by the U.S. federal government, pooled across 19 content categories, 1946–98	Tabulated from the Policy Agendas Project
U.S. executive orders	Annual percentage change in the number of executive orders issued by the president, pooled across 19 content categories, 1946–98	Tabulated from the Policy Agendas Project

(continued)

Table 7.1. *Continued*

Distribution	Description	Source
Public budgets: congressional budget authority	Year-to-year percentage changes in budget allocations, U.S. congressional budget authority, 1947–96, pooled across 62 OMB subfunctions	Tabulated from the Policy Agendas Project
Public budgets: outlays	Year-to-year percentage changes in total U.S. budget outlays, 1800–1994	U.S. Bureau of the Census

the argument we developed in chapters 3 and 4 concerning implicit indexes, but the "news"—that part of the information flow that people attend to— is likely to be leptokurtic. Elections and asset markets (stock and bond markets) are both characterized by very low decision costs (generally the buyer or voter has control over the decision) and low transaction costs.

The Agenda Size Problem

Before moving to our analysis, it is worthwhile to consider one complication in our data series. Is the policy agenda space constant, or can it expand and contract in time? This is an important theoretical issue that has the potential of introducing considerable confusion into the discussion. We know that *measures* of agenda access change empirically in postwar America. For example, the number of hearings Congress has conducted in any given year has varied from 766 (in 1947) to 2,232 (in 1979). In 1960, Congress conducted but 769 hearings, and in 1998 only 1,206. Similarly, the *New York Times* published considerably more stories in the 1970s than in the 1950s or in the 1990s. While we do not observe secular trends in these agenda-size indicators, we do see large differences in the overall size of our agenda indicators in different periods of history. Should we adjust for variations in the size of the agenda space or not?

In what follows, we study shifts in policy effort across the nineteen major topic areas of the Policy Agendas Project datasets. In all cases, we use percentage changes, but those percentage changes can be based on counts or proportions. For example, if we examine hearings on macroeconomics, we could take the number of hearings in 1950 minus the number of hearings in 1949, divided by the number of hearings in 1949. Or we could take the proportion of hearings on macroeconomics in 1950 minus the proportion of hearings in 1949, divided by the proportion of hearings in 1949.

This difference matters. Figure 7.1 shows the frequency distributions for

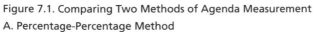

Figure 7.1. Comparing Two Methods of Agenda Measurement

A. Percentage-Percentage Method

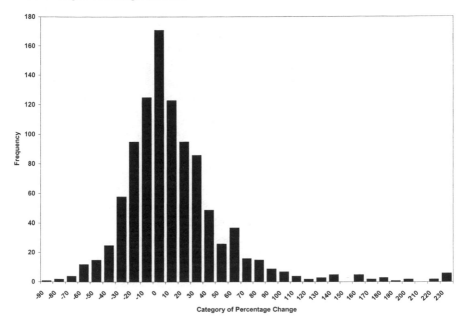

B. Percentage Count Method

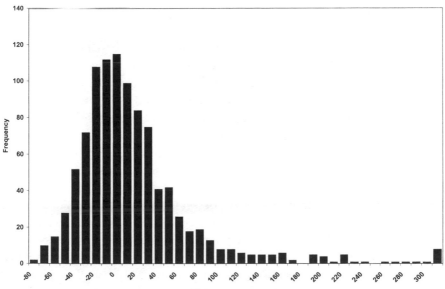

the total number of hearings held by Congress, 1947–98, using these differing approaches. If we base the distribution on proportions or percentages—that is, if we assume that the agenda space is constant (Part A of the figure— the percentage-percentage method), then the distribution is more symmetric (and clearly leptokurtic). If we base it on counts (Part B of the figure—the percentage count method), it is leptokurtic but is in addition more heavily skewed toward the positive side.

Which approach is most appropriate depends on one's objectives. It is evident, for example, that expanding the capacity of government allows the intrusion into new issue areas without necessarily withdrawing from the old ones. Generally, in the analysis to follow, we focus on changes in proportions, because we are fundamentally interested in shifting priorities. In other work, we might be interested in raw numbers, since the overall workload of government, the carrying capacity of our institutions, is an interesting question in itself. We leave that, however, for another time. The general findings, in any case, are robust with respect to method (though they do differ in some important details). By analyzing changes as we do, with percentages, our analysis here is consistent with that presented in figure 4.14.

Kurtosis in Policy Distributions

All of the distributions we study here are first-difference change scores, or percentage changes; our theory applies to changes. For all distributions, we pool the time series change scores across the basic units; that is, for example, in using the Policy Agendas datasets we first calculate the percentage change in attention to a given topic (using our nineteen major topics) from year to year, over the roughly fifty-year period of the study. Then we combine the nineteen different series into a single frequency distribution, so we have about a thousand cases, roughly speaking, for most of our analyses. Some of our series, as we will show, have longer historical coverage, and some use units other than our nineteen content categories. For example, in elections, the units are the electoral constituencies, and the frequency, of course, is not annual but every two, four, or six years, depending on the election. For the stock market data, we use daily returns of the Dow Jones Industrial Average over more than a century. Figure 4.14, which uses OMB categories of spending, shows about sixty categories over fifty years, with about three thousand total observations. In any case, all our data are organized in as similar a manner as possible and reflect a consistent organization: percentage changes combined across time and categories to produce a single frequency distribution of percentage changes in outputs. (See the appendix to this chapter for a discussion of measurement and analysis strategies employed here.)

There is no ideal method for comparing distributions regarding their punctuations, so we settled on a three-stage approach. First, we ran a standard statistical test, the Kolmogorov-Smirnov test, on all the distributions; then we examined the sample kurtosis for each distribution; finally we moved to a direct parameter-estimate approach. The K-S test compares the values of a distribution of data to a theoretical probability distribution (for example, the normal distribution). The null hypothesis that the underlying probability distribution is either normal or lognormal is easily rejected for all the distributions we studied. With this test, we reject the incremental model for decision making for all policy distributions under study.

Armed with this information, we examine the standardized kurtosis values for each of the distributions we studied. These results are presented in table 7.2.

Table 7.2 generally supports both of our hypotheses. First, all distributions suffer from what finance economists term the "excess kurtosis problem" (Mills 1995)—each and every one of the values exceed that expected from the normal distribution. We can test the statistical hypothesis that the observed sample kurtosis exceeds the expected theoretical value of 3, and reject it in each and every case.[1] So our data strongly confirm the generalized punctuation hypothesis: incrementalism and proportionate response characterize none of these series.

We can directly assess our second hypothesis, the institutional friction hypothesis, as well. The table divides the distributions into three groups: those assessing final *output commitments* (the budget distributions), those indicating *public policy processes,* and those independent of policymaking institutions (here termed *input distributions*). The policy process distributions include statutes, executive orders, CQ stories, House and Senate hearings, and

---

1. Kurtosis is defined statistically as the fourth moment around the mean; the variance and skew are the second and third moments. A unit-free measure of kurtosis somewhat analogous to the coefficient of variation for the variance (the standard deviation divided by the mean) was developed by Karl Pearson; it is the raw fourth moment divided by the square of the variance (Anscombe and Glynn 1983). Its formula is

$$k = \frac{\Sigma(X - \mu)^4/n}{(\Sigma(X - \mu)^2/n)^2},$$ where μ is the mean.

The sample kurtosis is distributed normally with variance equal to 24/n in the limit (Anscombe and Glynn 1983) around the theoretical mean of 3. Kurtosis has suffered from difficulties in interpretation (Finucan 1964; Moors 1988) and is flawed as an empirical measure (Balanda and MacGillivray 1988; Groeneveld 1998). But it is the best direct comparative measure we have.

Table 7.2. Sample Kurtosis Calculated on Raw Data

Distribution	Kurtosis	SE(K)
Budgetary series		
Budget authority	85.29	.100
Budget outlays	59.55	.342
Policy process series		
Statutes	23.81	.159
Executive orders	9.75	.151
CQ stories	23.54	.165
House hearings	29.28	.154
Senate hearings	28.42	.154
House bills	29.09	.0015
Senate bills	15.97	.024
Policy input series		
New York Times stories	10.18	.162
House elections	3.67	.035
Senate elections	4.52	.137
Presidential elections	5.85	.00022
Dow Jones Industrials	7.63	.00087
Averages		
Budgets (2)	72.42	
Policy process (7)	22.84	
Input series (5)	6.37	

Note: Policy data distributions were calculated using the percentage-percentage method. Presidential elections kurtosis estimate was calculated on grouped data; SE was estimated from entire sample. DJIA kurtosis estimate was averaged across four time periods; SE estimated from entire sample. Policy distributions include statutes, executive orders, CQ stories, hearings, and bills. Input distributions include newspaper coverage, elections, and markets. We have eliminated change data of more than 1,000 percent because of the extraordinary sensitivity of the sample kurtosis to extreme values.

congressional bill introductions.[2] Input distributions include *New York Times* coverage, elections, and markets. We see great differences in the average sample kurtosis—over 72 for the budget distributions, almost 23 for the policy process distributions, but only 6.37 for the input distributions. The kurtosis measures generally order the distributions according to institutional friction. This provides very strong support for institutional friction being the root cause of disproportionality in policy outputs.

2. Bill introductions, made available to us by Scott Alder and John Wilkerson, cover a much shorter period—1973–98; hence, the frequency distributions are less satisfactory and may cover only a unique historical period. Nevertheless, the distributions generally conform to expectations.

There are, however, several "out of order" distributions within these groups. The most glaring of these is the kurtosis for executive orders, which falls closer to the values characteristic of the input distributions than to the policy distributions. Also noteworthy is that the kurtosis for statutes is less than that for hearings. For the input distributions, elections seem to exhibit less kurtosis than markets, and the House, Senate, and presidential elections do not fall in the order we expected. Kurtosis is a finicky statistic, not always reflective of the concept we want to measure, though it is the best single indicator of peakedness of a distribution. But there are additional ways—more complicated, unfortunately—that allow us to look at these series in more detail. We turn to these analyses now.

A More Precise Test: Direct Parameter Estimates

Probability distributions differ in kurtosis. A normal distribution displays less kurtosis than the exponential, which in turn has less kurtosis than the Paretian distribution. Kurtosis essentially measures how "wild" the distribution is, that is, how many cases are far out in the tails compared to how many are in the central peak. We can assess this with greater accuracy in the following manner.

If we can figure out what underlying probability distributions characterize several empirical frequency distributions, we can rank them according to their shapes. It is technically not possible to study all possible probability distributions, but we can do so for two important classes of distributions—the double exponential (or Laplace) and the double Paretian. The distributions are termed "double" because change can occur in a positive or a negative direction. These distributions may be arrayed along a continuum from thin to heavy tails (or from "mild" to "wild" randomness, in Mandelbrot's [1997, 1999] terms), with the normal being mildest—the thinnest tails and hence fewest punctuations—the exponential being wilder than the normal, and the Paretian the wildest of the three, with the heavy tails and more probable punctuations.[3]

Each probability distribution is actually a family of distributions depending on certain parameters. The normal distribution is completely characterized by its mean and variance (higher moments—skew and kurtosis—do not vary within the normal family). Skew and kurtosis do vary within the other two families of curves. A Paretian distribution becomes more and more wild

---

3. Theoretically, the Paretian is so punctuated that its variance is infinite. This applies to the theoretical distribution; in empirical practice all moments may be estimated.

as the absolute value of the exponent decreases, essentially fattening the tails of the probability distribution and weakening the shoulders, as we illustrated in figure 6.6. Similarly, the slope parameter for the exponential assesses wildness—the shallower the slope, the more punctuated the distribution (and the more cases in the tails).

We present below selected frequency distributions and their associated scatter plots used to estimate the type of probability distribution with the highest likelihood of generating the empirical frequency distributions. Paretian and exponential distributions may be estimated by examining the fit of the frequency distribution (frequencies versus category midpoints) in log-log and semi-log plots respectively.[4] We plot the category midpoints against the number of cases in each category, yielding a simple scatter plot, just as we did in figure 6.6 in the previous chapter. If the log-log or the semi-log plot fits the data, then the points will appear in a straight line (that is, for the Paretian, the log-log plot will show a straight line; for the exponential, the semi-log plot will show a straight line; and for a normal distribution, either of these two transformations of the data will show an obvious drop-off). Any curvature in the plots clearly shows that the underlying distribution does not fit the distribution.

Once we've presented the data in these scatter plots, the question of interest is simply whether the transformed data array in a straight line (and what is the slope of that line). Standard ordinary least squares regression procedures can be used to compare directly the goodness of fits, and these are presented in tables 7.3, 7.4, and 7.5. These goodness-of-fit tests can then show statistically whether the series are normal, exponential, or Paretian. That is, the R^2 statistic should be close to 1.0, indicating that the straight line really does characterize the transformed data. If so, we know that the data are Paretian or exponential. Further, the slope estimates from the regressions can tell us how many cases are far out in the tails rather than in the central peak. Lower regression coefficients indicate "flatter" lines, reflecting more cases out in the tails: greater relative "wildness" in the data, higher kurtosis. Observing the plots also tells us if the observations in the tail fall below or above the re-

---

4. For the Paretian, $y = aX^b \rightarrow \ln(y) = \ln(a) + b\ln(X)$; for the exponential, $y = ae^{bx} \rightarrow \ln(y) = \ln(a) + bX$, where X represents the category midpoints of the variable of interest, and y represents the frequencies associated with the midpoints. As is common practice, we use the cumulative frequencies to estimate the plots. Each side of the distribution is cumulated from its extreme (tail) to the middle category. This makes no difference in the estimation procedure, and displays the fundamental aspects of the distribution by stabilizing the "chatter" at the tails of the distributions.

gression line, indicating that they are less punctuated or even more punctuated than the distribution to which they are being compared. Although this
set of procedures is admittedly complex, it gives us a complete way of testing
how "wild" each of these distributions is. This is a much stronger test than
the simple kurtosis test we presented above, and it shows roughly similar results for our data. But its greater precision allows a more satisfactory ranking
within the three general categories (input, process, output). The greater the
institutional costs, the "wilder" the series, generally speaking.

Policy Processes

We expect to find more pronounced punctuations in policy commitment
distributions than in agenda-setting distributions. Early in the policy process,
when proposals struggle to gain agenda access, cognitive costs are high, but
institutional costs are reasonably low. Scheduling a hearing indicates that policymakers are taking the topic seriously—the topic has accessed the policy
or governmental agenda—but it requires low costs. Figure 7.2 shows the frequency distribution for Senate hearings, along with the log-log and semi-log
plots for the distribution. The hearings data are skewed toward the positive
side. The slopes for the left side of the scatter plots have been reversed in sign
for purposes of comparison.

The fit for the log-log plot (in the lower right part of the figure) displays a
distinct downward curvature, indicating that the fit is not good; basically the
distribution is less "wild" than the Paretian. The semi-log plot, shown in the
lower left quadrant, fits much better: The observations fall almost perfectly
along a straight line, indicating that the exponential distribution fits the data
well. The slope estimates for the two tails are distinctly of different absolute
magnitude; this indicates that punctuations are more common in a positive
direction than in a negative one. Both are relatively straight indicating that
both the positive and negative distributions are exponential rather than normal. (If they were normal, they would curve downward in the semi-log presentation just as they do in the log-log presentation.)

Figure 7.3 depicts the frequency distribution and the associated scatter
plots for lawmaking. That is, rather than dealing with hearings, it deals with
statutes. The frequency distribution is not as well structured as the other policy distributions, but a long tail is clearly present, and the right tail displays
excellent fit. The left tail fits less well, a phenomenon that characterizes all of
the policy frequency distributions. Moreover, the strong central peak is not
as much in evidence in the distribution—it is overshadowed by the extended

Figure 7.2. Yearly Percentage Change in Senate Hearings by Major Topic, 1946–99
A. Frequency Distribution

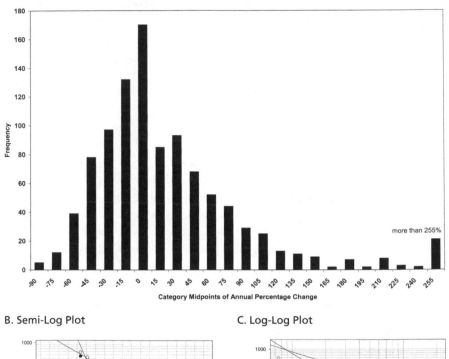

B. Semi-Log Plot   C. Log-Log Plot

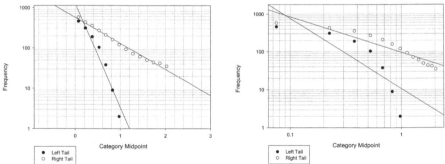

tail. This is characteristic of exponential distributions as the parameter increases in absolute magnitude. One interpretation of this finding is that when major statutory change occurs, it tends to shift activity from the existing set of policy concerns to new ones.

All of the distributions we studied except for government budgets were best approximated by a double exponential probability distribution. In almost all cases, the fits were exceptionally good, although the right (positive

Figure 7.3. Yearly Percentage Change in Statutes by Major Topic, 1948–98
A. Frequency Distribution

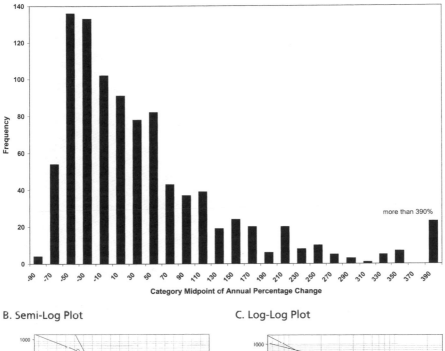

B. Semi-Log Plot   C. Log-Log Plot

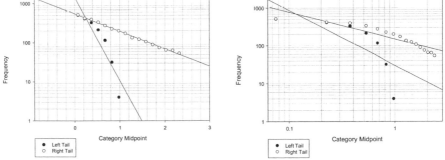

change) tails for the policy distributions display better fits than the left (negative) tails.[5] Table 7.3 presents the exponential fits for policy data (except government budgets), as well as for the elections data. Because of differences in measurement, the market, elections, and policy data are not directly compa-

5. In the case of bills, we estimated only the positive tail because of peculiarities of the distributions.

Table 7.3. Exponential (Semi-Log) Fits for Policy and Election Frequency Distributions

Distribution	N Total # (Categories by Year)	Parameter estimate (Right Tail/ Left Tail)	R^2 (Right Tail/ Left Tail)	Pseudo Standard Error (Right Tail/ Left Tail)
Statutes (1948–98)	17,041	−.448	.995	.0013
	(950)	2.137	.838	.0466
Executive orders	3,659	−.507	.932	.0054
(1945–2000)	(1,045)	2.238	.820	.0845
CQ article lines	12,580	−.538	.999	.0019
(1948–94)	(874)	2.238	.928	.0623
CQ stories	12,580	−.550	.975	.0037
(1948–94)	(874)	2.781	.893	.0541
Average for decision		**−.511**		
making		**2.348**		
House hearings	41,977	−.575	.960	.0049
(1946–99)	(1,007)	2.774	.960	.0272
Senate hearings	24,149	−.647	.983	.0047
(1946–99)	(1,007)	2.586	.949	.0272
House bills	107,448	−.602	.995	.0041
(1973–98)	(475)	—	—	
Senate bills	40,477	−.551	.988	.0052
(1973–98)	(475)	—	—	
Average for		**−.593**		
agenda setting		**2.680**		
NYT stories	34,149	−.885	.991	.0035
(1946–94)	(911)	2.850	.936	.0429
House elections	19,387	−1.451	.992	.0013
(1898–1992)		1.480	.992	.0013
Senate elections	1,277	−1.920	.983	.0099
(1920–98)		1.993	.999	.0028
Presidential	110,003	−2.480	.985	.0013
elections		2.173	.998	.0005
(1824–1992)				
Average for inputs		**−1.684**		
		2.124		

Note: N's refer to the number of cases studied for each distribution. For the policy distributions, the raw data were transformed into changes across categories, yielding a lower number on which the frequency distributions were based. These N's are in parentheses. The parameter estimate is the estimate of "b" in the equation for the exponential distribution in note 7.4. Estimates are unstandardized regression coefficients for semi-log plots for each distribution. Pseudo standard errors are standard errors adjusted for the actual N's involved in the calculation of the coefficients. Only positive slopes were estimated for the bills data due to the skewed nature of the distributions.

rable to each other, but each indicator can be compared to others within sets; therefore, we present them separately. But all can be assessed by how well the goodness-of-fit statistic indicates that they fit the exponential distribution rather than some other, such as the normal. The policy output data can be ranked by using the parameter value—lower values indicate more extended tails (that is, more punctuations).[6]

The first lesson from table 7.3 is simply that all of these policy series fit very well with an exponential model. What can we say about the differences among the series? We noted above that the slope parameters can be used to assess the degree of "wildness" in the series: the steeper the slope, the less wild the series. As hypothesized, the systemic agenda, measured by the *New York Times* coverage of politics and government and other input processes, displays more moderate change than distributions assessing later stages in the policy cycle. Examining policy processes separately for two categories, agenda setting and decision making, we find the expected results. The policy agenda, measured by the introduction of bills and the scheduling of hearings, ranks after the input variables. The data suggest somewhat different processes at work in House and Senate, with House hearings slightly more punctuated than Senate hearings. This can be due to constitutional facets that require hearings in certain categories—appropriations, for example. In any case, the difference is not large, and both fit the general pattern. Similarly, there are differences between the chambers on bill introductions.[7]

Next in order of punctuation comes decision making. Inside-the-beltway specialized coverage by the *Congressional Quarterly* is wilder than press coverage or hearings. *CQ* coverage is clearly indexed to the lawmaking activities of Congress, with more emphasis on the "downstream" activities related to lawmaking than on the "upstream" activities of agenda setting. As hypothesized, statutes are the most punctuated of all the policy distributions. Lawmaking requires the cooperation of three separate policymaking institutions and, as a consequence, can be exceptionally sticky. Presidential executive orders occupy a position between the agenda-setting variables and the statutes. Presidential attention must be engaged in order for him to issue an executive

6. There are difficult statistical issues associated with direct parameter estimates. First, cumulated plots will not yield independent errors, but the error seems to be trivial (Sornette 2000:141). Second, the number of cases is not properly represented by the number of points plotted. We report "pseudo standard errors" to indicate that we adjust these for the actual number of cases studied. This is not entirely correct, either, because the extreme values are estimated by fewer points than the points closer to the center of the distribution.

7. Parameter estimates suggest the Senate is more punctuated in bill introductions, but kurtosis estimates suggest the opposite. This is one area where the two techniques diverged.

order, but the president commits the nation to a policy change with a signature (Mayer 2001). While the president need not secure the cooperation of
other branches of government in the process, he must deal with intrabranch
cooperation among affected agencies, the Office of Management and Budget,
and the Justice Department.

Table 7.3 also presents some averages for the decision-making series, the
agenda-setting series, and the input series. The slope parameters for both
positive and negative directions of the change distributions are ordered exactly correctly—from an average positive tail slope of $-.511$ for decision making, to $-.593$ for policy agenda-setting processes, to -1.684 for input series.
The input series are therefore less punctuated than the agenda-setting series,
which are in turn less punctuated than the decision-making series. This is
very strong confirmation for our hypothesis. We will see in the next section
that as we move to budgets the punctuations become even more extreme; indeed our budget series fit the Paretian distribution, not the exponential. In
sum, institutional costs can be seen to transform the series by adding friction
to them, producing the characteristic pattern of doing very little even in the
face of changing inputs, then overreacting when pressures finally rise above
some threshold.

Public Budgets

Next we examine resource commitment—the special case of congressional budget authority. Figure 7.4 presents scatter plots for U.S. congressional budget authority, pooled across OMB subfunctions, for 1947–2000.
We have focused on policy subfunctions, eliminating financial transactions,

Figure 7.4. Real U.S. Budget Authority, FY 1947–2000, Pooled across OMB Subfunctions
A. Semi-Log Plot   B. Log-Log Plot

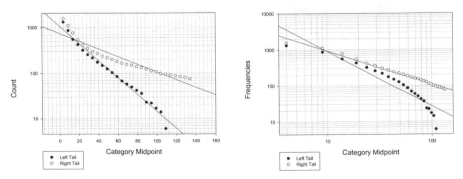

Figure 7.5. Real U.S. Budget Outlays, 1800–1994

A. Frequency Distribution

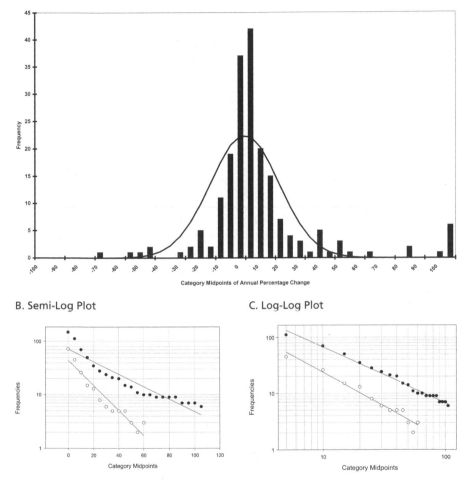

B. Semi-Log Plot   C. Log-Log Plot

and have adjusted for inflation. (The data underlying figure 7.4 are the same as those in figure 4.14, presented earlier.) Figure 7.5 presents the full set of graphs for annual changes in aggregate U.S. budget outlays, 1800–1994 (we do not have category-by-category spending totals going back to 1800, unfortunately; these data relate to the size of the entire federal budget). Table 7.4 describes the log-log fits for the two budget series we examined. In each case, the Paretian fits better than the exponential. For U.S. budget authority, available only for the modern era, an exponential fits the left, negative change tail better than the Paretian. That is, cuts are less punctuated than increases.

Table 7.4. Goodness-of-Fit Measures for Paretian Distribution for Government Budget Data

Budget Distribution	N	Exponent Right Tail/ Left Tail	R²	Pseudo Std Error
U.S. budget authority	3,024	−0.924	.990	.00038
FY1947–2000 (all		1.525	.875	.0314
policy subfunctions)				
U.S. outlays 1800–1994	195	−0.996	.988	.00005
		1.205	.954	.0817
U.S. budget authority	3,024	−.019	.984	.0002
(exponential fit)		8.149	.885	.0002

Note: Parameter estimates are for "b" in the equations in note 7.4.

The Paretian distribution displays "wilder" randomness than the exponential; hence, the budget distributions are both more stable and more punctuated than any of the distributions estimated in table 7.3. This is exactly what the theory of institutional friction predicts; budget stability is maintained through the formal institutional friction of American political institutions and through the interconnecting net of subsystem activities noted by the original incrementalists.

Growth and Retrenchment in Public Policy

A close look at the semi-log plots for the policy distributions suggests a slight upward curvature for the right (positive change) tail. This is suggestive of a "stretched exponential," which may be viewed as more leptokurtic than the pure exponential (Laherrère and Sornette 1998). (This is also the case for the stock market data.) On the other hand, the left side (negative change) of the policy distributions curve down in the semi-log fit, indicating a "truncated exponential," one less leptokurtic than the pure exponential. The downward curve is not a consequence of the constrained range of the data due to our use of percentage changes; the end point of these tails occurs prior to the theoretical minimum of −100 percent. It is a real phenomenon.

In essence, policy expansions are more punctuated than retrenchments. The budget and policy data support a general proposition: there seems to be a rush as government enters new domains of activity, taking on new responsibilities, but there is a more cautious approach in withdrawing from previously supported activities. In particular, there is less evidence of the large lurches when dealing with withdrawal of attention as we see in positive changes, when attention surges into new areas. Our data clearly make the case, however, that retrenchments do indeed occur, though they are somewhat less dramatic than the areas of growth.

We have conceived of institutional friction as imposing stability but being subject to occasional punctuations. We generally associate it with distributional kurtosis. But there may be an element of institutional friction associated with skew: Affected interests may be able to retard retrenchment punctuations more than they can prevent expansion punctuations.

Elections

We round out our study of the role of institutions in information processing with a brief look at elections and markets. Elections in general should be characterized by less institutional friction than policymaking processes, and our distributional analysis shows that is indeed the case. Figure 7.6 presents the results for House elections; similar results were obtained from the analyses of Senate and presidential elections. As is the case for the policy distributions, the exponential is the proper fit for this distribution. The slopes for each side of the double exponential are similar in absolute value, indicating that change is about as likely in one direction as the other—strikingly different from policymaking distributions.

Within elections, presidential contests are least punctuated, while House contests are most (see table 7.3), as we expected because of the greater amounts of information available in the high-salience elections. The slope coefficients for House elections, -1.45 and $+1.48$ (for the positive and negative sides of the distribution) are significantly more flat than those for the Senate (-1.92, $+1.99$) and the presidency (-2.48, $+2.17$). The steeper slopes for House elections indicate that they are characterized by long periods of very little deviation in the voting patterns for the incumbent, punctuated by occasional large swings. Missing is the moderate adjustment that is expected with the normal. It is well known that legislators may make themselves safer than might be predicted by the policy attitudes of the represented, but our approach offers a method of comparison not available when we examine distributions in isolation. It is likely that information in presidential elections leads to more frequent updating, and hence to more moderate change, than in House elections. For the sake of space we do not present the Senate and presidential election results in a figure as we do for the House in figure 7.6, but these series fit the exponential just as the House data do. The more visible elections have steeper slopes (as seen in table 7.3), indicating relatively fewer punctuations, as compared to the House elections.

Figure 7.6. Election-To-Election Change in House Vote Margin by District
A. Frequency Distribution

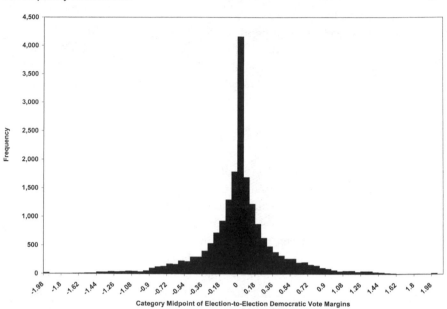

B. Semi-Log Plot   C. Log-Log Plot

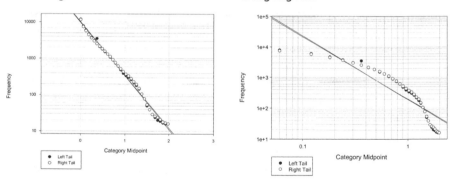

Markets

Markets, in theory, should be the most friction-free of the major political
and economic institutions in America; in fact, in theory they should be perfectly efficient. Figure 7.7 presents the results for U.S. stock market returns
(on a daily basis) as a composite diagram across 100 years of the Dow Jones

Figure 7.7. DJIA Daily Percentage Returns, 1896–1996

A. Frequency Distribution

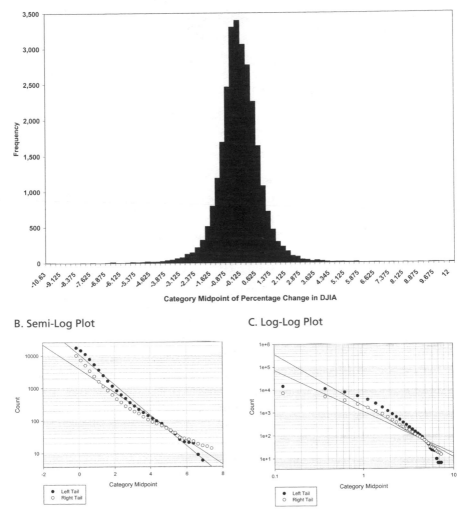

B. Semi-Log Plot

C. Log-Log Plot

Industrial Average. We estimated exponential fits for daily returns for the Dow Jones Industrial Average for four separate periods and for the entire series, 1896 through 1996. Table 7.5 presents these results.

Financial economists have studied the kurtosis associated with stock returns (beginning with Mandelbrot 1963, 1964). Direct empirical estimates of the distributions have been rarer than time series studies, and occasionally

Table 7.5. Exponential Fits for Dow Jones Daily Returns, Various Periods, 1896–1996

Dow Jones Industrial Average	N	Parameter Estimate Right Tail/Left Tail	R^2 Right Tail/Left Tail
1896–1921	7,244	−1.33	.997
		1.15	.992
1921–46	7,463	−0.83	.992
		0.64	.942
1946–71	6,469	−1.73	.968
		1.56	.965
1971–96	6,418	−1.43	.997
		1.47	.983

analysts have rushed to conclude that stock markets follow Paretian or power functions (Peters 1991, 1994). Table 7.5 shows that stock markets, like much political data, follow an exponential probability distribution (see also Sornette 2002). The upward curvature is suggestive of the "stretched exponential."

The parameter estimates for the U.S. stock market would place the market squarely within the political input series, where our theory would place it, based on its relatively low friction compared to other institutions. It is an efficient information-processing device, even if not perfectly so as in the "efficient market thesis," which predicts a normal distribution of market returns (Cootner 1964; Samuelson 1965; Maikel 1996). The implicit index theory developed in this book is a generalized model of the efficient market thesis— rational adaptation to multiple input streams predicts a normal change distribution. When cognitive and institutional costs affect choices, change distributions will be leptokurtic. Because of the absence of decision costs and generally low transaction costs, leptokurtosis in the stock market is a function of cognitive factors, not institutional ones. With costs of trading reduced to very low levels, the leptokurtosis we observe has more to do with attention shifts, emotional mobilization, and inappropriate mimicking than institutional arrangements.

We divided the stock market performance into somewhat arbitrary periods and found pronounced temporal effects. The period 1921–46 was characterized by much more extensive punctuations than any of the other periods. We leave the particulars of these findings to others, but we note that the general operation of institutions does not preclude considerable contextual effects. If an institution operates differently in one time period, it could just as clearly operate differently in varying cultural contexts—an observation as true of politics as of markets.

Dynamic Processes in Institutions

The distributions we have studied order themselves clearly into four groups: the *input distributions* (elections, markets, and news coverage), with relatively low kurtosis and shorter tails; the *agenda setting distributions* (congressional hearings and bill introductions), with higher kurtosis and somewhat extended tails; *decision making distributions* (CQ coverage, executive orders, and statutes), with even higher kurtosis and more extended tails; and *budget distributions*, with very high kurtosis and both relatively high stability and thick tails.

The finding of so many exponential distributions among those we studied is intriguing. Technically, statisticians categorize the exponential distribution as (relatively) thin-tailed, and some use the exponential as the dividing point between thin- and thick-tailed distributions. In addition, in the case of the exponential, peakedness and stretched tails (a better term than "thick tails" for the exponential) are inversely related. Empirically, that means that within the exponential family of distributions, major changes or punctuations must be compensated for by "giving up" some stability or peakedness. That is not the case for the Paretian, where both stability and punctuations can increase at the expense of the shoulders.

As the parameter for the exponential increases, then, the tail becomes more "stretched out," and there are relatively more extreme changes. That is at the cost of stability. Both stability and punctuations occur relatively less in any exponential distribution than in Paretian distributions, but the exponential parameter is an important governor of the extensiveness of punctuations within the exponential family. As the exponential parameter decreases, there are relatively more punctuations, and relatively less stability. That seems to be the dynamic characteristic of most policymaking distributions, even statutes. It suggests that policymaking systems following an exponential path are more adaptive to incoming information than systems following a Paretian path.

In any case, this analysis allows us to begin along a path that has never been tried before: to analyze the degree to which policy institutions are efficient or heavy with friction and institutional costs. We can do this now with reference to the shape of the output distributions that they generate. We've shown clearly that these are not normal in any of our series, thereby confirming our most important hypotheses and uncovering the mystery of the shape of figure 4.14. But in this new type of analysis, more work can be done in developing the best measures of peakedness, heavy tails, and other elements reflecting these friction-based processes. Future analyses will need to refer to kurtosis, exponential, and Paretian distributions as essential characteristics of adaptive institutions and leave behind the metaphors of "comparative statics," "gridlock," and "veto points."

A second issue relates to the causal dynamics that underpin the distributions we have studied. We have relentlessly pursued the notion that political change is affected by institutional friction, and it is clear that there is considerable evidence for the hypothesis. That cannot be the whole story of punctuated political distributions, however. As we noted in the previous chapter, heavy tails in frequency distributions can be caused by policy cascades. In such situations, cases are interdependent. Such "chain reaction" dynamics are most in evidence in the budget data. Clearly, program budgets are not completely independent, but neither are they solely dictated by macrobudgeting concerns. More generally, any process that induces interdependency (such as the familiar monitoring and mimicking behaviors observed in markets and in lobbying) results in "thick-tailed" distributions. We cannot address here just how these cascading processes are intertwined with friction-related institutional costs, but we believe that this is ought to be a major avenue of future research in policy processes.

While our direct parameter tests indicate that the double exponential fits both the elections data and the stock market data, the distribution for elections is more central peaked than in the stock market data. This means that the punctuations for the stock market are relatively more extreme, and the central stability relatively less rigid. Election swings are bounded, of course, while stock market returns are not (a stock can increase by 500 percent, but the Democratic share of the two-party vote cannot, practically speaking); this may account for some of the difference. But other factors may be at work. Both institutions aggregate individual choices in a straightforward manner, but Tip O'Neill's dictum that "all politics is local" suggests that elections for the House of Representatives, at least, are less subject to mimicking and cascading than stock markets. As markets become more linked, they could be more subject to cascades even as information is more and more widely available, but that should operate against election punctuations. One fruitful line of inquiry would be to examine more thoroughly the "anchoring" effect of local forces in congressional elections. It stands to reason that election distributions will be more strongly anchored by the incumbency effect, something that does not exist for markets.

Conclusions

In this chapter, we have demonstrated the following:

1. All of the distributions display distinct positive kurtosis that exceeds that of the normal distribution.
2. If we order institutions in terms of the institutional costs they impose on taking collective action, then the associated output distributions are increasingly leptokurtic.
3. Where institutionally imposed costs are very low, positive kurtosis is still in evidence.
4. All of the distributions are best approximated by the exponential, except for budgets, which are Paretian. As the Paretian is more "wild" than the exponential, this confirms our hypothesis that as we move down the policy stages we see increased signs of friction and institutional costs. These are apparent in the shapes of the change distributions across all our series.
5. In the case of policy change, entering new policy domains is more punctuated than withdrawing from old ones.

Such empirical regularities require a general approach, based in how institutionally imposed costs and the cognitive limitations of participants act to affect how information coming from the environment is processed. This moves us to a high level of abstraction, one focusing not on the details of how institutions deal with one policy at a time, but rather one that allows direct comparisons among institutions themselves. In the case of U.S. national policymaking institutions, our approach implies that "gridlock" is an incomplete description of policy processes and that institutions with higher costs display a greater tendency to lurch between stability and punctuations. But we have also shown that not all institutions are created equal; some are more efficient than others. And we have provided a method for others to apply to other institutions of government as well.

In the United States, institutions add friction to human choices in a predictable way—they cause greater stability but more severe change when it does occur. The right balance between stability and change is elusive; too much stability can lead to major disruptions, even revolutions, when change occurs, whereas hyperresponsiveness to incoming information may not allow for any continuity and future planning (B. D. Jones 1994); some degree of stability is helpful in policy institutions. Indeed, our entire constitutional structure and most parliamentary rules are designed to induce some equilibrium patterns out of preferences that may change more quickly than policy ever should. Moreover, because decision costs, unlike transaction costs, impose policy choices on the unwilling, ensuring that major policy shifts are based on large majorities seems normatively justifiable. In sum, we are trying to assess the impact of institutional friction in the policy process; by no means do we believe that a frictionless process would necessarily be preferable to what we currently enjoy. It is good to know what we have, however. And in this chapter we have demonstrated that we have some institutional processes that are very heavy with friction.

Why do the governmental processes we have examined here display less extreme behavior than natural phenomena? The earthquake and sandpile models we described in chapter 6 show Paretian distributions, but for the most part human-created institutions are characterized by exponential ones. Many scientists claim that Paretian or power distributions characterize a wide range of physical phenomena. There have been dissents (Lahèrrere and Sornette 1988), but these studies have found stretched exponentials, close to the extreme values of the Paretian. With the significant exception of positive change in government budgets, we report none of the extreme distributions found in natural sciences. Why are the distributions we describe less wild? A possible answer may be found in the openness of the system examined. Forest fires are far less likely to be catastrophic if regular lightning strikes ignite fires; if fires are contained, and fuel builds (that is, the system is more "closed" to inputs), then the likelihood of extreme fires may increase. Limiting a system's sensitivity to inputs make it more subject to punctuations. Similarly, dikes on rivers may prevent moderate floods but inadvertently increase the (still small) probability of major floods. We have noted that "exponential" policymaking systems in effect give up peakedness in order to achieve punctuations. Paretian policymaking systems can give up shoulders for both peakedness and punctuations. It is likely, then, that exponential policy systems are more adaptable to changing real-world circumstances. That certainly seems to be the case from the distributions we have studied in this chapter.

In human systems, intervention may act to move a previously well-behaved system into a more punctuated one (as in the case of forest fires or river engineering, where human interventions may have removed the moderate changes and thus increased both the peaks and the tails of these distributions), but the opposite may also occur. The key may be to think of tuning a system toward regular disruption, suffering dislocations but avoiding catastrophe. This notion has been advanced for policymaking subsystems (B. D. Jones 1994), and Robinson (2004) suggests that bureaucracy can lead to more adaptability, presumably by adopting rules that tune in information from the environment. This kind of system may be better modeled by the exponential than the Paretian.

In any case, the empirical regularities that underlie political (and perhaps economic) change are so pervasive that a general approach is warranted. At present, an information-processing approach that is sensitive both to the cost structure imposed by institutions and to the cognitive limits of actors seems most promising. And the tools we have laid out here can be used to study outputs from any institution. They require only hard work and many observations. We hope that others will use these tools to assess the relative performance of government and other institutions at the local, state, and international levels. The payoff could be a better understanding of the consequences of institutional design.

Appendix

In this chapter, our measures are change scores—either first differences or percentage changes—usually pooled across subcategories. In this appendix we detail the measurement strategies used here. Particularly important for the policy data are the different ways to calculate percentage changes; each is legitimate, but each has different theoretical implications.

For presidential elections, we pool across counties; for House elections, across election districts; for Senate elections, across seats. Electoral data are swing ratios (calculated as the election-to-election differences in the Democratic percentage of the two-party vote across House elections [by district] and Senate elections [by seat]). For the policy data, we calculated percentage changes across the Policy Agendas major topic codes (Baumgartner, Jones, and MacLeod 1998). In the project's datasets, a wide variety of policy-related events (i.e., congressional hearings, statutes, *Congressional Quarterly Almanac* stories, *New York Times* stories, and executive orders) are coded into one of nineteen major topic categories. When we calculate year-to-year change in attention to each topic and then aggregate across topics, the resulting distribution illustrates the patterns of change. The total number of cases in each distribution is thus calculated by multiplying the number of topic categories by the number of years in the series. This essentially measures how a focus of attention shifts from one policy category to another. Similarly, budget authority data was pooled across Office of Management and Budget subfunctions. The Dow Jones Industrial Average and the U.S. budgetary outlays were not pooled; we have just one observation in each time period for these series (daily for over one hundred years for the DJIA; yearly since 1803 for the out-lays data).

We calculate our year-to-year percentage-change scores in the amount of attention paid to each major topic using the following formula:

$$\frac{\text{count at time 2} \ - \ \text{count at time 1}}{\text{count at time 1}}$$

Thus, if there were twenty-four hearings on health care in 1946 and twelve in 1947, the year-to-year change would be $-.50$. We use this method because it enables us to capture both change in attention to issues *and* the overall growth of the agenda over time.

We could also choose a relative measure of change, for example, calculating the percentage of the total agenda constituted by each issue area in each year and then calculating difference or percentage change scores:

$$\frac{\text{percentage at time}_2 \ - \ \text{percentage at time}_1}{\text{percentage at time}_1}$$

For example, if health constituted 10 percent of the agenda in 1946 and 12 percent in 1947, we could measure the amount of change as $0.12 - 0.10 = 0.02$ or as $(0.12 - 0.10) / 0.10 = 0.20$. These two approaches actually have different theoretical implications. The first, the *percentage-count* method, allows for growth in the total size of the policy agenda. It does so by basing change on what has occurred before within the policy arena. The second, the *percentage-percentage* method, treats the agenda space as constant through time. It bases change both on what went before in a policy arena and on what is happening in other policy arenas. We generally prefer the first, because expanded capacity of government seems to imply a growing capacity to process issues, but we use the second for the direct tests of kurtosis, since the skewed distributions from the percentage count method cause estimation problems.

The results we report here are robust with respect to the choice of methods for calculating change—this does not influence the functional form of the aggregate change distributions. The specifics of the parameter estimates, however, are affected. The positive and negative tails of the policy distributions are approximately symmetrical for the percentage-percentage method, but for the percentage-count method the positive (growth) tail is more punctuated.

Notes on the Efficient Market Thesis

Markets for assets such as stocks and bonds in modern capitalist economies impose few transaction costs (and no decision costs) on participants. Informational inputs should be efficiently translated into outputs (returns). This notion has been around for a century. In 1900, Louis Bachelier articulated what was to become the *Efficient Market Thesis* (EMT). If market returns (defined as the difference between prices at $time_2$ minus prices at $time_1$) were independent, identically distributed random variables, then they would follow a random walk (dubbed Brownian motion by Einstein five years later). The modern literature may be dated to the early 1960s, when Eugene Fama formalized the EMT (Cootner 1964). Samuelson (1965) formulated the problem as a martingale, which implied that "information contained in past prices is instantly, fully, and perpetually reflected in the asset's current price" (Campbell, Lo, and MacKinlay 1997:30). This formulation implies that, given the available information, the conditional expectation of future price changes is zero.

The EMT, as codified by Fama (1970), implies that market returns ought to follow a random walk (perhaps with drift), and hence be normally distributed (by the Central Limit Theorem). The problem is that market returns don't display such behavior. Rather, market returns in many empirical studies display pronounced positive kurtosis (and less pronounced skew) in comparison to the normal (Lux 1998; Peters 1991, 1994). This anomaly has led researchers to postulate different underlying distributions and stochastic process to account for the empirical findings, but there has been a tendency to avoid full discussion and examination of the substantive interpretations of these deviations (Lux 1998) or to claim that somehow they are rational (Hirshleifer 1995). It is hard, however to escape the interpretation that markets are just not fully efficient, that this inefficiency is rooted in the cognitive capacities of actors, and that these cognitive costs result in leptokurtosis (Plott and Sunder 1982; Shiller 2000).

PART III

SIGNAL DETECTION AND THE INEFFICIENCIES
OF AGENDA SETTING

To this point we have focused on the mechanics of disproportionate information-processing in policymaking settings. Starting with some fundamental concepts from bounded rationality, organizational theory, and the formal analysis of American political institutions, we built a theory of how informational signals from the environment are transformed in the process of government. Numerous conflicting signals deluge policymakers, and they find ways to cope with this "information-rich environment" through selective attention—generally ignoring many signals and focusing on others, juggling various policies as time allows. Being subject to mimicking, cascading, informational sieves, and especially the friction that comes from institutional rules, all human institutions produce disproportionate responses; they are not perfectly efficient. These characteristics are inevitable consequences of human cognitive architecture and institutional design.

The allocation of attention imposes "cognitive costs" on the process of complex decision making. These are not the same as "information" or "search" costs. Decision makers encounter search costs when they know they need to find solutions to problems. Cognitive costs occur when problems are recognized as needing attention. Attention allocation is fundamental to choice. *Policymakers prioritize problems by allocating attention to them.* The attention capacity of individuals is severely limited—so limited that one can focus on only one thing at a time. This is reflected in the agenda-setting process, because organizations, including policymaking organizations, also have severely constrained serial processing capacity.

All of this occurs in any formal organization, or in any policy subsystem. But in the American system of Madisonian democracy, formal procedures compound the disjoint and episodic decision-making process imposed by human cognitive architecture and organizational dynamics. Institutional costs interact with cognitive costs to produce an output stream that is severely punctuated. As a consequence, the response of governments to signals from the environment indicating potential problems is both highly punctuated and highly uncertain. This uncertainty stems both from inherent measurement error in any indicator and the process of interpreting, analyzing, and responding to these signals. Disproportionality compounds uncertainty, leading to the characteristic leptokurtic output patterns that we demonstrated in the previous section.

The implications of all this for how we understand how governments operate are profound. Agenda setting must be inefficient in this fundamental sense: we cannot expect a one-to-one correspondence between the intensity of a signal and a governmental response, or even a one-to-one correspondence between the strength of the signal and government attention to the problem. There are two key issues: whether the problem in the environment is detected and, if so, how that problem is prioritized. In the next three chapters we explore in some detail these implications. First, in chapter 8, we study the relationship between three well-established problems that government has been called upon to address—the economy, poverty, and crime. All three share an uncommon characteristic; they have numerical indicators of the severity of the underlying problem: inflation or unemployment for the economy; the poverty rate; and the crime rate. So we can assess directly in these cases whether responses are proportionate to inputs; we know what the inputs are. We find considerable sensitivity to the problems of economics and crime, but the responses to poverty actually display an inverse relationship to the severity of the problem. One reason for disproportionality is attention shifting: policymakers can shift attention to some other issue during times when an indicator is below some threshold. But the ability to get back to a pressing issue can be limited when there are lots of other issues competing for agenda space. In chapter 9 we examine the phenomenon of issue crowding: the unavoidable fact that time spent on one problem necessarily subtracts from time available for addressing others.

These two chapters demonstrate conclusively that information processing in politics is disproportionate, and that a major reason for this is the limited issue-carrying capacity of policymaking institutions. But we still don't know exactly how the various competing signals from the environment are weighted—just that they are and that we can detect a higher priority for some issues (the economy) than for others (poverty). We can never know with any degree of certainty how this weighting occurs, and the reason is inherent to democracy. The very openness of the process (ideally) allows for the interplay of standard political forces such as interest groups and political parties, but it also allows for the airing of arguments. Policy arguments, part and parcel of the democratic dialogue, weight policy priorities.

Our focus on attention gives us a new way of thinking about representation, and we explore this in chapter 10. If attention shifts in government, is that because priorities have shifted in public? One might hope so.

8

Agenda Setting and Objective Conditions

Attention allocation affects the choice of issues, the choice of issue characterizations, and the choice of solutions. Attention is a severely constraining
factor in politics—a bottleneck through which all matters must squeeze. As
a consequence, attention allocation must be disproportionate. This raises an
important issue: just how are problems in the environment translated into
policymaking responses?

Any judgment on this issue presupposes that the analyst has a method
of weighting the importance of various problems independent of the political process. One approach is simply to relate objective indicators of a problem
to policy responses, tracing the association through time. There are, however,
serious problems with this. This single-issue approach makes the unstated
assumption that other issues do not compete with the issue of interest, or at
least that the competing issues are constant in their severity across time. This,
as we have already shown, is not defensible.

Moreover, there are no readily available indicators for many of the issues
facing policymakers. What indicator can be used to assess the need for business promotion and regulation—a major activity of all governments? The
former could be related to the state of the economy, but the short-term relationships between business promotion and economic growth are tenuous at
best. In the case of business regulation, the relationships between indicators
and policy attention are even more tenuous. One measure could be concentration of economic power in sectors of the economy, and these are regularly
collected. Another could be the emergence of issues in corporate governance,
or in sustained financial market manipulation; there are no reliable indicators
for these kinds of problems. Finally, calls for deregulation could be associated with lackluster economic performance. One reason that this and many

other issues become fodder for political debate is that measuring progress toward an agreed-upon goal often cannot be assessed in a simple, quantitative
manner.

Three Issues in Comparative Perspective

The connection between problem and measurement is not always so elusive.
Some issues are unambiguously related to quantitative indicators. With appropriate caution, we can examine policy responses to the severity of indicators in the policymaking environment on an issue-by-issue basis. Here we
will look at three issues with very different characteristics: macroeconomics,
social welfare, and law and crime. Each is easily associated with a set of readily observable indicators. In each case, we pursue a similar strategy. First, we
examine the factors that lead to the issue's rise on the agenda, by developing
an *agenda-setting equation* relating the objective indicator to agenda access—
the number of hearings Congress had on the issue. Then we develop a *lawmaking equation* that relates the public policy response to the indicator. Our
study in the previous chapters of institutional friction implies that we will
have greater success in the former enterprise than in the latter, and that is
indeed the case. In each case, the success of the agenda-setting equation in
explaining outcomes is far superior to the lawmaking equation. If the analysis presented in previous chapters is accurate, there should be no single and
proportionate relation between problem and solution. Further, since these
three issues are chosen precisely because widely shared indicators of the nature and severity of the problem exist, then any lack of correspondence cannot be for a lack of indicators. Other dynamics must explain it.

These dynamics are related to issue intrusion, described in chapter 3. Signals in politics neither detect nor weight themselves; this is a function of democratic political processes. For example, we ask the question of whether an
issue is more heavily weighted in the decision-making process—in the sense
of generating more congressional hearings—when citizens express concerns
about the matter. Do issues intrude when citizens are anxious about a matter? It turns out that citizen anxieties are very important in economic policymaking, sporadically but intensely important in crime and justice policy, but
not at all important in welfare policy.

Let us first examine the major patterns of government responses to our
three issues. Figure 8.1 diagrams the number of congressional hearings devoted to each topic. A strong wave of interest in government public affairs
occurred in the United States from around 1964 through 1980 (we'll discuss

Figure 8.1. Three Issues

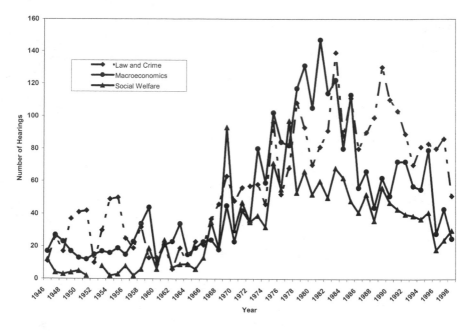

this phenomenon in more detail in the next chapter), but only social welfare seems to have been caught up in this general process. It peaks earlier (in
1969 and again in 1977) than do economics and crime. Attention allocations
to the three issues do not peak at the same time, so they cannot all have been
driven by the broad-scale social movement toward governmental activism
that gripped the United States beginning in the 1960s. Of these topics, only
social welfare reaches its high point (in terms of the number of hearings) during this period. Congressional interest in both economics and crime increased
during that period, but each peaked later—in 1981 for economics and in 1983
(and again in 1989) in the case of crime.

We can use rough objective indicators in each of these three cases. In the
case of social welfare, a rough-and-ready indicator would be the proportion
of families falling below the government poverty line, an arbitrary but useful
standard. In the case of crime, we can use the FBI's crime indices, calculated
from crimes reported to police departments across the country. The often-
noted problem with this index is that many crimes go unreported, so criminal justice experts have supplemented these data with victimization surveys.
There are numerous indicators of the health of the economy, but over the
longer run they tend to correspond reasonably well (but they may not over
periods of months, which is why economists developed leading, coincident,

and lagging indicators of the strength of the economy). Economic problems themselves differ—inflation and unemployment are both signs of economic ill health, but they are inversely related. In any case, no matter what the accuracy of these various indicators, they are in fact widely used by policymakers, widely reported in the press, and widely understood to reflect the severity of the underlying problem. So they provide us with a good opportunity to explore the linkage between the inputs and outputs of government.

Our focus is, as usual in this book, the relationships between the governmental agenda and public policy commitments. It has been more common in the agenda-setting literature to focus on the relationships between the governmental agenda, the media agenda (in the sense of what topics are covered by the mass media), and the "public agenda" (the salience of policy problems for the mass public; see Soroka 2002). For us, the media and public agendas are exogenous to the policymaking process. They influence policymaking though the highlighting of issues—designating some important and others less important. In effect, they influence the weighting of information streams in the policymaking process. That, of course, is not the whole story of governmental agenda setting. Specialized publics and interest groups are important here, too.

It is possible that the relationship between an objective indicator of conditions and the governmental agenda is mediated by public and media attention. As a consequence, we have examined the coverage of the three issues in the media and the salience of the issue in the mass public. In the former case, we use the Policy Agenda Project's *New York Times* database, which is a sample of stories in the *New York Times* coded according to our standard coding scheme. In the latter case, we use the Gallup Poll's Most Important Data series, accordingly coded. We tabulated the proportion of responses to each poll that indicate an issue to be the most important problem facing government.[1]

For each issue, the agenda-setting equation includes the number of hearings across time as a dependent variable. As independent variables we in-

---

1. The Gallup MIP data are the most important long-running time series indicating the salience of issues to the American public. Nevertheless, there are several important issues in using these data. In the first place, we have no rankings of problems, only the number of times respondents indicated a topic was most important. Second, across time Gallup used different wording for these questions. Finally, the polling is not consistent across years. Some years were heavily sampled, and some were not. Since 1945, only one survey was conducted in 1951, 1952, and 1954, and no surveys were conducted in 1953 and 1955. We interpolated for the missing years. For a full discussion in comparative perspective, see Soroka (2001). We have coded all Gallup MIP polls according to our policy agendas coding scheme. See Feeley, Jones, and Larsen 2001.

clude (1) an objective indicator of the problem; (2) a perceived indicator of the severity of the problem by the public (the Gallup Poll's Most Important Problem ranking); (3) a measure of the generic liberalism of the public (Stimson's [1999] public mood measure); and (4) a measure of the conservatism of Congress (Poole and Rosenthal's [1997] Nominate scores). For crime, we also added *New York Times* coverage, because the literature on crime and the media indicates an important media amplification effect. We also explored the president as an agenda setter, to no avail; thus, we do not report those results in what follows.

Economics

We first take up the issue of economics. Does the attention of policymakers match the intensity of the economic problem? If so, by what transmission process does the connection get established? We first establish the existence of a correspondence between objective economic conditions and governmental attentiveness. Then we examine three potential transmission devices: *signal detection,* by which the attentiveness of the public to the economy influences the attentiveness of government; *public opinion,* by which the general direction (liberal to conservative) of opinion influences policymaking attention; and *congressional ideology,* in which the more liberal members of Congress are more aggressive in pursuing governmental solutions to economic problems.

There are many measures of economic activity, and for the annual tabulations we use, most are highly correlated. We studied several measures, particularly change in inflation-adjusted gross domestic product, the unemployment rate, and the inflation rate (which is not particularly correlated with the other two indicators). Because politicians are supposed to be sensitive to the salient concerns of citizens, we also examined the Gallup Poll's Most Important Problem data (what we call the MIP series, or the MIP data), tabulating the proportion of responses noting economics as the most important problem; we pooled these responses across polls on an annual basis.

Figure 8.2 graphs three series: the unemployment rate, the proportion of responses from the MIP data indicating that some aspect of the economy was the most important problem facing government at the time, and the number of hearings that we coded as centrally involving macroeconomics. Again we divide each value for a series by its maximum value to facilitate trend comparisons.

The series show a great deal of correspondence. The three series all peak within a three-year period; interestingly, hearings peaks first, followed by

Figure 8.2. Economics and Agenda Setting

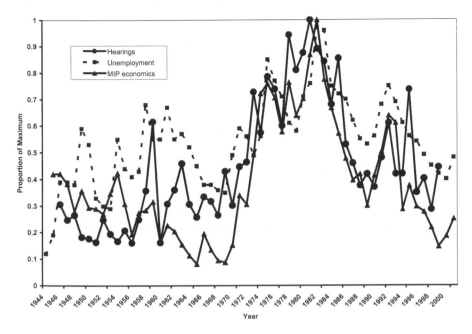

MIP, and then unemployment. (Unemployment is what economists call a "lagging indicator"; that is, unemployment is one of the last indicators to move down when a recession is ending.) That hearings peak before either of the other two measures is probably indicative of the extraordinary sensitivity of the political system to downturns (see, for example, Erikson, Stimson, and MacKuen 2002).

Perhaps more interestingly, hearings and the sensitivity of the public to economic concerns seem to be more tightly intertwined than unemployment is with either of the other two. In the 1950s and 1960s, in particular, unemployment rates are out of phase with citizen perceptions and with hearings. This may well be due to the agenda-crowding effect: in that period; the cold war, the Vietnam War, and the civil disorders in urban America competed with the economy for primacy on the public agenda. This is a critical point: as we noted above, divergences between objective indictors may have little to do with lack of political responsiveness and everything to do with prioritizing the agenda space in the face of competing demands. It is dangerous to infer too much from a lack of correspondence between indicators and policy responses without an examination of other issues that compete for scarce agenda space.

Figure 8.3. Hearings and the Law Index for Macroeconomics

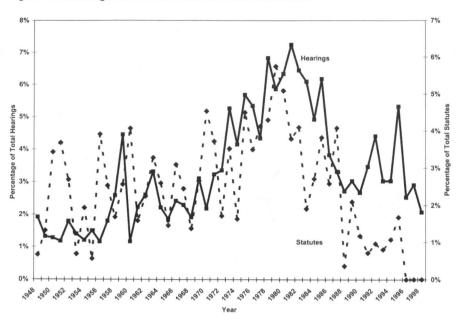

To assess the influence of economic conditions on lawmaking, we constructed an index composed of the most important statutes concerning economics, all statutes on economics, and the *Congressional Quarterly* coverage
of economics (the latter tracks legislative activity in Congress). The lawmaking index assesses intensity of legislation but not the content of that legislation. A discussion of the index may be found in the appendix to this chapter.
Figure 8.3 diagrams hearings on economic affairs with our law index. The relationship between hearings and legislation is clearly in evidence. Both hearings and legislation peaked in 1981, as President Reagan pushed through major tax and expenditure changes. One thing that does not seem to occur is a
flurry of hearings with no subsequent legislation. This might be expected if
hearings were solely symbolic responses to the economic pain of the public.
However, it seems clear that President Reagan and his allies in Congress were
able to take advantage of public concerns about the economy to move though
Congress a package of tax cuts and spending limitations. If Democrats had
continued to control the levers of government, doubtless the solutions to economic distress would have been considerably different. The solution adopted
can be very influenced by partisan control as parties exploit public anxieties
with their favored policy proposals.

A Model of Economic Effects

The problem with simply examining time series to discern how two series ebb and flow together is that the eye can be fooled. By being a little more rigorous, we can eliminate much of the guesswork. We do this by setting up a model of how the U.S. government has responded to economic change since the Second World War, using the basic framework set out above. Our basic model has two fundamental components: the *agenda-setting equation* and the *lawmaking equation*. The agenda-setting equation relates attention allocation to economics in Congress (assessed by the number of hearings conducted on macroeconomics) to objective economic conditions, the public's perception of these economic conditions, and political considerations—the extent to which public opinion is liberal or conservative, and the extent to which general congressional ideology is liberal or conservative. So the equation estimates the effects of signal detection (the extent to which hearings are affected by the state of the economy), on the one hand, and political bias (the direction of public opinion and partisan politics in the legislature), on the other. The signal detection component is itself divided into a direct component (the state of the economy) and a mediated component (the perceptions of the public concerning the economy). The agenda-setting equation allows us to compare the relative roles of signal detection and standard political forces. It also allows us to compare the relative roles of direct and mediated signal detection. Exact specification of the model and empirical estimates are presented in the appendix to this chapter.

The lawmaking equation is more difficult to specify. First, and simplest, policy cannot be enacted unless attention is directed at the problem. So we will need to include policymaking attention (assessed by the number of hearings) in the model. Second, the configuration of policymaking institutions can act to add a nonlinear component to the translation of inputs into policy outputs—in addition to the signal detection nonlinearities—as we demonstrated in great detail in part 2 of this book. Disproportionate information-processing is affected first by signal detection and then by the complexities of American institutions. We model this by squaring the number of hearings, implying that very intense congressional interest is necessary to generate lawmaking activity. And, of course, political variables can enter the policymaking process directly and independent of their effects on agenda setting. We also postulate that all objective indicators of a problem are filtered through the agenda-setting stage of the process—that is, there will be no direct effects of objective conditions on policymaking once the agenda-setting effects of the

objective indicators are controlled. Finally, we lag the agenda setting (hearings) variable by one year, under the assumption that a softening-up process
is necessary to overcome institutional friction. So the lawmaking equation
includes a time-delay factor and an intensity-delay factor. That is, the agenda-
setting effects are delayed in time, but they also must be quite strong to generate a lawmaking effect.

The details of model estimation are in the appendix, but we can summarize them in a straightforward manner. For the agenda-setting equation, we
found statistically significant effects for only two of the variables we entered
into the model: public perceptions of economic problems (the MIP economics question) and congressional ideology (Poole-Rosenthal Nominate scores).
The more liberal the members of Congress, the more economic issues were
a focus of hearings, over and above public concerns with the state of the economy. These two variables, however, did an exceptional job of predicting congressional attention to economic matters: adjusted R^2 was .80.

All of the objective effects of the economy are filtered through public perceptions. The most important result from the model estimation is the absence of objective economic conditions in explaining agenda access for economic matters; the system responds only when signals about the economy
are weighted by citizen anxieties. Moreover, the connection between economic conditions and MIP is affected by the kinds of nonlinearities we expect
from disproportionate information-processing. The simple linear correlation
between the unemployment rate and the MIP question for economics was .71,
but when we square economic conditions (the unemployment rate), the correlation with MIP increases to .78. Squaring the independent variable models
threshold effects (see fig. 6.2).

In chapter 3 we showed how issue intrusion destabilizes the policymaking process. Weights of input streams can shift episodically when policymaking attention is directed at one input source, generally to the exclusion
of others. We left unanswered how an issue might become salient enough to
disrupt, but now we begin to supply an answer. In the case of economics, salience weights are almost certainly affected by citizen anxieties; indeed, if we
are to believe the regression equations, Congress pays attention to economic
signals only when citizens believe the economy to be underperforming.

Laws directed at macroeconomics are much harder to predict, generally
because of the institutional friction that we discussed in full in the last chapter, but also partly because a satisfactory measure of lawmaking on macroeconomics proved hard to devise. Nevertheless, the results generally suggest
that more hearings on macroeconomics lead to more laws, and more liberal

Figure 8.4. Summary of the Model Linking Economic Conditions to Governmental Response

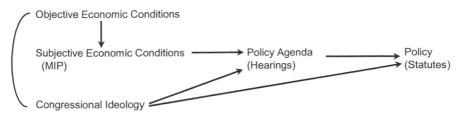

congresses pass more laws. Actually, hearings don't predict laws, but hearings squared do. In the case of macroeconomics institutional friction adds a nonlinear component to the processing of signals (a linear model of lawmaking yielded insignificant results). At low levels of congressional attention to economics, little lawmaking is accomplished; but at high levels of attentiveness, with congressional committees scheduling numerous hearings, a virtual explosion of lawmaking occurs. This explosion is far in excess of what would be predicted proportionately from the hearings. This is exactly what we expect from our model of disproportionate information-processing and institutionally imposed decision costs.

Figure 8.4 summarizes the connections implied by the model we have estimated. The model for agenda setting is simple: economics is a focus when the public is concerned and when Congress is more liberal (and more Democratic). Also, significant nonlinearities affect the connections between agenda setting and lawmaking—just the kind of disproportionate information-processing we expect.

In general, then, there is clear evidence that objective economic conditions generate congressional attention, but they do so only through the mediation of citizen perceptions. These economic conditions also lead to lawmaking on the subject, filtered through both the perceptions of citizens and the agenda-setting effects of scheduling hearings. Political ideology of legislators also plays a role, but there is no evidence that the ideological positions of citizens play a part in either agenda access of economic matters or lawmaking on the subject. Stimson's measure of general public liberalism did not influence agenda setting or lawmaking either simultaneously or through lags.

In sum, during the postwar period Congress evidenced great sensitivity to the state of the economy. Signal detection was were entirely mediated through the perceptions of citizens. Hearings predicted laws, indicating that hearings were not simply symbolic exercises but were intimately bound up in the policymaking process. In the case of the economy, signal detection (in the sense of stimulating congressional hearings) is facilitated—that is, economic issues are weighted more heavily—when citizens express their perceptions that economic performance is subpar. Nonlinear threshold effects show up in the relationship between objective economic conditions and citizen anxieties about the economy, and in the relationship between hearings and lawmaking.

Crime

Crime concerns citizens because it makes their lives less secure. So we might expect sensitivity in signal detection with respect to crime on an order similar to that for economics. Like economics, the measurement of crime is multifaceted, and indicators are plagued with problems. The most widely used measure, the Federal Bureau of Investigation's index of criminal activity, is based on the Uniform Crime Report, tabulated from reports by police departments across the country. The FBI index has been criticized, because it relies only on reports and because of the standard inefficiencies of bureaucratic agencies that collect statistics. Also available are victimization surveys, conducted since 1973. Because we expect politicians to be responsive to the issues that are salient to citizens, we also examine Gallup's Most Important Problem tabulations.[2]

As in the case of economics, we estimated agenda effects and lawmaking effects in separate equations. Policymaking processes play out somewhat differently for crime than for economics, but there are some broad similarities. Model estimation for the agenda-setting equation presented in the appendix shows considerable direct impact for violent crime, and a role for general public opinion such that as opinion moves in a conservative direction, Congress holds more hearings on crime. On the other hand, the model shows no effect for the MIP data, nor does it show any media effects. Signal detection is occurring, in that more hearings occur when crime is rising, but the weighting system is more complex than for economics.

If we examine the patterns graphically, we discover a consistent but more complex story. First, let us examine figure 8.5. There we tabulate the FBI violent crime rate and the number of congressional hearings on law and crime.

___

2. Crime is not nearly as salient as economics across time—or, more precisely put, fewer respondents point to crime-related issues as most important. So the series are more plagued with the "potential unrecorded second choice" problem than is economics.

Figure 8.5. Accessing the Crime Agenda: FBI Violent Crime Index and Congressional Hearings on Law, Crime, and Justice

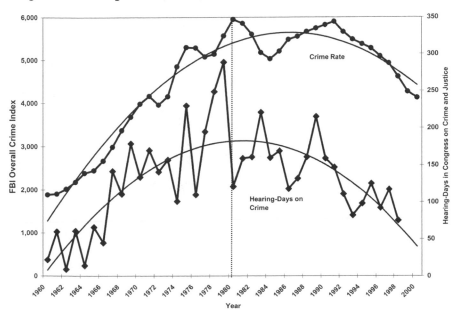

Source: Crime rates, Federal Bureau of Investigation, 2002, Uniform Crime Reports.

As indicated in the crime agenda-setting equation, congressional hearings are more tuned to the reported crime rate than to citizens' estimates of salience.[3] Somewhat perversely, the MIP data and hearings are inversely related. The time path for MIP data (not shown) is basically ∪-shaped, displaying a double peak (one in 1968 and one in 1999), while hearings are ∩-shaped, peaking in the 1980s at exactly the time that the MIP data are at their lowest values. Hearings continued to rise almost in lockstep with the reported rate. All three indicators declined together after 1990, but the hearings began their steep decline before the crime rates did (whether these are based on crime reports or victimization surveys).

One might suspect that the media were involved, amplifying concerns about crime, but the agenda-setting equation indicates otherwise—*New York Times* stories on crime are not related to hearings. This is, however, not the en-

3. Hearings very closely track the reported rate but are less correlated to victimization rates. Violent-crime victimization rates are close to their peak in the early 1970s (when tabulation of this measure began), when the reported crime index was still rising. Victimization rates and reported rates declined together after 1990.

Figure 8.6. Crime Ratchet

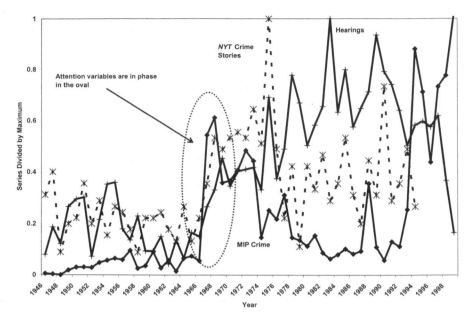

tire story. Figure 8.6 suggests a somewhat more complex explanation. There we plot hearings, MIP crime, and *New York Times* coverage of crime, plotting each series relative to its maximum value for ease of comparison. The figure shows a remarkable pattern. Before the mid-1960s, hearings and newspaper coverage were trending downward relatively, while the crime index was trending upward. Suddenly in 1966 the three series came into phase with one another, then ratcheted upward during the late 1960s. Crime as the most important concern leaped from 5 percent to 50 percent of its maximum value in 1967, a year of intense disorder in many American cities. The three series stayed at high levels during the mid-1970s and then fell out of phase with one another. Each series went its own direction, with hearings continuing to rise and *NYT* coverage and MIP crime concerns dropping dramatically.

We were unable to develop a satisfactory model of lawmaking for crime, but an examination of budget allocations is instructive. Figure 8.7 presents results. Budgets climbed beginning in 1969 and peaked in 1975. Budgets resumed their climb in 1982, the early Reagan years, and continued unabated until the end of the twentieth century. Budget allocation for crime and justice was in phase with the crime rate until the latter began to decline in the early 1990s; budget allocations continued to rise.

The MIP, hearings, *NYT*, reported crime rates, and budget series all dis-

Figure 8.7. Violent Crime Index, Hearings on Law and Crime, and Congressional Budget Authority for Law, Crime, and Justice

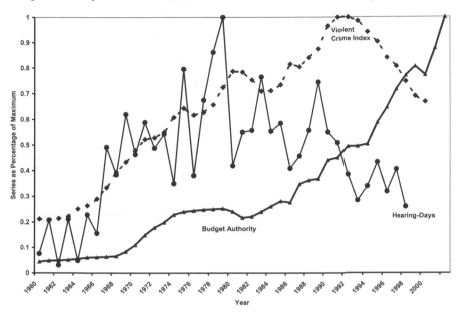

Source: Violent Crime Index, Federal Bureau of Investigation, 2002, Uniform Crime Reports.

play the hallmarks of a positive feedback process during the late 1960s. All series fall into phase for a few years, a pattern not characteristic of them throughout the postwar period. While this phase compatibility was probably triggered by the urban disorders of 1967–68, that is not the whole story. The crime rate began its quarter-century accelerated rise in 1963; the riots were over by 1969. Public concern (indexed by the MIP) and *NYT* coverage dropped after the mid-1970s as concerns turned to other items. Hearings and budgets stayed in phase with the crime rate until 1989.

The probable story line is as follows. The urban disorders of the 1960s focused attention on the crime problem, and government responded. As attention declined (relatively at least), the issue remained on the governmental agenda, driven by the interests of professionals in law enforcement, the scrutiny of specialized publics (such as victims' rights groups), and the decision of the Republican Party to pursue a "law and order" strategy that seems to have resonated. These forces probably drove the governmental agenda until the 1990s, but budget allocations continued to rise throughout the 1990s.

The pattern is classic. Public and media agendas are most sensitive to trends and visible, dramatic events, but once the event fades, public and media coverage fades, supplanted by other issues. The governmental agenda is similarly sensitive to the focusing event but continues to be affected by the extent of the problem even when attention fades. The internal dynamics of this continuation is the operation of interest-group politics. Interest groups do not disappear when media and public attention fade. When the intensity of the problem fades, interest groups demanding action lose one of their powerful allies: the facts. Crime not only begins to get less coverage but generates fewer and fewer dramatic stories. But budgets have been locked into place by the creation of agencies and programs for the agencies to implement. They continue to grow long after the media, the public, and Congress itself have lost interest. When dealing with an issue like crime, professional law enforcement groups can also argue that the massive government spending programs are working and therefore should be continued precisely *because* the crime rate is lower. Creativity comes into play, not just a simple relation between objective indicators and government response.

Why are agenda setting and policymaking in criminal justice only occasionally sensitive to environmental signals about the severity of the problem? The answer is in the juggling act that must be performed by government in responding to multiple streams of information. The signal detection function is simply not as efficient regarding crime as it is regarding economics. There must be an extraordinary confluence of circumstances to drive crime to the level of political salience occupied by economics. These interactive effects add more complex nonlinearities than we observed in the case of economics, but they are consistent with what we expect from what we expect from considerations of disproportionate information-processing. Citizens are threatened by crime but seemingly, in postwar America, are not as threatened as they are by economic malaise, and this generates a more complex policy dynamics.

Social Welfare

Finally, we take a very brief look at social welfare. This is a complex policy arena, and we have no intention of doing full justice to it. It is likely, however, that signal detection in Congress is attenuated regarding social welfare in comparison to either economics or crime. Most Americans (especially those who vote) are not threatened by a fall into dire poverty, at least since the Great Depression. They may be concerned about social welfare, but more because they care about how government treats the less fortunate than because they believe themselves to be threatened. Such indirect effects are recipes for

Figure 8.8. Poverty Rate, Welfare Hearings, and Congressional Budget Authority on Income Security

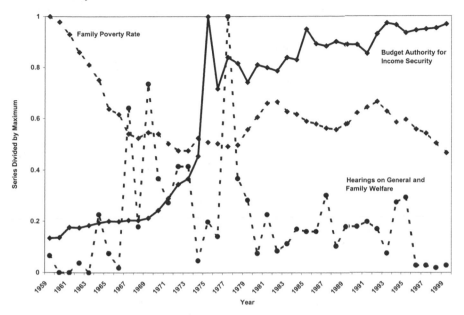

Sources: Poverty rate from Joseph Dalaker and Bernadette Proctor, 2000, *Poverty in the United States, 1999,* Current Population Reports, Series P60-210 (Washington, DC: U.S. Census Bureau). Congressional budget authority and welfare hearings from the Policy Agendas Project. See True 2004 for details of congressional budget authority. General and family welfare hearings is a combination of the Policy Agendas codes 1300 (general) and 1302 (poverty assistance for low-income families).

interest-group politics, and interest-group politics are less efficient in forging linkages between problems in the environment than is the electoral politics that seems to forge the link for economics and (sporadically) crime.

Figure 8.8 graphs the poverty rate (from the Bureau of the Census), hearings on general and family welfare (from the Policy Agendas Project), and congressional budget authority for income security. We can look at that figure to make one or two simple but important points. First, as the poverty rate for families declined dramatically in the early 1960s, the federal government became very interested in the matter. Unlike the cases of crime or economics, the key indicator of the problem was improving when the issue came to the fore. Second, serious budget allocations followed this interest. The great jump in 1975 marks major welfare reforms, including the introduction of the Supplemental Security Income (SSI) Program, and expansions in food and housing assistance programs. Since that year, income security expenditures of the federal government have not grown in inflation-adjusted terms.

After the burst of interest and policy commitment, the poverty rate stagnated, then even rose briefly from 1978 through 1982. Yet neither hearings nor budgets followed. Conservatives would say that the welfare programs established during the period of Lyndon Johnson's Great Society and following were failures, and that the rise in poverty was to be expected. Liberals would say that economic problems just overwhelmed the good intentions of government. In any case, neither group got the matter on the agenda until the late 1980s, when welfare reform rose as a major issue.

We can add a final "perversion" to the strange set of relationships between public problem and governmental response. The relative extensiveness of public concern for social welfare issues as indicated by the Gallup MIP polls corresponds neither to the poverty rate nor to governmental attention. There was some concern in the late 1960s, but the most sustained period of interest in this problem was from the mid-1980s to the late 1990s. This could well have been mostly a concern over Social Security, and not relevant to the kinds of welfare policies we have examined in this section. In fact, very few Americans cite poverty as *the* most important problem facing the nation. The high point for this concern came in 1995, when a scant 12 percent cited it. The highest point for crime was 1994, at 27 percent. More than 50 percent of the public regularly cited the economy as the most important problem, with the high point coming in 1982, with almost three-quarters of responses citing it. Defense and international affairs similarly generated regular public concern, especially during the early years of the cold war and during the Vietnam conflict. These high-profile issues that affect almost every citizen generally crowd out other more specific issues, such as social welfare or the environment. In any case, we can infer that the expansion of welfare policies in the 1970s occurred without the issue reaching the high levels of salience characteristic of war, the economy, and crime.

The irony of welfare policy is that major welfare initiatives came about as the poverty problem was declining in intensity, and interest by government officials declined when the problem stopped getting better and actually worsened. All of this happened without the deep concerns of the mass public that characterized economic and crime policies. Maybe things would be different if more poor people were integrated into the political process, or if there were more policy professionals constantly affecting the process as there are in the case of crime and law enforcement. The key point here is that there is nothing inevitable about the relations between the severity of social problems and governmental response.

A substantial portion of the perverse relationships between problem and action is resolved by the agenda-setting equation for welfare. Results presented in table A8.6 show the dominance of congressional ideology in determining agenda access for social welfare matters. Liberals are interested in promoting social welfare; conservatives are not. Ideology trumps problem severity in this case. Similarly, lawmaking, while poorly explained overall, is related only to ideology. This suggests an intense, but primarily "insider," policy debate in a policy subject to competing conceptions (Burstein and Bricher 1997; Burstein, Bricher, and Einwohner 1995). In welfare policymaking, the ideological stances of lawmakers, the demands of advocacy groups for the poor, and policy recommendations by professionals, government officials, and private "think tanks" are more important than objective conditions of poverty in the nation or the concerns of the mass public. Signals concerning the state of welfare are weighted according to the abilities of groups and political activists to push it to the agenda, and that seems quite disconnected to the magnitude of the problem.

Conclusions

In this chapter, we traced three issues addressing problems whose underlying conditions can be assessed with reliable indicators that have been collected over long periods of time—economic policy, crime and justice, and welfare. Each displayed a somewhat different pattern from the others. Across the postwar period, both economic and crime policies responded to objective conditions. But their mechanisms of accessing the agenda and gaining policy response were very different. Economic policy tracks public concern better than it tracks any of several indicators of economic health. Policymaking attention is simply and directly related to the extent to which people see economics as the major problem facing the nation, but laws addressing economic matters are not simply related to attention to the problem. Crime surged to the public, media, and governmental agendas in the late 1960s, and budgetary commitments quickly followed. But when media and public interest waned, governmental attention and policy commitment continued. Both economics and crime are affected by complex nonlinear dynamics associated with disproportionate information-processing.

Just when it looks as if government responds, even if in a disjointed and sometimes indirect manner, to the severity of the problem, we turn to social welfare policy. Social welfare turns the indicator problem on its head: when the problem is improving, interest and commitment by government increase. When it worsens, interest and commitment decrease.

If we move from social welfare policy through law and crime to economics, signal detection of problems in the environment improves. So we might ask how these policy arenas differ. It is probable that the extent of threat to the mass public, and hence the activation of public opinion, is the difference. So we can predict with more certainty governmental response from the intensity of the signal when the threat is extensive and can result in electoral changes than when it is not. But this is of no help in knowing when issues will reach the agenda in the absence of such mediation. Even in the case of crime the response is highly contingent on a positive-feedback effect kicked off by visible events.

These findings shed bright light on the process of issue intrusion. Issue intrusion involves reprioritization; as it pushes onto the policymaking agenda, it pushes aside other previously important matters. An issue intrudes when a problem is severe and when the signal indicating the severity of that problem is weighted heavily. Our findings here suggest that this is a complex process, because it can have several sources—including the anxieties of general citizens, the vividness of particular events, and the activities of interest groups and policy advocates.

In one important respect, the findings in this chapter mimic our studies of budgetary change in chapter 4. We had to tell a different story, and hence develop a different model, for each of the three policy areas we studied. Each makes perfectly good sense, and we learned a great deal about the processing of signals in developing and testing these models. But they do not generalize. Prediction is frustratingly difficult because of its contingency, and generalization is elusive. In different issue areas we see different patterns, each of which makes sense on its own, but we detect no single pattern that characterizes all policy areas. A general model of policymaking will not emerge from the study of any single policy area.

Appendix: Models and Results

For each of the issues we studied, we estimated a similar model consisting of two equations: an agenda-setting equation and a lawmaking equation. We have tried to keep the presentations as similar as possible, but the issues are not identical, so the models are slightly different. However, these findings prove to be robust with respect to the addition of many other variables; we do not report results for variables that added nothing to the predictive power of the equation and did not alter the magnitude of coefficients for other variables, though we did extensive robustness testing.

The general model we estimated for each of the three issues is written as follows:

$$A_t = \alpha + \beta S_t + \gamma O_t + \lambda P_t + \eta R_t + \varepsilon_t,$$
$$L_t = \alpha + \delta A_{t-1} + \phi P_t + \psi R_t + \varepsilon_t,$$

where

A = Governmental agenda (hearings)

L = Lawmaking

S = Public Priorities (Most Important Problem tabulation)

O = Objective economic indicators (unemployment rate, poverty rate, or crime rate)

P = Public opinion. This is an index derived from a dynamic combination of public opinion polls across the period. See Stimson 1999.

R = Conservative ideology in Congress (NOMINATE score). This is an index of ideology based on the roll-call voting behavior of congressmen. See Poole and Rosenthal 1997.

In the case of crime, we also included *New York Times* stories as an indicator of media agenda setting. The literature on media and crime suggests a strong linkage between vivid stories on crime and governmental and public response.

Table A8.1 shows the various indicators of each of the above components.

Table A8.2 presents the ordinary least squares regression estimates for our final model for macroeconomic policymaking. The fit is excellent, and there are no autocorrelation problems in a straightforward OLS fit.

Table A8.3 presents the OLS estimates for our final model for lawmaking on economics. The lag for the law index was necessary to correct for significant autocorrelation, even though the lag is not significant in the final equation and does not change the magnitude or significance of the other coefficients in the model in any appreciable way. The nonlinear threshold dynamics associated with institutional function is modeled with the squared term in the lagged hearing variable.

For comparison purposes, we estimated a linear form for the lawmaking model. The adjusted coefficient of determination was .370, compared to .434 for the nonlinear model.

Table A8.4 presents the regression results for hearings on crime and law. The dependent variable is a count by year of hearings from our major topic

Table A8.1. Indicators for Variables Included in the Model

	Economics	Crime	Welfare
Objective indicator	Unemployment rate	FBI Violent Crime Index[d]	Percent families below poverty line[e]
Public priorities	MIP (Economics)	MIP (Crime)	MIP (Welfare)
Public opinion	Public mood[a]	Public mood	Public mood
Congressional ideology	NOMINATE first dimension[b]	NOMINATE first dimension	NOMINATE first dimension
Agenda access	Number of hearings, Policy Agenda, topic 1	Number of hearings, Policy Agenda, topic 12	Number of hearings, Policy Agenda, topic 13
Lawmaking	Lawmaking Index[c]	Number of Laws, Policy Agenda, topic 12	Number of Laws, Policy Agenda, topic 13

[a] Stimson 1999.
[b] Poole and Rosenthal 1997.
[c] An index constructed to attempt to weight properly the complexities of lawmaking in economics, which is confounded by many small "adjustment" statutes. While it is arbitrary, it captures the process better in a single measure than the entire set of statutes passed on economics, yet it does not rely on a handful of "important" statutes alone. The index is 6 × (important statutes) + 3 × (CQ coverage) + number of statutes. (CQ coverage is used here because it tracks major statutory activity so well.)
[d] Source: FBI Uniform Crime Reports.
[e] Source: Dalaker and Proctor 2000.

Table A8.2. Estimating the Agenda-Setting Model for Economics

Variable	Coefficient	Standard Error	t-value
Constant	27.75	44.95	0.62
MIP economics	125.23	31.30	4.00
Unemployment rate	2.53	3.13	0.81
Congressional ideology	−212.87	65.77	−3.24
Lag (Liberal mood)	−0.53	0.75	−0.71

$R^2 = .800$; Adj. $R^2 = .780$
$F = 40.99$; DW = 2.05

Table A8.3. Estimating the Lawmaking Model for Economics

Variable	Coefficient	Standard Error	t-value
Constant	30.71	7.22	4.25
Lag (Law index)	0.116	.116	0.87
Lag (Hearings^2)	0.0019	.001	2.92
Congressional ideology	−204.3	82.72	−2.47

$R^2 = .468$; Adj. $R^2 = .434$
$F = 13.51$; DW = 1.76

Table A8.4. Estimating Agenda Setting for Crime

Variable	Coefficient	Standard Error	t-value
Constant	135.74	71.35	1.93
FBI Violent Crime Index	82.07	28.62	2.87
MIP crime	−36.01	60.37	−0.596
NYT stories	0.30	.43	0.691
Lag (Liberal mood)	−2.04	1.01	−2.01
$R^2 = .762$; Adj. $R^2 = .711$			
F = 14.96; DW = 2.16			

Table A8.5. Estimating the Lawmaking Equation for Crime

Variable	Coefficient	Standard Error	t-value
Constant	17.75	3.40	5.21
FBI Violent Crime Index	−13.75	9.55	−1.44
MIP crime	−2.26	21.64	−0.12
NYT stories	−0.12	20.31	−0.11
Lag (Hearings)	0.005	0.67	0.82
$R^2 = .141$; Adj. $R^2 = .026$			
F = 6.29; DW = 2.95			

Table A8.6. Estimating Agenda Setting for Welfare

Variable	Coefficient	Standard Error	t-value
Constant	7.42	45.05	0.17
Family poverty rate	−84.59	27.68	−3.06
MIP welfare	−10.33	14.74	−0.70
Congressional ideology	−216.86	89.79	−2.42
Lag (Liberal mood)	1.05	0.82	1.28
$R^2 = .354$; Adj. $R^2 = .280$			
F = 4.80; DW = 2.41			

code 12, law, crime, and family issues. A lag for hearings was necessary due to autocorrelation problems. The objective indicator of crime and public opinion (lagged) are related to agenda access, the latter such that conservative opinion leads to more agenda access. Table A8.5 presents results for a lawmaking equation for crime, using a simple count of laws categorized as focusing primarily on law, crime, and courts. As the table indicates, no satisfactory lawmaking equation for crime could be developed.

Table A8.6 presents the regression results for hearings on family welfare.

Table A8.7. Estimating the Lawmaking Equation for Welfare

Variable	Coefficient	Standard Error	t-value
Constant	−0.008	6.60	−0.01
Family poverty rate	−6.03	4.07	−1.48
MIP welfare	1.23	2.23	0.55
Congressional ideology	−25.17	13.74	−1.83
Lag (Liberal mood)	0.15	0.12	1.24
Lag (Laws)	−0.26	0.17	−1.52
$R^2 = .171$; Adj. $R^2 = .050$			
$F = 1.41$; DW = 2.00			

The dependent variable is a count by year of hearings from our major topic code 13, social welfare. We summed hearings on general and family welfare, excluding Social Security, disability, and other categorical welfare programs. Table A8.7 presents results for a lawmaking equation for welfare, using a simple count of laws categorized as focusing primarily on general and family welfare. Liberal ideology leads to more laws on welfare, but the relationship is not impressive.

9

The Inefficiencies of Attention Allocation

Sometimes problem severity is matched fairly well by government attention and subsequent action (as in the case of economic policy); sometimes it is not (as in the case of welfare). When people detect a mismatch between policy and problem, they often tend to attribute the discrepancy to "political influence"—the influential get attention to their favored problems, while the less influential do not. Of course, who is "influential" depends on where you stand. Liberals see the wealthy as influential; conservatives see the "liberal pro-government establishment" as influential. Nevertheless, both factions use the same underlying causal theory. In this chapter, we note that one needs no theory of influence to explain inefficiencies if there are many problems needing action that compete for agenda space. No political system can balance the intensity of policy attention with the severity of problems so long as the agenda space is constrained. And, of course, collective action cannot occur before collective attention is directed at a problem.

The bottleneck of agenda setting in processing inputs leads to severe inefficiencies in the allocation of attention to problems. By "inefficiencies" we mean slippage in the transmission of signals in the environment into public policy outputs; they invariably occur when information processing is disproportionate. We have reviewed many reasons for this in the previous chapters. But let us recall that attention is not a resource that can be allocated in small increments. A person is either attentive or not. Similarly, a political system is either attentive or not. The dreary implications of this are somewhat alleviated by the ability of organizations to use subunits to process inputs in parallel. Policies are assigned to subsystems that attract the interested (they attend) and leave out the disinterested (they pay attention to something else). But major policy changes need the attention of the major policymaking branches.

As a consequence the bottleneck of agenda setting cannot be entirely escaped. And, as many authors including ourselves (Baumgartner and Jones 1993), have pointed out, devolving policymaking fully to self-governing subsystems has many drawbacks. It is government by the self-interested and relies on a shift in issue salience to bring it back to the purview of the policymaking branches.

Attention allocation is not the only reason for a mismatch between problem severity and policy outputs. Other reasons include the futility of any public action in some areas (that is, some important social problems simply have no apparent solutions, so attention is not often focused on them); the operation of institutions, such as is inherent in the American system of separated powers, which thwart policy response; and the explicit calculation in the decision stage that the problem is not worth the effort given other competing claims. But as we shall see in this chapter, the allocation of attention is a major reason for the problem-response mismatch in the policymaking process. It takes a lot to get the attention of policymakers, but once attentive to an issue they can change policy in large increments, as we saw in previous chapters. How the scarce resource of attention is allocated among numerous competing priorities, all of which are characterized by numerous streams of uncertain and more or less reliable information, accounts for much of the disjoint and episodic nature of policymaking.

Attention allocation affects political outcomes via three distinct mechanisms:

- Attention is allocated to government rather than private affairs;
- Attention is allocated among the various problems that could be addressed by government;
- Attention is allocated among the various solutions that could be proposed to solve the chosen problem.

Attention Allocation: From Private to Public

Collective attention does not have to be directed at public concerns. Many observers have noted that public attentiveness to government and politics is not consistent, and some have argued that broad cycles of interest in public affairs characterize the United States (Huntington 1981; Schlesinger 1986)). It is not fully clear whether these alleged cycles are driven by broad public interest or by activists; nor is it clear whether interest is stimulated by the press of issues

Figure 9.1. A Wave of Public Policy Interest

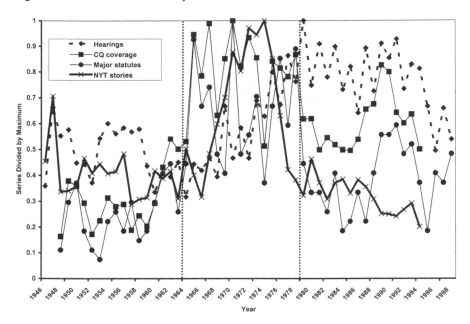

The four policy trends are each divided by their highest value so that all series could be plotted on the same graph. They are the total number of hearings, CQ coverage, *New York Times* stories, and major statutes.

or whether interest stimulates the raising of issues for public debate. In any case, pressing issues and general political interest can feed off each other in a positive feedback system, yielding more government activity than could be predicted from new information and fresh issues alone.

In figure 9.1, we graph several indicators of attentiveness to political affairs: *New York Times* coverage of public policy matters, congressional hearings, *Congressional Quarterly* coverage, and a tabulation of major statutes passed during the period. Hearings, CQ stories, and *NYTs* policy stories are total counts of these series (not percentages, as we have sometimes used in previous chapters; here we want to know about raw totals). Each of these series is an indicator of how much attention is devoted to politics and public policy (as opposed to other matters) by the institutions responsible for producing public policy or reporting on the public policy process. In these series "demand" for policy is not separated from "supply"—that is, coverage of the public policy process by the *New York Times* and by *Congressional Quarterly* could be directed at problems governments face (and thus assess the information flow into the policy process) or be directed at what government is doing to address those problems (and hence assess the "supply" of policies in response to information). For our purposes here, it does not matter. What is critical is the extensiveness of focus on government.

Each series is divided by its own maximum value in order to facilitate comparison. A value of 1.0 indicates the year in which the series signals the highest level of attention (e.g., the greatest number of stories). Clearly in evidence is the explosion of interest in the mid-1960s, a continued interest in matters political until the early 1980s, and then a substantial drop-off in the intensity of interest in all of the arenas. Every series peaks in that period.

Whatever generated this period of intense interest cannot easily be explained by economics or demography or other such background variables. The ascent of political interest is too rapid, and the decline too drastic for such variables to explain the phenomenon. The increase in interest in government and politics is more complex than this simple overview suggests; in particular, our analysis of budgets in chapter 4 shows the turn toward government happened considerably earlier than this cursory analysis suggests. But the bulge was real, and it had enormous public policy consequences for the country.

The number of hearings peaks later than the other series, and it maintains itself at a relatively high level until the very end of the series. Indeed, there are no sustained declines in the number of hearings until the 1994 Republican election victories that led to the control of both houses of Congress. It is probable that Congress continued to grapple with policy problems generated by the enactment of legislation through oversight of the bureaucracy and hearings to adjust problems in the original statutes passed in the burst of activity in the 1964–1980 period. Still, even the hearings series shows that what goes up can come down: there is nothing inevitable about some trend toward "more government."

Political Dynamics

What governs this process of attention allocation at the most aggregate level? Why would some eras generate a more intense turn toward government than others? The simplest notion is that public opinion has taken a liberal turn (whether this turn is cyclic or not) and the more liberal party (that is, the Democrats) mobilize this opinion. That is, the agenda is set by parties and by opinion, as it should be in a democracy.

A second thesis, however, is that the nature of issues matters. We get more government because we have more challenging issues during one period than another. Some have argued that we get more government because external crises, such as war and depression, have stimulated policy responses. At a more modest level, the allocation of attention may well be caused by the existence of problems, and some periods of history are more fraught with problems (e.g., the 1930s, the 1960s) than others (e.g., the 1990s). And, as we have seen, more attention tends to lead to more policy action.

We address the first question, the extent to which democratic political dynamics governs attention, here. We introduce two measures that are important indicators of political dynamics. The first is the simple size of the Democratic coalition in Congress. We simply take the percentage of Democrats in both houses of Congress, and follow that measure across time. We ignore all of the subtleties and complications here—who was president, whether there was divided government, and whether the Conservative Coalition was still in place (the alliance between Republicans and southern Democrats that was important between the 1930s and the 1980s). We just want to know whether electing more Democrats leads to a turn toward more government. The second measure is James Stimson's (1999) measure of the aggregate level of liberal public opinion in the country. This measure also ignores the subtleties—the particular issues that were important, the particulars of the various polling methodologies across time, and variation in the quality of the polls themselves. It reaches for an aggregate.

We plot these two measures of political dynamics along with an average of the five measures of public policy interest. These are the four presented in figure 9.1—hearings, *CQ* coverage, *NYT* stories, and major statutes—plus the number of total statutes passed. These separate series are clearly causally interrelated, but for now we simply ignore these complexities. While individually these series point to different particular aspects of the policymaking process, in the aggregate they indicate a broad-based shift from private to public affairs. It might be thought of as capturing a general interest in public affairs by the media and political elites (and the aggressive use of government in pursuit of that interest). These measures are plotted in figure 9.2.

Each series peaks in a different year. The high point of policymaking attention is, by our measure, 1970. The period of most intense interest lasted from 1970 through about 1978. On the other hand, liberal opinion peaked in 1961, while the size of the Democratic coalition in Congress reached its postwar peak in 1965–66, when, following President Lyndon Johnson's landslide victory over Barry Goldwater, more than 60 percent of the total seats were in the hands of the Democratic Party.

A period of Democratic dominance is evident in the graph. It ran roughly from 1958 (when Democrats won seats in a severe recession) to 1978 (when Republicans won seats during a period of "stagflation" and foreign policy

Figure 9.2. Political Dynamics

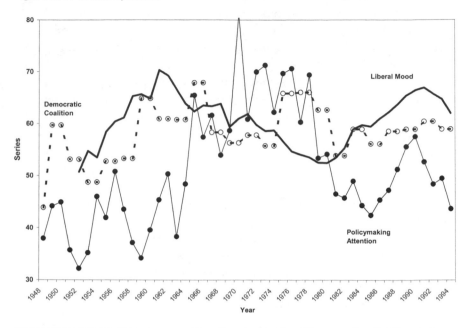

Average policymaking attention is an average of five policy series—hearings, *CQ* coverage, *New York Times* stories, total statutes, and major statutes, each divided by the highest value of the series, averaged. Liberal mood is the aggregate liberal public opinion in the country as reported by Stimson 1999. The size of the Democratic coalition is the percentage of Democrats in both houses of Congress.

challenges with the taking of American hostages in Iran). That period is certainly associated with a more intense turn toward government. Moreover, it is intriguing that liberal public opinion peaked just before the clear shift upward in the 1960–65 period.

The prevailing view of aggregate public opinion is that it works on government policy somewhat like a thermostat (Stimson 1999; Wlezien 1995). There is a feedback effect from government activity into public opinion. Too much government, and the public becomes more conservative. Too little, and it becomes more liberal. Certainly, mood declines as government attention grows, but it proved impossible to develop a straightforward regression model of our aggregate attention measure as a function of public opinion, the size of the Democratic coalition, and the state of the economy. It is possible that attention to government is generated by factors not captured by the basics of political dynamics; in any case, this issue must remain unresolved for now. All we can say for sure is that a wave of policymaking interest occurred during the 1960s and 1970s, and that its relationship to traditional political dynamics is complex.

We have only scratched the surface here. There is more to be done in exploring the role of political parties and public opinion in setting the general policymaking agenda. It is not surprising that general public opinion and the general turn toward political affairs are intertwined, albeit in complex ways; indeed, that is what John Kingdon (1994) was trying to capture by his notion of "public mood." People in Washington refer to it very often, according to Kingdon, though they do not have in mind particular survey results when they do so. The sense that there is a broad public mood cannot be simply reduced to public opinion alone. Rather, it reflects complex interactions among public opinion, elite ideas, and the focus of the media.

If ebbs and flows in the extent to which government has dominated public debate are linked in mysterious ways to standard political dynamics, then perhaps the nature of public problems accounts for them. At least at the aggregate level, this seems a fruitless search, because there is little reason to think that somehow the period of high attention was dominated by more severe problems than in other periods. It is more likely that political dynamics dictated the broad social mobilization that characterized this period, even if we can't capture these dynamics easily. Generally, there is no reason to assume that attentiveness to governmental issues even at the highest levels of aggregation is proportionate to the severity of the set of problems facing the country. Less severe problems can generate lots of public interest due to contextual factors; "understandable complexity" characterizes broad-level attention as well as the smaller budgetary categories of chapter 4.

Attention Allocation: Issues

Generalized attention toward government is only a small piece of the policymaking puzzle. Given that attention is directed away from private toward public affairs, what problems are chosen for activity? Four aspects of the allocation of collective attention to issues are critical. These are as follows:

1. the *total resources* devoted to detecting problems in the environment;
2. the particular *issues* addressed when attending to problems;
3. the specific *components* of an issue addressed when attending to a particular issue; and,
4. the *intensity* with which components are addressed.

Figure 9.3. Issue Attention, Attribute Attention

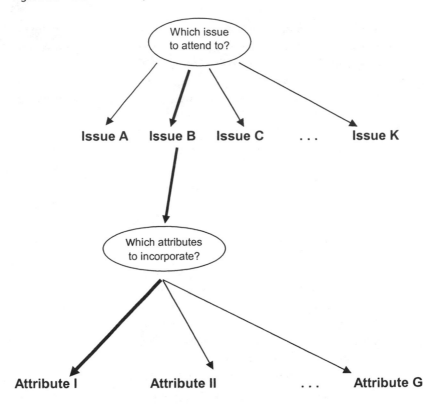

These aspects of attention allocation are the system-level analogues to the first two stages of policy choice depicted in figure 2.1. This is the "front end" signal detection and interpretation system that precedes explicit policy choice. For convenience, we reproduce these two stages in here in figure 9.3. Congress must choose, as individuals must choose, which issues to address. Once an issue is chosen, Congress must decide which attributes of that issue to focus on. Often these "choices" are so automatic that we don't recognize them explicitly; we assume the choice of issues to be more or less obvious, and the definition of a problem can be so bound up with partisanship, or our "values," or our professional or organizational perspectives that we miss the "choosing." We stress again that the stages of choice in government are analytical devices; participants in the process often do not consciously follow them. That participants overlook their importance does not make them any less important in information processing.

Resources

All organizations are characterized by varying amounts of *slack*—how in total they allocate their scarce resources. Organizations don't have to run at 100 percent; indeed one major critique of government is that too much of the time is spent wasting time rather than accomplishing goals. Slack resources may not be deployed in attending to policy issues, and attention can take different forms. Gathering information on issues can interfere with enacting policy, for example. In Congress, time devoted to hearings can detract from time spent in floor debate and action. Figure 9.4 diagrams the number of hearings conducted by each house of Congress between 1946 and 1999. Clearly, there is considerable ebb and flow in the legislative resources devoted to hearings. Congress reached a plateau in hearing activity in the mid-1970s, at around 1,700 hearings, a plateau that continued until the mid-1990s. Corresponding to the Republican takeover of both houses of the legislature was a substantial reduction in the total number of hearings. That drop characterized both bodies, but the House considerably more than the Senate.

This represents a major withdrawal of resources directed at detecting and

Figure 9.4. Number of Hearings Conducted, 1946–99

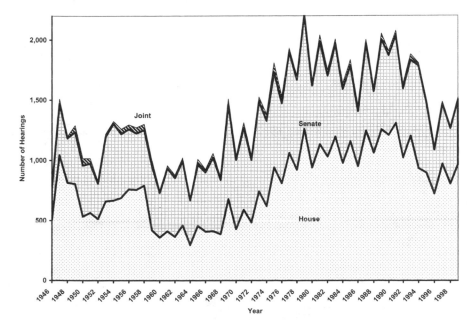

interpreting information from the environment. Some have argued that the more resources devoted to detecting problems in the environment, the more problems will be found that demand action. This is almost certainly true—we have reiterated the organizational dynamics that predict exactly that. Others argue that this attenuation has been costly in terms of the ability of government to address important and pressing issues. Both sides of the argument have merit, but we should not ignore the fact that the signal detection capacity of government is not constant, nor has it increased linearly with the size of government or wealth of society. It responds to the political debate and the balance of partisan control.

Within the constraints of the total resources available, these resources are allocated across the various issues of concern. These issues ebb and flow in the attention of policymakers. Figure 9.5 displays the allocation of attention by Congress to the major policy topics addressed since the Second World War. Again we use hearings as our indicator of attention. We have combined the Policy Agendas major topic categories into six "supercategories"—economics, human services and law, infrastructure development and the envi-

Figure 9.5. Allocation of Congressional Attention to Major Policy Topics, 1947–98

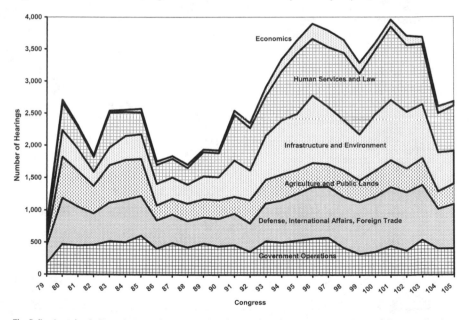

The Policy Agendas major topic categories were combined to generate these "supercategories" as follows: economics, major topic 1; human services and law, topics 2, 3, 5, 6, 12, 13, 14; infrastructure and environment, topics 7, 8, 10, 15; agriculture and public lands, topics 4 and 21; defense, international affairs, and foreign trade, 16, 17, 18, 19; government operations, 20.

ronment, agriculture and public lands, defense and foreign affairs, and government operations. The graph is called a *stacked area graph,* and it treats the agenda space as variable across time. (That is, it presents the total numbers of hearings for each topic over time, also showing the changing overall levels of activity in the aggregate by the size of the combined categories in each year. All hearings are included, so the overall height of the graph reflects the total number of hearings in each period.)

The issue space grew rapidly between the 90th and 95th Congresses (1967–68 to 1977–78). The agenda space stayed about constant from the 96th through the 102nd Congresses (1979–80 to 1993–94), then declined dramatically with Republican control. The policy agenda space became more crowded during the period of issue growth by the robust expansion of three of these supertopics: economics, human services and law, and infrastructure and environment. These "new issues" augmented the traditional governmental concerns in foreign affairs, economics, and government operations. As the nation turned attention to public matters, Congress addressed more and more problems, adding complexity to the agenda space. Then during the 1980s and 1990, the issue space contracted, with great declines in the category of human services and law, and to a somewhat lesser extent, infrastructure and the environment.

Variation in attention to issues cannot be solely a function of the severity of problems. There is no indication that the severity of problems represented by human services and the environment declined upon President Reagan taking office. Clearly political dynamics affects the willingness of political leaders to devote resources to signal detection. It should not be surprising that the issue space contracted as Republicans gained national power after 1980; after all, their major complaint was that the government was too big and intrusive. And, of course, the shrinkage of capacity after 1980 was selective. While defense, foreign affairs, and economics did not shrink after Reagan's election, the standard domestic package of human services, infrastructure, and the environment shrank substantially. On the other hand, issues don't go away easily after they get incorporated into the policymaking apparatus; agencies have been created, and Congress must oversee them. We saw in chapter 7 that retreats from policy areas are typically less dramatic than the emergence of new ones, but we can see here that they do, in fact, occur. And sometimes the reasons for these retreats are high-level ideology as reflected in election outcomes.

Both the magnitude of policymaking attention and the concentration of that attention on particular issues have varied across the postwar period. Moreover, there has not been some sort of inexorable growth of the agenda, nor is the capacity to examine problems simply and directly related to the severity of problems that government faces. Political dynamics matters in agenda control. One may see these political dynamics—debates between the parties and among candidates for office, interest-group actions, and pressures from broad social movements and public opinion—as, in effect, weighting or prioritizing the myriad of potential problems facing public officials. This weighting is part and parcel of the disproportionate information-processing dynamics we have been describing in this book. In the next chapter, we explore in detail this weighting function in regard to representation and public opinion.

Issue Components

Issues are themselves complex. Policymakers may be concerned with particular components of issues at the expense of others, and this attention may vary over time. In chapter 3 we noted how attributes underlying issues can become relevant, causing a reinterpretation of the issue, and here we trace the changes in the components, or attributes, of a major issue across a long time span. We are unable to examine all issues addressed by modern government here, or even a fair sampling of them. But issues have their own separate dynamics. To get a flavor for these distinct dynamics, which are nevertheless bound up with national trends, we will examine the issue area of the regulation and promotion of financial institutions and domestic commerce, one of the most important functions of modern government.

This issue broadly includes business promotion, on the one hand, and business and financial regulation, on the other. It is clear that these are two aspects of a general policy area—how government makes policies that affect businesses. They may be seen as issue attributes, because they indicate two basic orientations about how government addresses business. Congress seldom treats such policies holistically. Rather it "splits"—it distinguishes between small businesses and large businesses, and between types of regulatory activity, antitrust activity, and so forth. It seldom, if ever, decides to act in two stages: first deciding whether to devote resources to the area of domestic commerce; then second, deciding whether to promote or regulate. More typical would be a demand for regulation stemming from a corporate scandal, or a call for subsidies for small businesses with no consideration of the broader arena of government–business relations. Attention allocation is disaggregated, disjoint, and contextual, generally detracting from "comprehensive and coherent" policymaking and often frustrating professionals seeking coherent, coordinated policy solutions to problems. But that is the way it is in all areas, not just this one.

The Policy Agendas content coding scheme provides two major topics focusing on economic and business regulation: macroeconomics (topic code 1), which deals with broad aspects of economic growth and decline and the state of the economy in general, and domestic commerce, banking, and financial regulation (topic code 15), which deals with the particulars of regulating the financial system, consumer credit, and other business issues. Let us take the latter to illustrate the ebb and flow of issues within this important general category.

An excellent indicator of the allocation of effort to an issue by Congress is the number of days the legislative branch assigns to the study of an issue. Figure 9.6 depicts the allocation of attention to components of this critical issue across time as a percentage area graph. It treats the agenda space occupied by business-related issues as a constant and examines the ebb and flow

Figure 9.6. Allocation of Attention to Business Regulation and Promotion

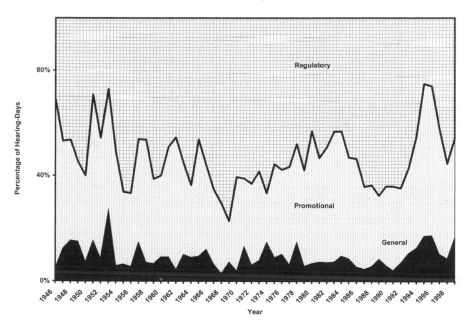

The subtopics for Policy Agendas topic 15, banking and financial regulation, were combined to generate the categories. Business promotion includes small-business issues, disaster relief, and patents and copyrights. Business regulation includes antitrust, financial and banking regulation, consumer finance regulation, and consumer safety.

of the proportion of the components of business regulation across time. (That is, rather than presenting the raw numbers of hearings as in figure 9.4, this one presents them as proportions of the yearly total. Further, we use days of hearings here, which has the advantage of giving greater weight to those hearings that go on for a long time as compared to those that occur in just one session and are then complete.)

We have divided the panoply of business-related issues into those that regulate and those that promote business activities. We classified hearings involving antitrust matters, consumer finance and safety issues, and financial and securities regulation as "regulatory," while we classified hearings on small business, disaster relief, and patents and copyrights as "promotional." Now we can examine the ebb and flow of regulatory and promotional activities across time.

Regulatory activities expanded at the expense of promotional activities between the end of the Second World War and 1970. Although there were some year-to-year variations, from the late 1940s through the mid-1950s business promotion occupied around 60 percent of the agenda space. That proportion steadily declined until it reached a nadir in 1969 of under 20 percent. This is the postwar high point of interest in business regulatory activities. After a rebound, a new period of interest in regulation at the expense of promotion occurred in the mid to late 1980s; then promotion came to the fore once again in the 1990s.

We have simplified the picture here by dividing components into only three fundamental categories. A closer examination of subcategories shows clearly that within business regulation, financial regulation occupies more of the business-related agenda than in the 1950s, antitrust regulation considerably less. During most of the postwar period, antitrust issues occupied between 10 and 20 percent of the agenda, but after 1990 it fell to less than 5 percent, and has not recovered since.

The Intensity of Attention

Given that a particular issue is addressed, how intense is the scrutiny of that issue across time? In studying attention intensity, we treat the size of the agenda space as a variable, expanding and contracting as the decision-making body adds or subtracts resources available for the study of the issue in question. This can vary across time far more for issue components than for total information-processing capacity, because resources can be shifted away from some issues and toward others. Such a shift, if accompanied by a change

Figure 9.7. Intensity of Attention Allocation to Business Regulation and Promotion

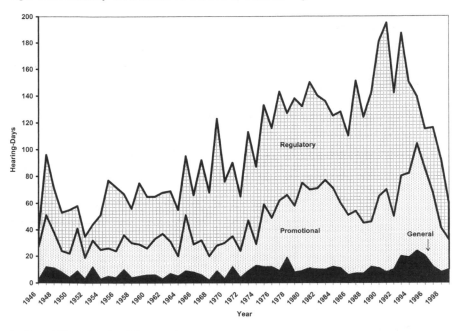

See figure 9.6 for explanation of the categories.

in the relative resources devoted to issue components, is a sure sign that an issue redefinition is under way.

Figure 9.7 graphs the level of congressional commitment to investigating business and commerce, not as a constant, but as variable across time, using a stacked area graph (that is, raw numbers rather than annual proportions).

The ebb and flow of the size of the agenda space is striking. If we had stopped our data collection around 1992, we may have concluded that there was an inexorable drive toward more and more business regulation. The size of the agenda space devoted to business and finance had grown steadily since 1946, with the number of hearings tripling between the late 1940s and the early 1990s. Moreover, the trend was clearly toward less concentration on business promotion and relief and more toward regulatory and consumer protection activities. In the long term, it would seem that the national government had redefined its relationship with business, regulating it more and promoting it less. Hidden in this total is the deregulatory push in the 1980s and early 1990s, but this could be viewed as a continuation of the same inexorable trend that has involved government more and more in the affairs of business.

Change in the intensity of interest in business matters after 1992 make this a wrongheaded generalization. After 1992 the entire agenda space devoted to business issues rapidly contracted. Quite simply, Congress lost interest in both business and consumer issues after 1990. We cannot say, from figure 9.7 alone, if the total of resources devoted to the process of examining policy issues declined or if congressional attention moved on to something else. Looking at figure 9.5, however, we see that the decline in business-related issues was part of the general constriction of the policymaking agenda during the 1990s.

It is not obvious from glancing at figure 9.7, but reexamining figure 9.6 indicates that the shift away from business-related issues after 1990 affected business regulation disproportionately. Congress continued to conduct many hearings on issues of business promotion; business regulation suffered greatly, however. Put simply, Congress lost interest in studying the regulation of business during this commerce-friendly period. Clearly this was an important, but perhaps underappreciated, issue redefinition, and, as later events were to prove, a very important one. The sudden shift of congressional interest away from the regulation of business contributed to the economic bubble of the late 1990s, and exacerbated the subsequent corporate governance crises. We discussed the consequences of this in some detail in chapter 3; as we saw these were quite substantial. But they are not unique. Attention shifts, underreaction, and overresponse are normal parts of the policy process.

There are both methodological and substantive lessons from this brief study of congressional attention to business issues. The major methodological lesson, related to the issue of "agenda size," is that we can study agenda processes via two straightforward graphical devices. One is the percentage area graph; it treats the agenda space as a constant through time. The other is the stacked area graph; it treats the agenda space as variable across time. We use the former to study variability in proportions, so it is useful in studying the allocation of attention to issue components. We use the latter to study variability in the intensity of that allocation of attention. We learn something different from each of these.

The substantive lesson is that there has been considerable variability in the total size of the agenda space devoted to business issues across time, with the peak occurring in the late 1980s and early 1990s. The components of regulatory activity have also varied across time, with the late 1960s being the time that Congress devoted the most intense effort toward business regulation, and the mid-1990s being the period in which it devoted the least.

Solutions

Attention dynamics also influence the choice of solutions. All intelligent systems—from artificial life to human cognition to human-created organizations—face what Allen Newell (1990; see Jones 2001:58–60) calls *the preparation-deliberation* trade-off, as we discussed in chapter 2. When faced with a threatening situation, a person or an organization may either (1) search the problem space (trying to understand the problem better) or the solution space (trying to forge new solutions) to find the best ways to react; or, alternatively, (2) reach back into previously prepared solutions that are stored in memory and apply them to the current situation. Reaching back to pull out previously stored solutions requires attention, but not as much as doing a comprehensive search for all possible solutions. Government, similarly, relies in part on memory to generate solutions. New solutions are not searched out every time a problem emerges. The government agencies, congressional committees, interested organizations, and states and local officials that form Washington's policy communities supply the "memory" of solutions, and urge them on government. Often, solutions are associated with large agencies or service providers that have massive investments in the provision of a particular solution. As we noted in chapter 2, solutions are often associated with those particular agencies that have a history of providing them (and the equipment, personnel, and technical expertise to do so). Moving from solution to solution is not seamless; massive investments like these are not simply thrown away as we switch from one solution to another. The same characteristics of friction that relate to shifting attention from issue to issue relate to how government might shift from solution to solution. Many powerful political actors will struggle to maintain their part in the process. But, just as we described a friction model in chapters 6 and 7 relating to this process generally, we can expect that the choice of solutions would also be characterized both by a strong status quo tendency as well as an occasional willingness to try something dramatically new. In any case, selective attention is critical. This applies to the search for solutions just as it does to problems.

Conclusions

In this chapter we have developed two themes regarding the notion of inefficiencies in the allocation of collective attention to public problems. First, policymaking institutions can allocate limited space to any given problem at any one point in time. Agenda bottlenecks are unavoidable. Second, the capacity to address problems can to some degree expand and contract across time. In the United States a major wave of interest in public affairs crested during the decade and a half from 1964 thorough 1979, and this wave of interest stimulated the development of governmental capacity to address problems.

Because the capacity to respond to multiple issues at any one point in time is strictly limited, issues can develop much faster than government can add the capacity to address them. Numerous potential problems press the limited agenda space at any time, causing some problems, perhaps most problems, to be "crowded out," as policymakers balance the competing claims of so many issues. This "crowding and balancing" act ensures inefficiencies in the allocation of attention—if we measure policy efficiency as a proportionate response to a problem facing government. We have demonstrated the mechanisms of crowding and balancing in this chapter by focusing on a few cases. Similarly, in chapter 8 we noted that attention was disproportionate to the severity of problems and that a single model did not apply across the three cases studied there. In all, combined with our earlier emphasis on the inefficiencies of government attention more generally, we have demonstrated that attention dynamics play an important role in explaining the underlying inefficiencies of government response. These inefficiencies are not pathologies, but necessary and unavoidable characteristics of how complex organizations deal with massive amounts of information, huge numbers of potential issues, and great numbers of conflicting preferences. The process goes by fits and starts. It could not be any other way.

As the U.S. government has grown in the period from 1947 to present, as we have shown here, it has not been characterized simply by an inexorable trend toward "more" government. Rather, there was a clear period of intense activity when many new issues rose onto the public agenda and during which the intensity and the number of simultaneous actions of government increased dramatically. This watershed period of the Nixon era, roughly speaking, constituted a period of great change for U.S. government and how it functioned. However, subsequent trends have made clear that attention is selective; issues can recede from attention just as they rise in attention.

A theory of government response must include a theory of government attention, and a theory of attention must include a theory of how diverse inputs are weighted. Politics prioritizes inputs by weighting their saliences. The weights are provided not solely by the severity of the problem, but also by politics. We turn to this issue in the next chapter, where we develop a model of political representation based not on opinion congruence, as it has been typically studied, but on attention congruence: are the issue priorities of the mass public and government similar?

1 0

Representation and Attention

Problem solving is a critical component of competent government, and problems cannot be solved without attending to them.[1] Solving problems requires information—some system for detecting and interpreting signals of varying uncertainty and urgency in the environment and responding appropriately to them. But problem solving is not the sole, or even the most cited, standard for judging democratic government. Much more of the political science literature has centered on representation than on information processing and problem solving. Obviously, the two need not be at odds; surely the opinions of the public are critical in assessing the nature of problems facing a government. But they need not exactly correspond, either.

In this chapter we add a new approach to the study of representation. We see representation as part of a democratic signal detection system that alerts policymakers to the anxieties and wishes of the public. It is an important component of the process by which signals about changes in the environment are prioritized for policy action—that is, how the numerous signals get weighted in the model of choice detailed in the first section of this book. The process of representation helps representatives appreciate how the public views information, and, as a consequence of potential electoral sanctions, it highlights this information in the decision calculations of representatives. It is an information-processing device that detects and prioritizes.

This view of representation suggests numerous lines of research, but we simply ask the most basic of questions: whether the policy priorities of the public—those issues that members of the public consider to be the most im-

1. This chapter is a modification of Jones and Baumgartner 2004. Chris Wlezien, Jim Stimson, Robert Shapiro, David Lowery, and Hank Jenkins-Smith provided useful comments.

portant ones facing the country—are reflected in the activities of Congress. Because people attend to issues they think are important, we ask, Do the public and the Congress attend to the same issues at the same time? In this chapter we first address the issue of agenda correspondence between the American public and Congress. Then we address whether the policy outputs of the government correspond to public priorities—but first things first. Policy actions cannot be taken unless attention is directed at the matter, but many policy actions can be blocked by the ponderous operation of American political institutions.

Interestingly, this is not a question ever addressed systematically in the political science literature. Most scholarship on representation focuses on the correspondence in the policy positions of representatives and the represented—for example, how closely do the liberal to conservative positions (termed "ideal points") on domestic issues match? This is *positional policy congruence*—it asks only how the policy positions of the government and the governed correspond. Important debates in this field have centered on whether such representation takes place at the individual or the collective level. Of interest here is the question of whether the policy preferences of the public are reflected in the preferences and activities of their representatives, either individually for each constituency or collectively for the nation.

We have no quarrel with this approach, and it has led to important understandings about the democratic process. But this approach is incomplete, because it neglects priorities among issues. How representative is a legislative action that matches the policy preferences of the public on a low-priority issue but ignores high-priority issues? Logically one would expect that for position representation to occur, attention would be focused on similar issues.

The range of issues pressing on government and the public is huge, but the attention capacities of both the general public and government are constrained quite severely. The public holds lots of generalized positions on issues, but only a few of those issues will be relevant at any particular time— that is, people will attend to only a limited number of issues. Under the positional approach, representatives can get high marks even while ignoring the priorities of the public. We might judge congruences to be high if representatives ignore those issues the public considers most pressing but match public preferences in less salient matters. Failure to act on those issues seen by the public as most important should be reflected in our models of representation, but it is typically absent from traditional approaches.

While our focus on the question of allocation of attention is new, several studies have traced public and government concerns over time or at the macro level as we do here (Erikson, Stimson, and MacKuen 2002; Erikson, Wright, and McIver 1993; Page and Shapiro 1992; Stimson 1999). While none of these works has dealt specifically with issue attention, our findings lend more credence to these works, since we find that Congress and the public show impressive correspondence in their issue priorities. With this congruence of attention in place, conditions are ripe for positional representation to occur. If we had found the opposite, no attention congruence, then findings about positional congruence would be called into question.

The Public Agenda

By "the public agenda" we mean the set of policy issues to which the public attends. We do not include the policy solutions that may be entertained by political elites or by segments of the mass public. Public opinion tends to be vague when it comes to technical issues or complex solutions, but there is little doubt that people have a strong sense of what issues the government ought to be addressing (or to quit addressing, because public opinion in America includes a fine sensitivity to being overgoverned).

To assess the policy priorities of the mass public, we have coded the answers to the "Most Important Problem" (MIP) question in hundreds of polls conducted by the George Gallup organization into the policy content categories developed by the Policy Agendas Project. We are fortunate that for many years the Gallup organization has asked the same or a very similar question of the American public: "What is the most important problem facing the nation today?" This question addresses the public's issue priorities, ignoring policy positions and preferences for solutions. As such, it is almost ideal for studying agenda correspondence. However, there are a number of potential pitfalls in using these data as a temporal measure of policy attention by the public. These include variability in question wording, in the number of respondents per poll, and in the tabulation of the answers on this open-ended question (Soroka 2001). Also problematic is the variability in coverage of polls across the years. Perhaps more problematic are interpretative issues. As Wlezien (2003) has emphasized, the concepts of "salience" and "importance" are not equivalent. Demanding a response on the single most important problem when problems are few and minor (the late 1990s?) and when they are numerous and intense (the late 1970s?) always yields a ranking, but these may not be equivalent. In fact we will see that the public's attention is considerably more focused than that of Congress, but our measure of congressional atten-

Figure 10.1. Policy Issues on the Public Agenda

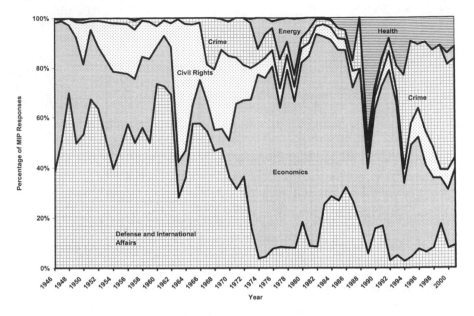

tion is not limited only to the single most important problem, since Congress is divided into committees, each of which can pay attention to different problems simultaneously.

Despite these issues, the Gallup MIP questions are the sole source we have for assessing the attention of the public to issues. Potential gains far outweigh the pitfalls, so we proceed. To translate the raw totals of Gallup's polling into our policy content system, we took two steps. For each poll we took the percentages for each policy category. Then we aggregated these polls on an annual basis, taking the average values in those years where multiple polls were conducted.[2]

Figure 10.1 shows the most important issues as seen by the public in the postwar period. The figure is a stacked area graph, so that the total area of the graph represents the total public agenda space during the period (or 100 percent of the responses). Similarly, the region for each policy area represents the proportion of the public rating that issue as the most important problem over time. We have combined our defense and international affairs categories,

---

2. There are a number of technical issues we had to address in constructing this dataset, including the handling of multiple responses, variability in question wording and the sampling density of polls across the years. See Feeley, Jones, and Larsen 2001. Most problematic is the absence of polls in 1953 and 1955; we interpolated data for these years.

since these matters, as important as they are to government, tend to blur in the public's mind.

Two things stand out from the figure. First, it is clear that the particulars of attention vary considerably over the postwar period. Civil rights occupied a prominent place in the priorities of the general public during the 1950s and 1960s but dropped from the agenda in the 1970s. Crime was prominent in the 1970s and again in the 1990s. Economic concerns were paramount in the 1980s.

Second, it is evident from the figure that the public agenda is dominated by concerns of national and economic security. In some years these two issues so dominate the public agenda that there would seem to be no room for public discussion of anything else. In 1948, 78 percent of all responses fell into these two categories, and in 1983 the total was 83 percent. The low point was in 2000, with only 20 percent of the public concerned about one or the other of these issues as the most important problem facing the nation. The events of September 11, 2001, and the economic malaise beginning that year have transformed the situation, but our analysis stops with the turn of the twenty-first century.

The public agenda space is constrained, and it is dominated by national and economic security. Occasionally, other issues will displace these two major concerns of the public, but, with the exception of civil rights in the 1960s, clusters of issues tend to displace the "big two." The impression one gets from figure 6.1 is the solid dominance of international and economic security as the key priorities of the general public, with an occasional "spike" of other concerns. These other concerns tend to occur together, because the absence of economics and defense opens somewhat of a "window of opportunity" for these other concerns to move up in the collective attention of Americans. These windows are relatively rare.

The Congressional Agenda

As in chapter 9, we assess the congressional agenda by using congressional hearings from the Policy Agendas Project. Figure 10.2 shows the proportion of hearings in each of the nineteen major topics as defined in the Policy Agendas Project (these include defense and international affairs separately).

Figure 10.2 shows that the congressional agenda is much more diverse, at any given time, than the public agenda. This is partly an artifact of the measures. The public agenda, as we have noted, is measured by the answer to a question about "the most important problem" facing the nation, whereas the

Figure 10.2. Policy Issues on the Congressional Agenda

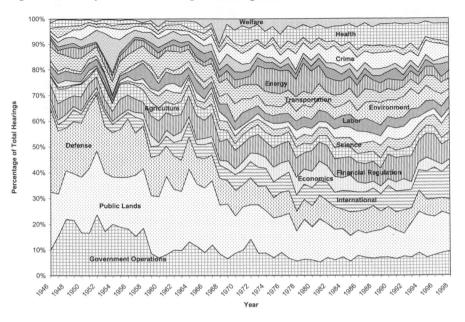

congressional agenda is based on hearings activity. As there are scores of committees in Congress and each can hold hearings simultaneously, it is normal that the congressional agenda should be more diverse than the public's response to the Gallup question.

Still, there are sound reasons to compare the two series. First, different members of the public can have diverse opinions about the most important problem. Figure 10.1 shows that at many times there are a number of issues that gain considerable mention by different respondents as the most important problem; there need be no consensus on this. Second, congressional committee chairs are able to see important issues rising in public concern, and the jurisdictions of their committees are not so rigid that they have no leeway to address issues that they see on the horizon. Agriculture Committee hearings can focus on foreign trade issues, worker safety, unemployment and poverty, or the environment, since all of these may affect farmers; the Commerce Committee can hold hearings on a wide range of topics affecting business. In short, while the congressional data show much greater diversity in attention because of the division of labor and the organizational structures of Congress, we can nonetheless evaluate changes in the relative priorities of the public and the Congress through a focus on these two measures of attention.

Agenda Congruence

We know that the agenda space of government is constrained, and we know that many forces other than public opinion clamor for space on the governmental agenda. Just how do the concerns of the American public match the governmental policy agenda across the postwar period? If the represented and their representatives prioritize national problems differently, then representation cannot occur. It may not occur even where such correspondence exists, because serious policy action may be blocked by the complexities of the American political system, or in the case where leaders hold views opposite to those of the public. But congruence between the public and the governmental agendas is an unavoidable precondition without which representation cannot be said to occur.

Table 10.1 is a first step, and we believe a major first step, in the study of the congruence between public and government agendas. It matches the policy priorities of the American public with the congressional policy agenda. Congressional attention to a policy area is the proportion of total hearings in a given year that centered on that policy category. For both sets of data we have combined defense and international affairs, and dropped government operations and public lands from consideration, because so much of congressional consideration of these topics is housekeeping in nature. The table covers the years 1946–98 and shows truly impressive congruence.

Hearings activity is a "front end" component of the policymaking process. That is, it responds more easily to changing information flows than do the later stages of the policymaking process. As a consequence, it is reasonable to expect a reasonably rapid response in hearings activity to citizen concerns, and we matched public opinion and hearings for the same year. So we adopted a stringent standard: to count as agenda congruence, we demanded that public and congressional attention occur at the same time. If hearings are scheduled a year after an increase in public attention to a topic, our approach will not count it.[3] Table 10.1 shows the simultaneous correlations between public and congressional attention across the nineteen topics listed in the rows and columns.

In Table 10.1, the rows are the MIP categories, and the columns are the corresponding hearings categories. Listed along any row are the correlations

3. More sophisticated modeling is possible, but right now we concentrate only on the yearly agenda correspondences between the public and Congress. We use correlations because it is not possible to presume directionality. Correlations can be affected by differential variances or trends (non-stationarity); the use of proportions for each variable guards against both.

Table 10.1. Agenda Correspondence: Correlations Between the Proportion of MIP Responses on a Topic and the Proportion of Congressional Hearings on the Topic

MIP Proportion	Proportion of Congressional Hearings by Major Topic, 1946–1998															
	Econ	CRts	Heal	Agri	Labr	Educ	Envir	Ener	Tran	Crim	Welf	Hous	Com	Def&Ir	Scien	FgnT
Economics	**.81**	−.23	**.45**	−.18	−.02	.20	.33	**.75**	−.25	**.41**	**.39**	.29	.06	−.29	.02	**.32**
Civil Rights	−.29	**.27**	**−.39**	.23	.07	−.03	−.23	**−.36**	.20	**−.32**	−.11	−.18	−.02	−.01	−.09	−.30
Health	−.02	−.18	**.59**	**−.29**	.10	.24	**.62**	−.04	**−.36**	**.38**	.12	.13	**.35**	−.28	**.42**	**.51**
Agriculture	−.22	−.09	−.28	.15	−.22	**−.30**	−.30	−.15	.21	**−.35**	−.22	−.17	−.28	**.68**	**−.35**	−.23
Labor	−.27	−.04	**−.34**	.17	−.11	**−.35**	**−.38**	−.23	.18	**−.43**	**−.33**	−.04	**−.37**	**.74**	**−.45**	**−.39**
Education	−.13	−.20	**.34**	**−.34**	.12	**.35**	.25	−.19	−.18	.25	.03	−.23	**.38**	−.14	**.55**	.16
Environment	.12	−.15	**.57**	**−.39**	.04	**.33**	**.63**	.08	−.20	**.41**	**.35**	.15	.27	**−.36**	.23	.26
Energy	**.49**	−.19	.13	−.09	−.10	.06	.10	**.76**	.05	.09	**.36**	.12	−.03	−.28	−.00	.04
Transportation	−.22	.22	**−.31**	.16	**−.35**	**−.42**	**−.31**	−.04	−.15	−.25	**−.32**	−.24	**−.39**	**.32**	**−.42**	−.32
Crime	.07	−.21	**.39**	**−.42**	.04	**.36**	**.35**	.01	−.18	**.41**	**.38**	.00	**.41**	**−.35**	**.46**	.03
Welfare	.21	**−.33**	**.75**	**−.50**	.21	**.51**	**.72**	.08	−.31	**.62**	**.41**	.12	**.61**	**−.48**	**.59**	**.47**
Housing	**−.30**	−.13	−.27	.18	−.21	**−.31**	**−.35**	−.16	.18	**−.35**	**−.32**	.13	**−.39**	**.67**	**−.53**	**−.31**
Commerce	−.27	.09	−.13	.19	**−.39**	−.17	−.15	−.14	−.02	−.13	.22	−.08	−.07	.24	−.24	−.10
Defense & Inter	**−.62**	**.39**	**−.78**	**.44**	−.08	**−.35**	**−.69**	**−.59**	**.38**	**−.63**	**−.49**	−.22	**−.39**	**.40**	**−.36**	**−.39**
Science & Tech	−.18	−.02	**−.35**	**.32**	**.37**	−.23	−.29	−.19	.29	**−.34**	−.29	**−.35**	−.22	.10	−.00	−.14
Foreign Trade	.10	−.21	**.63**	−.25	.21	.30	**.66**	−.03	**−.34**	**.44**	.14	.08	**.40**	−.27	**.44**	**.61**

Note: Correlations in **bold type** are significant at .05 for a one-tailed test for diagonal elements, and a two-tailed test for off-diagonal elements (N = 52). Those in *italics* are significant at .10. Defense and International Affairs are combined. Government Operations and Public Lands are omitted.

between an MIP topic and the hearings on the various major topic categories. Listed down any column are the correlations between a hearing topic and the various categories of MIP responses. Along the diagonal are the correlations among the same policy topics: the congruence scores.

For those accustomed to standard correlation matrices, the matrix of table 10.1 may initially be confusing, since the cells above and below the diagonal are not equivalent. The diagonal cells represent the correspondence of public and congressional attention. These are the correlations between public and congressional attention *to the same topic*. Cells above and below the diagonal show the correlation between the proportion of hearings on the topic listed in the column heading with the proportion of the public saying that a given problem is the most important one facing the nation, as indicated in the row headers. In short, by looking along the diagonal we can see the correspondence in public and congressional attention. Looking in the cells off the diagonal, we see spillover effects and trade-offs. Spillovers are positive correlations: when public attention focuses on health care, for example, we see that Congress pays increased attention not only to health care, but also significantly more to the environment, crime, science, and foreign trade. Trade-offs are negative: looking again at the health care example, more public concern for health care is statistically related with *less* congressional attention to agriculture, transportation, and defense.

Let us look a little more carefully at the meaning of entries in the table. The cell in the third row and first column of the table is the correlation between the proportion of MIP responses indicating health as "the most important problem facing the nation" and the proportion of congressional hearings on the topic of macroeconomics; the value is −.02. The cell in the first row and third column is the correlation between the MIP responses on economics and hearings on health; the value is .45. So hearings on health are related to public concern about the state of the economy, but hearings on macroeconomics are not related to public concern about health.

The diagonal entries are most critical: they are the relationships between similar MIP and hearing categories, and hence most directly indicate representational behavior. We cannot say *why* the correlation occurs. The correlation could be a result of responsive behavior on the part of representatives; it could result from people becoming attuned to governmental activity and responding to it; or it could be the case that both the citizenry and its representatives are reacting to a similar empirical set of circumstances. Only detailed case analyses can indicate that. Nor can we say whether the policy outputs of government match citizen priorities. The second issue is enormously complicated because of the operation of American institutions—they act to deter a seamless match between citizen preferences and policy outputs. But we can say that, whatever the mechanism, the diagonal entries in table 10.1 indicate the extent to which the citizenry and the representatives have similar policy priorities. And, in general, the entries along the diagonal of table 10.1 show an impressive correspondence.

In table 10.1, note that the agenda correspondences for economics and national security (defense and international affairs) are both robust, as are the cases for the less publicly dominant issues of health, education, the environment, energy, and foreign trade. Notable for their absence in agenda correspondence are the classic policy subsystem issues of agriculture, transportation, labor relations, commerce (including regulation), housing, and science and technology: congressional hearings in these areas apparently are not in response to broad public concern in these lower-salience issue areas. The modest correlations for civil rights, crime, and welfare are surprising, given the media play that they have received. The case of civil rights is interesting, since during the McCarthy era Congress devoted considerable hearings energy to suppressing people's civil rights and liberties—an important reminder that attention congruence does not guarantee positional agreement.

Agenda Correspondence and Agenda Congruence

Table 10.1 is a matrix of elements in which each cell entry assesses the correspondence between a potential policy priority of the public and the appearance of that item on the governmental agenda. As such, it can be an important theoretical tool in the study of policy dynamics. We term it the *agenda correspondence matrix*. Correspondence is not the same as congruence. Congruence occurs when Congress and the public attend to the same issue at the same time. Correspondence occurs when Congress and the public attend to any two issue pairs simultaneously. So congruence is a subset of correspondence.

Any particular diagonal element is where an issue priority of the public matches the identical element on the governmental agenda. The size of the correlation indicates the magnitude of the correspondence. For example, the correlation between the public's concern for economics as the most important problem facing the nation and the hearings Congress conducts on the state of the economy is .80. This is a strong relationship between the two priorities, public and governmental, across time. Thus these diagonal elements assess raw *agenda congruence*.

What about the other elements in the matrix—for example, when the public is prioritizing "health" and the government is focusing on "welfare"?

These off-diagonal elements have different interpretations depending on whether they are positive or negative in sign. A negative coefficient indicates an *agenda trade-off*. Because the agenda spaces of the government and the public are constrained, admitting one issue to the agenda necessarily means that there is less room for other issues. While the system of committees in Congress allows the parallel processing of multiple issues, this system is not infinitely expandable. Agenda trade-offs are entirely consistent with policy congruence. Indeed, in a system in which the governmental agenda responds only to the concerns of the public, and those concerns shifted in unison, we would find a matrix with only positive elements in the diagonal and only negative or zero elements in the off-diagonal cells.

A positive correlation in off-diagonal elements, on the other hand, indicates *agenda crowding* or *policy spillovers*. Agenda crowding occurs when the public prioritizes one issue and Congress attends to another. For example, say that public concerns are correlated: As the proportion of the public focusing on crime increases, so does the proportion of Americans with concerns about the economy. Congress may well respond to the economy concern, or the crime one, but potentially not both. If so, we would see a higher correlation off the diagonal than on the diagonal. Unlike negative correlations, indicating agenda trade-offs, positive correlations are indicative of attenuated responsiveness, or of related issue concerns. It is, of course, possible that both the public and governmental agendas juggle multiple issues—as is clearly the case in figure 10.1 for the 1990s. But some crowding must occur, and so agenda crowding may be an indication of less responsiveness, or of greater responsiveness to some concerns than others.

All crowding is not the same, however. Some crowding comes as *displacement:* one issue displaces others. Look for a moment at the row in Table 10.1 for defense and international affairs. Reading across that row, there are a number of significant negative correlations. As defense declines in importance on the public agenda, a cluster of domestic issues have the opportunity to rise on the congressional agenda—economics, health, education, the environment, energy, crime, welfare, domestic commerce, science, and finally foreign trade. With so many powerful negative correlations, it is clear that a decline in public concern with international security issues opens up the agenda for much more proactive governmental attention to a great number of domestic policy priorities. Naturally, the opposite is also true: public concern with defense and security issues correlates with much lower levels of congressional activity in these same policy areas.

A second form of crowding comes as *spillovers*. Attacking one issue legislatively may have serious implications for a second. For example, addressing health care may require a reexamination of budget and tax policies. Spillovers also may be a result of political ideology or of the general public mood. Issues may cohere because either elite or mass opinion coheres. Or a general concern of the public—say on economics—can translate onto the congressional agenda as specific action on energy supply or prices (and, indeed, the correlation between public concern on economics and hearings on energy is .75).

The correlations in the diagonal of the matrix presented as table 10.1 are the critical elements in assessing agenda congruence. Because these correlations are based on samples, we can use statistical significance as a standard to evaluate their strengths.[4] In eleven of the sixteen cases on the diagonal, the connection is positive, and ten of these are statistically significant. Furthermore, none of the significant correlations in the diagonal is negative. On no issues do Congress and the public systematically move in different directions. When the public is very concerned about an issue, Congress generally is discussing it.

This is not the whole story of significance. We would be unimpressed if all of the correlations in table 10.1 displayed the same proportion of significant correlations as the diagonal. In fact, the strong on-diagonal findings survive a more stringent test of their significance. The details are in appendix 10.1 at the end of this chapter.

V. O. Key (1961) used the analogy of opinion dikes to describe the relationship between public opinion and public policy. Opinion, he thought, did not dictate policy, but it did constrain it. Our finding that congressional attention never moves against public attention is testament to Key's insight. Of course, the fact that a problem reaches both public and governmental consciousness implies little about the nature of the solution, or even whether Congress will enact one at all. Much of the struggle within government can be about solutions, as policy entrepreneurs race to take advantage of the "window of opportunity" that has presented itself when a problem has reached the public agenda. But an examination of the data presented above means that the notion that somehow sinister forces set governmental agendas in opposition to the public is incorrect. At least when it comes to what Congress considers, there is a close correspondence with the priorities of the public. The public may or may not be bamboozled and misled, but it seems to be a coconspirator in the agenda-setting process, not an omitted party.

---

4. This is not so straightforward. We use the number of years, fifty-two, as the operative estimate for degrees of freedom, but we aggregated hundreds of Gallup polls and over 60,000 hearings in preparing table 10.1.

Policy Congruence

Thus far we have examined *agenda congruence* between the American public and the U.S. Congress. We turn now to an examination of *policy congruence* between the priorities of the American public and the actual policy outputs of government. As we have noted, making laws is far more complex than setting agendas because of the operation of American institutions. Moreover, simply because a problem has accessed the governmental agenda does not mean that a ready solution is at hand. So we expect far weaker associations between public priorities and policy outputs, but it would be disappointing indeed if the U.S. policymaking system worked independent of such priorities.

To examine policy congruence, we prepared matrices like that presented in table 10.1 for two important output measures: all statutes passed in the United States between 1948 and 1998, and those statutes we rated as the most important statutes (1948–1998). The list tabulates the most important 576 statutes as determined by discussion of the statutes in the *Congressional Quarterly;* the method used to isolate these statutes is described in appendix 3.

In Table 10.2, we present correlations between the MIP series and two types of statutes: all statutes (not counting commemorative laws) and those rated as the most important statutes of the postwar period. In addition, we show the correlations between public opinion and hearings (from table 10.1, for comparative purposes), and between hearings and our two measures of statutory activity. Essentially, the columns in table 10.2 are similar to the diagonals in table 10.1: they represent congruence, not spillovers or trade-offs.

The data show substantial associations between statutory output measures and the priorities of the public. In column 2 we present the correlations between MIP responses and all noncommemorative statutes; in column 3, the correlations between MIP responses and major statutes. For all noncommemorative statutes, in column 2, seven of the sixteen issues reach statistical significance (at the appropriate one-tailed test; we reject policy congruence for a negative correlation). For major statutes, similarly, in column 3, seven of sixteen do so, against the ten for the hearings. However, the correlations for the two output measures are much smaller in magnitude than the impressive correlations for hearings.

Lawmaking is considerably "downstream" from the priorities of the public. Hearings are relatively easy to schedule. Laws are not passed without hearings; so accessing the governmental agenda is a precursor to lawmaking. But of course it could be easy to dismiss hearings as simple exercises in symbolic politics—much sound and fury, signifying nothing. The relationship

Table 10.2. Correlations between MIP and Governmental Activity, 1946–98

Major Topic	Hearings– MIP	MIP–All Statutes	MIP– Major Statutes	Hearings– All Statutes	Hearings– Major Statutes
Economics	*.81*	*.30*	*.49*	*.44*	*.45*
Civil rights	*.27*	−.20	*.26*	−.29	−.07
Health	*.59*	*.36*	.22	*.64*	*.34*
Agriculture	.15	.06	−.13	.13	−.04
Labor and employment	−.11	−.18	*.45*	.20	.15
Education	*.35*	*.26*	.11	*.52*	−.01
Environment	*.63*	*.28*	.06	*.55*	.04
Energy	*.76*	*.38*	.25	*.43*	.14
Transportation	−.15	.10	−.11	*.38*	−.07
Law and crime	*.41*	.22	*.24*	*.31*	*.19*
Welfare	*.41*	*.30*	−.11	*.51*	.11
Housing	.13	.07	*.59*	.22	−.08
Commerce and finance	−.07	−.16	−.15	*.53*	.13
Science and technology	.00	−.09	.09	*.42*	*.28*
Foreign trade	*.61*	−.18	−.04	−.19	−.11
Defense and international	*.40*	*.53*	*.27*	[.46]	[.28]
Defense				*.69*	*.38*
International				*.48*	−.05
Government operations				*.43*	.08
Public lands				*.39*	.01

Note: Correlations in *italics* are significant at .05 for a one-tailed test, ***bold and italics*** for significance at the .01 level (*N* = 52).
*General appropriations laws from major topic 20, Government Operations, have been added to major topic 1, Macroeconomics.

between hearings and laws is complex, but it is very easy to send the simplistic version "hearings as symbolic politics alone" to the waste bin.

The last two columns in table 10.2 do exactly that. Columns 4 and 5 tabulate the correlations between congressional hearings and our two measures of lawmaking: noncommemorative statutes and major statutes. We introduce none of the complexities of lawmaking, ignoring for the moment the "stickiness" of American political institutions, the clear tendency of Congress to pass more laws in the second session of any given Congress, and the oft-noted need for policy entrepreneurs to "soften up" the system for a new policy idea. Nevertheless, the connection between hearings and statutes is impressive indeed. Of the nineteen correlations of issue topics between hearings and statutes (here we expand coverage to our full major topic coding system), fourteen are statistically significant. If Congress investigates, Congress legislates. Of course, much of this hearing–statute connection takes place in the continual adjustment process that characterizes much lawmaking. Hearings are often held because of the prior existence of statutes. Nevertheless, the connections between public attention and hearings, and between hearings and statutes, strongly suggest the general sensitivity of the lawmaking process to public priorities.

The connections between major statutes and hearings are, however, considerably attenuated. While there are convincing connections between public attention and congressional hearing activity, and between public attention and major statutory activity, there are fewer convincing associations between hearings and major statutory activity. This may well be due to threshold effects—extraordinary events, partisan majorities, or mobilizations are necessary to gain passage of major acts. Clearly, public opinion is not the only thing that explains the passage of major legislation. But our look at the linkages between public priorities and congressional responses shows some clear linkages.

Representational Agenda Spaces

Both the public and congressional agenda spaces act as severe constraints on representational behavior, because both are limited in their carrying capacities. We generally have argued that the congressional agenda space has a larger carrying capacity for issues, because the committee structure allows specialization. On the other hand, as Page and Shapiro (1992) have pointed out, there may not be a single public opinion on any given issue. Rather, "parallel publics" may have different priorities at the same time, carrying these priorities through time.

This leads to a key question: are the structures of the public agenda and the legislative agenda congruent? Or are they so different that comparisons across them are meaningless? In particular, can the two disparate sets of data be represented in spaces of similar dimensions? If so, are the issues located in similar positions, relatively, in the two spaces? If the spaces are not congruent, then it could very well be the case that governmental and public attention-allocation mechanisms proceed according to quite different mechanisms, and we ought not be comparing them.

To address this question, we have conducted similar multidimensional scaling procedures on both sets of data. Multidimensional scaling is a technique that allows us to study the entire set of correlations among issues and recover the simplest structure that can account for those issues. We treated the correlations among issues as related to Euclidian distances, and recovered an issue space in the subsequent analysis, for both the public and legislative agendas. Details of the analysis may be found in appendix 10.2.

The public and legislative agenda spaces exhibit key similarities, but there are also critical differences. Both scale exceptionally well in two dimensions, but the congressional data exhibit slightly better fit. Moreover, the locations of issues in each space are roughly similar, but with some major differences on very important issues. Looking first at the public agenda space, depicted in figure 10.3, note that there is a tight cluster of almost exclusively domestic policy issues at the right side of the space. In public priorities, these issues are barely distinguished from one another. Naturally specialized publics distinguish among these issues, but the general public barely does—in the sense of allocating attention to them.

Only four issues "break out" of the tight domestic policy cluster, but they are the "big four"—the issues most dominant on the public agenda—economics, defense and foreign affairs, civil rights, and crime. In ranking the importance of issues, the public strongly distinguishes between economics and defense from the domestic policy cluster and from each other, but only weakly distinguishes crime and civil rights from the cluster.

Figure 10.3. Public Agenda Space

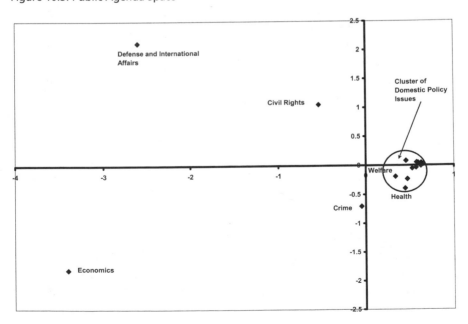

It is highly consequential that economics and defense occupy different poles of the y-axis. Because the agenda space is constrained, defense concerns crowd out economic worries, and vice versa. When neither is primary in the priorities of the public, then a panoply of domestic issues has the opportunity to access the agenda. As is evident in figure 10.1, these issues tend to "spike," rising quickly on the public agenda, and not infrequently falling as rapidly. They also tend to emerge on the public agenda simultaneously, accounting for the clustering in figure 10.3. This is not the case for defense and economics, which are enduring, and to a lesser extent civil rights and crime, which stayed on the public agenda longer and have emerged at different times than the other domestic policy issues.

The clustering of issues is most critical in understanding the public agenda space, but interpreting the dimensions that order the space can also be useful. We suggest that the x-axis sets priorities, with defense and economics of critical concern, and the other issues less so. The y-axis distinguishes domestic from international issues, but it also carries a "new versus old" component that corresponds to our earlier work with the hearings (see Baumgartner, Jones, and MacLeod 2000). The older issues of defense and civil rights are distinguished from the newer ones of economics, crime, and the domestic policy cluster. This does not mean that economics is a new concern; just that it occupied a less prominent position in public priorities before the 1970s.

The legislative agenda space, depicted in figure 10.4, is similar in dimensional structure and in the location of defense and international affairs. Domestic policy issues all fall in a limited range on the x-axis, as is the case for the public space, but they scatter impressively on the y-axis. Where the public lumps the domestic issues together, Congress splits them apart. The big difference between the public and legislative agenda spaces, however, comes from the location of economics. In the legislative space, it is indistinguishable from the other domestic policy issues. While we found that variation in the conduct of hearings on economics across time were extraordinarily sensitive to public reports of economics as the critical problem facing the nation, nevertheless the proportion of hearings on economics is not particularly impressive. As a consequence, economics falls with the other domestic policy issues.

We can see in figure 10.4 that the x-axis distinguishes between defense and international affairs hearings, on the one hand, and hearings on domestic policy matters, on the other. The y-axis clearly and unambiguously distinguishes between new and old issues, with the older issues having higher values (and hence located toward the top of the axis). Most particularly, the newer issues of health, energy, and the environment are distinguished from the older issues of civil rights, agriculture, transportation, labor, and housing.

Figure 10.4. Congressional Issue Space

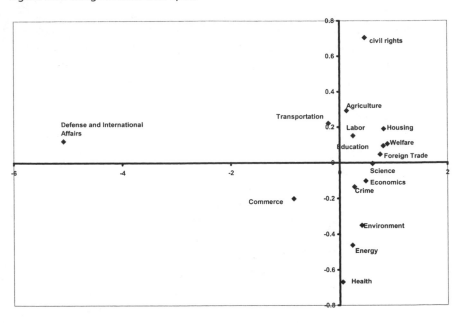

In summary, the public and congressional agenda spaces, while display-ing similarly low dimensionality, have critical differences with important pol-icy consequences. During the last half of the twentieth century, the general public has cared primarily about international and economic security, plac-ing lesser priority on other domestic policy issues. The legislative issue space is as simple dimensionally as the public issue space, but it is more complex in where issues are located in it. Where the public "lumps," Congress "splits."

The low dimensionality and the relative similarities of the two data series are worth consideration. Given the importance of economic and international security in the public agenda, it is clear that all other issues take a backseat, emerging only if and when these two primary concerns are low among the public. Congress, with its greater carrying capacity, can be attuned to more than only a few issues, and these issues spread out along the vertical dimen-sion, though defense and economics remain on a different dimension. As we saw, congressional organization also allows for continued attention to issues even when there is little public clamor over them. Our theories of government responsiveness clearly must work differently in the low-salience issues of housing, agriculture, and so on as compared to the higher-salience areas, such as health, energy, and others where public concerns more clearly make themselves heard. In any case, the diverse issues of the public and congressional agendas cluster into a small number of comprehensible dimensions, according to this analysis.

One important difference between the public and congressional agendas is in their respective "carrying capacities." It is true that the phenomenon of "parallel publics" means that the public agenda can include multiple topics—in the sense of different people having different priorities. But in reality the public agenda is often much simpler—it tends to collapse on one to three basic concerns at any one time. Congressional attention is directed at the same problems as the public's, as we have shown, but the legislature, as a formal institution with division of labor, has a greater capacity to process more issues simultaneously. This, in turn, means that other factors can affect congressional attention to issues. Interest groups, specialized publics, and policy analysts in and out of government can serve as information conduits to Congress.

Relative Carrying Capacities

The greater carrying capacity of Congress to process issues is important to understanding representation. Congress seems extraordinarily responsive to the concerns of the public, and as it homes in on these concerns, it tends to drop consideration of other issues—there are trade-offs. Nevertheless, Congress can crowd more issues onto its agenda than can the public. The right image here is that of two time traces for each issue—say, economics. They ebb and flow (in the case of economics) together, but one at a much higher level than the other, and one with much greater volatility. The proportion of the public who cite the economy as the nation's most important problem varies from 10.4 percent in 1965 to 78.7 percent in 1982. The proportion of hearings that Congress conducted on the economy (by the Policy Agendas Project tabulation) varied from 1.7 percent in 1951 to 7.2 percent in 1981.

Figure 10.5 displays these differences graphically. There we ranked the issue priorities for the public and Congress for the year 1981. Congress devoted just over 7 percent of its total hearings to economic and related matters (and another 7 percent to domestic commerce and finance), but fully 68 percent of the public saw the economy as the nation's most important problem. Domestic commerce and economics ranked third and fourth respectively in congressional attention (after the ever-present and necessary government operations and defense). The public divided its responses to the MIP query among

Figure 10.5. Issue Rankings, Public and Congressional Agendas, 1981

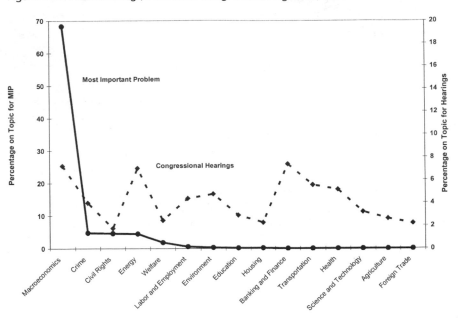

only ten issues (and only on six of these issues did more than 1 percent of the public mention the item), while Congress devoted hearing time to all topics.

Congress, in 1981 as well as in all other years, juggled more issues in its hearing processes than the public did in its attention to public problems. In no year during the postwar period did the public use more than eleven issue categories. Congress almost always employs them all.

Differential carrying capacity resolves the apparent paradox of the high degree of policy congruence reported in table 10.1 and the tendency of Congress to split apart domestic policy issues in comparison with the public, as we saw in figures 10.3 and 10.4. Congress is extraordinarily sensitive to public priorities (or perhaps Congress and the public are detecting similar problems in the real world), but Congress has plenty of room for more specialized interests on its agenda.

Conclusions

Do the public and the Congress attend to the same issues at the same time? Popular government seems to require some degree of agenda congruence between the two. Our results from this chapter suggest that the public is seriously involved in the agenda-setting process, not an ignored bystander. We can't say from our analysis here why agenda congruence occurs, but it certainly does.

Attention indicates priorities. If we study how people, or a political institution, allocate attention to issues, we are implicitly studying how they prioritize them. Here we have examined the priorities of the public, using the Most Important Problem data from the Gallup Polling Organization and the priorities of the legislature, using the data on congressional hearings and statutes from the Policy Agendas Project. The major conclusions from our analyses in this chapter may be summarized as follows.

1. *Agenda congruence:* There is an impressive congruence between the priorities of the public and the priorities of Congress across time.
2. *Policy congruence:* There is substantial evidence of congruence between the priorities of the public and lawmaking activities in the national government.
3. *Issue structure:* Although the priorities of the public and Congress are structurally similar, the location of issues within that structure differs between Congress and the general public in a manner that suggests multiple entry points for influencing the legislative agenda. The public "lumps" its evaluation of the nation's most important problems into a small number of categories. Congress "splits" issues out, handling multiple issues simultaneously.
4. *Differential carrying capacities.* The public tends to focus on a very constrained set of issues, but Congress juggles many more issues.

The analyses reported in this chapter have important implications for the study of representation. It is hard to imagine a mechanism by which positional representation could occur if Congress and the public typically do not have corresponding priorities. Agenda congruence is a necessary, though not a sufficient, condition for positional policy representation. Our finding that substantial agenda congruence does occur, and that there are both important trade-off effects and spillovers to related policy areas, gives us a greater understanding of the dynamics of representation in America. It also adds an important piece of the puzzle of information processing in democratic societies—the sensitivity of politicians to public opinion signals issue priorities. In effect, representation is one way that the complex, multiple streams of incoming information are weighted in the policymaking process.

Appendix 10.1: A Method of Assessing Significance of Agenda Congruence

The raw measures of agenda congruence—the number of significant correlations in the diagonal of Table 10.1—will be more meaningful if we can compare them to a standard. We develop here a way of interpreting the correspondence matrix of table 10.1 that allows more meaningful comparisons.

The correspondence matrix has a natural probability interpretation. If we count the number of statistically significant correlations in the diagonal, and divide that count by the total number of diagonal entries, we get an estimate of the probability that a significant correlation occurs. This probability is the probability of actual agenda matches relative to possible matches on the diagonal. The probability of agenda congruence indicates the extent to which Congress and the public are actually on the same wavelength in regard to policy priorities compared to all potential issue matches. How many times *does* a match between public and governmental agenda items occur out of the potential number of situations in which agenda matches *could* occur?

We use the term *agenda coincidence* to indicate any association between public attention and congressional attention. We can assess agenda coincidence by counting the total number of significant correlations in the entire matrix of figure 10.1. How many times does coincidence occur out of the potential number of situations in which coincidence could occur? This will serve as our baseline of comparison for agenda congruence. A significant positive entry on the off-diagonal indicates that when the public has a high priority for an issue, it actually gets something else. Of course, the congressional agenda may be more diverse than the public agenda, accounting for the large number of significant correlations. Nevertheless, the congressional agenda space is constrained, and trade-offs are unavoidable. Calculations are presented below:

Agenda congruence (diagonal entries)
    Number of cells on diagonal: 16
    Number of significant correlations: 10
    Probability of a significant correlation: $^{10}/_{16} = .625$
Agenda coincidence (total matrix)
    Number of cells: 256.
    Number of significant correlations: 125.
    Probability of a significant correlation: $^{125}/_{256} = .488$

The unconditional probability of a significant correlation between public and legislative priorities is .488—this is the probability of *agenda coincidence*. This is an important baseline, because so long as both the public and Congress have mechanisms for setting priorities, associations between priorities can occur from the operation of purely random processes. Moving from the unconditional probability of agenda coincidence to the conditional probability of agenda congruence (the probability of a significant correlation given that there is a topic match between Congress and the public) yields a difference of .625 − .488 = .137.

This is, however, too stringent a condition, because the agenda space is constrained and requires trade-offs. If Congress focuses on, say, health, it must sacrifice attention to other issues. Negative correlations in the off-diagonal cells are direct indicators of such trade-offs. If representation is occurring, we actually expect negative correlations in the off-diagonals because of this agenda bottleneck. Of the 125 significant correlations in the matrix, 67 are negative. These negative correlations may indicate the unavoidable trade-offs in the agenda-setting process. There are 56 positive correlations in the matrix, but 10 of these are in the diagonal. So there are only 46 positive correlations where the agendas of interest groups, specialized publics, or governmental agencies potentially crowd public priorities.

So we can add a final comparison: a measure of agenda crowding. Where correlations are positive and significant, issues are jostling for the same limited governmental agenda space.

Agenda crowding
    Number of cells: 256.
    Number of significant positive correlations: 56
    Probability of a significant positive correlation: $^{56}/_{256} = .219$
    Number of significant off-diagonal positive correlations: 46.
    Probability of significant off-diagonal positive correlation: $^{46}/_{256} = .180$
    Now the improvement from the unconditional probability of agenda crowding to the conditional probability of agenda congruence is
        .625 − .219 = .406.

The interpretation we give these calculations is as follows. Issues are metaphorically in a struggle for limited agenda space. Given that the public has a high priority for an issue, Congress will as well—there is actual agenda congruence ($r = .625$). If the public has a high priority for an issue, Congress will prioritize not only that issue but also certain other "spillover" issues, though with a lower probability ($r = .18$). The payoff for the somewhat tedious probability calculations is a much richer context for appreciating the extent to which Congress and the public are in synchrony in attending to critical policy issues.

Appendix 10.2: Multidimensional Scaling Results

We used a metric version of Shepard-Kruskal multidimensional scaling (Shepard 1962a 1962b; Kruskal 1964), which basically treated the correlations among issues across time as interval data, but we also analyzed the data assuming only an ordinal relationship between the correlations and recovered distances with no important differences. The multidimensional scaling algorithm compares the distance values from a hypothesized space with the empirical correlations among issues, using a measure termed "stress" to compare the two. The algorithm ceases searching (basically adding dimensions) when the improvement in stress falls below an arbitrary value (here .001).

The Public Agenda (Most Important Problem Data)

Goodness of fit. The squared correlation (RSQ) in distances is the proportion of variance of the scaled data (disparities) in the matrix that is accounted for by corresponding distances calculated from the recovered configuration.

Kruskal Stress 1 = .12417; RSQ = .989

The derived coordinates in two dimensions are presented below:

Topic Code	Category	Dimension 1	Dimension 2
1	M1ECO	3.3996	−1.8109
2	M2CIVRTS	.5372	1.0541
3	M3HEAL	−.4524	−.3944
4	M4AG	−.5815	.0491
5	M5LABOR	−.4615	.0788
6	M6EDU	−.5321	−.0523
7	M7ENV	−.5760	−.0381
8	M8ENERGY	−.4771	−.2347
10	M10TRANS	−.6551	.0207

Topic Code	Category	Dimension 1	Dimension 2
12	M12CRIME	.0478	−.7013
13	M13WEL	−.3418	−.1916
14	M14HOUSE	−.5965	.0442
15	M15COM	−.6558	.0214
17	M17SCI	−.6309	.0423
18	M18FGNTR	−.6285	−.0079
	MIRDEF	2.6047	2.1206

The Legislative Agenda (Hearing Data)

Kruskal Stress 1 = .05715 RSQ = .993

The derived coordinates in two dimensions are presented below.

Topic Code	Category	Dimension 1	Dimension 2
1	H1ECO	.7114	−.0565
2	H2CR	.5852	.5468
3	H3HEAL	.4996	−.5086
4	H4AGRI	.3324	.1855
5	H5LABOR	.4596	.0422
6	H6EDU	.9605	.0892
7	H7ENVIRO	.7099	−.2107
8	H8ENERGY	.5480	−.1749
10	H10TRANS	.0448	.0435
12	H12CRIME	.5687	−.0541
13	H13WELFR	1.0213	.1082
14	H14HOUSE	.9382	.2461
15	H15COMM	−.3947	−.4051
16	H16DEFEN	−2.5510	.8411
17	H17SCIEN	.8016	−.1293
18	H18FGNTR	.9178	.1078
19	H19INTER	.0306	−.6120
20	H20GOVOP	−4.1579	−.7470
21	H21LANDS	−2.0259	.6879

1 1

Conclusions

We began this book with an anecdote about the use and abuse of information in political settings. Information can be misused, misunderstood, and misestimated and is often misleading. But information is critical to all decision making and to politics. In the American political setting, information is abundant, and much of it is of excellent quality. In fact, for most issues most of the time, we have so much information that our problem is not how to gather more good information, but how possibly to sift through all the information available to us in order to comprehend it. The typical problem for decision makers is one posed by too much information, not too little. Where information is rich, it is difficult to know which bits of information are central, which are accurate, which are partially relevant, and which have nothing to do with whatever decision is at hand. Because of the complex nature of the issues, involving multiple dimensions of evaluation, constant assessment of how issues are to be prioritized is required. The problems of attention allocation across the various issues, and various dimensions of the issue that may be relevant, are much more fundamental than any lack of critical knowledge. The more common problem is to know which knowledge is relevant.

In this book we have examined the process by which the American political system processes information—detects signals in its environment, interprets those signals, prioritizes them according to their relevance and urgency, and produces public policy based on them. It is time to take stock of this enterprise.

Decision Making and Policy Choice

At the outset, we developed a model of decision making focusing on the boundedly rational nature of human cognition. *Boundedly rational* means two different things, apparently, to two different audiences. Some put the emphasis on the first word, stressing the limits, or the boundaries of human rationality. Others put the stress on the second word, emphasizing that humans do indeed weigh costs and benefits and make the choice that maximizes their expected utility, given what they know. In reality, human decision makers make the best use of the information that they can, but they don't always attend to the most pressing problems in complex environments. The range of information available is extremely varied and often of unknown relevance and accuracy. Priorities are hard to set, given the limits of human cognitive capacity.

Our model of individual decision making focuses on the various stages of a decision, from recognizing that there is a problem, to assessing the various dimensions of the problem, to sorting through the potential solutions, to making a choice. Similarly, we noted that organizations, which have the ability to devolve many decisions to subunits with specialized functions, nevertheless face many of the same problems of attention span that inevitably affect individuals. Both individuals and organizations are fundamentally affected by what we called the dynamics of "attention shifting." That is, they can attend to only a limited number of issues at once.

One important implication of the scarcity of attention is that it creates a preliminary stage of decision making, which is simply the decision to attend to one issue rather than to another. This is the way priorities are set—through the allocation of attention. Thresholds of importance come into play based on perceived urgency. We do not pay attention to issues in direct proportion to their importance; rather we pay little or no attention to a great number of issues that are below some threshold in order that we may devote our limited available attention to those issues that seem to be most urgent. These thresholds of urgency are not invariant; rather, they are context-sensitive. In the 1970s many domestic issues seemed more urgent, more pressing, than do similar problems today, a consequence of the path of public debate. So decision makers continually choose to focus among competing streams of information based on changing attentional thresholds.

The need to juggle competing problems is true of individuals who have to carve out so many activities and decisions in a twenty-four-hour day, and it is true of governments, which may have thousands of subunits and agencies available to make routine decisions on a daily basis, but where at the highest levels attention can still be focused on only a limited number of items. And this is true of organizational subunits within governments or other institutions, which themselves may have substantial range in their activities, each devolved to a specialized unit within the organization. Still, leadership and coordination require that at some point top-level attention be focused on certain issues, even if these are typically dealt with by specialized units. So the model of agenda setting and attention shifting we lay out applies across the board, from individuals, to small organizations, to larger organizations, to the entire government.

From this core, we have built an explanation for a wide range of dynamics associated with public policy in the United States. The system is greatly inefficient. By "inefficient" we mean that signals from the environment are processed disproportionately—the political system cannot respond in a proportionate manner to the intensity of these signals. These inefficiencies are not based on errors or pathologies. They will never be "fixed" or "corrected"; they must be managed and understood. They are part and parcel of human existence, and organizational processes simultaneously relieve them (by allowing substantial parallel processing) and aggravate them (by replicating in organizations the attention bottlenecks characteristic of humans). Governmental attention, like individual attention, shifts erratically, rarely smoothly. Issues surge onto the public and governmental agendas, just as they often rise suddenly to individual consciousness after a period "in the background."

Some items clearly require significantly more attention than others—they are objectively urgent. Reality is not "created," although it surely may be manipulated. Certainly we expect governmental leaders to be paying significant attention to these issues, leaving more routine ones to others at lower levels of the administrative structure. But there is no reason to expect that such delegation itself will be efficient. Political dynamics, not logic, weight signals from the environment.

So, from a cognitive base, focusing on the nature of individual cognition, we've moved up to develop a theory of governmental attention, and from there to a theory of the policy process. In doing so, we have not neglected the traditional aspects of political studies—the role of governing institutions and the dynamics of political parties, interest groups, and representation. But we have put all of these within a framework of information processing that has the potential to radically reorganize how we think about all of them.

Payoffs from the Approach

Several payoffs may be collected as a consequence of the information-processing perspective we have employed here. These include (1) a generalization of our punctuated-equilibrium model of governmental activity into a full theory of policymaking and an assessment of its validity; (2) an explicit linkage between the disparate literatures on policy processes and institutional analysis; (3) the solution to the old problem of incrementalism and an integration of it into a full theory of policy choice; (4) the development of a new perspective on representation, moving from an exclusive focus on the end to an appreciation of representation as a process of decision making; and (5) the demonstration of the power of the stochastic process approach in the study of American politics and public policy. After we discuss briefly these payoffs—findings from the analyses reported in this book—we turn to an examination of the implications of them for democratic governance.

The General Punctuation Hypothesis

We have laid out extensive and confirming evidence for a generalized form of the punctuated-equilibrium model of public policy that we developed in previous work (Baumgartner and Jones 1993). In our previous work we traced individual policies over time, examining the rare but important periods when smoothly functioning policy subsystems were either created, in a wave of policy enthusiasm based on widely shared hopefulness about the promise of some new policy idea, or destroyed, often in a roughly similar pattern of positive feedback and cascades of criticism. In this book we have adopted a more general approach, based first on the architecture of choice and second on the operation of institutions. An extreme status quo bias is generated by cognitive processes as well as by institutional "friction," but this equilibrium is interspersed with the occasional realization that new dimensions of evaluation need to be considered.

In this exposition, we focused not so much on individual cases studied over time (though we offered several illustrative examples), but on analyses of entire distributions of policy change. In each distribution that we studied, we noted the unusual "shape of change" that we first documented in our analysis of the federal budget, laid out in figure 4.14. Whether we then looked at hearings, newspaper stories, laws, executive orders, bills introduced in Congress, budget outlays, or elections, or even the stock market, in each and every case that we investigated, we found evidence of a similar pattern: extreme allegiance to the status quo coupled with great numbers of extreme outliers, a leptokurtic distribution. These findings, based on over 400,000 observations collected as part of the Policy Agendas Project, should put to rest any question of whether there is broad, system-wide support for the punctuated equilibrium theory. It is not limited to a single or a few divergent cases, but rather is a fundamental characteristic of the American political system. We explained these findings with reference to the interaction between the scarcity of attention and the operation of institutional rules, but whatever the explanation, we have documented its existence in a way that we believe cannot be discounted.

Policymaking and Institutions

Second in our list of payoffs is linking agenda setting with other parts of the literature on public policy and American national institutions. Through the 1980s, the literature on agenda setting consisted largely of three books: Schattschneider's *Semi-Sovereign People* (1960), which introduced the concept of conflict expansion; Roger Cobb and Charles Elder's *Participation in American Politics* (1983, originally published in 1972), which introduced the scientific study of agenda setting and honed the difference between the systemic and public agendas; and John Kingdon's *Agendas, Alternatives, and Public Policy* (1984), which extended the "garbage can" model of Cohen, March, and Olsen. To this mix we added *Agendas and Instability in American Politics* (1993), in which we first proposed the punctuated-equilibrium theory we push further in this book. The literature was considered a separate topic, an isolated part of the field of public policy, of interest perhaps to a broader audience but not well integrated into the rapidly diverging literature on American institutions.

The analysis of policymaking institutions, under the rubric of "neo-institutionalism," was becoming increasingly formal, based on careful analyses of the implications of formal rules and procedures. As a consequence, it became self-consciously static. The approach yielded great new insights into the operation of American politics, insights we incorporated into our analysis here as well as in *Agendas and Instability*.[1] But it was ultimately unsatisfying, because it relied on changes in preferences of actors—through electoral change generally—or through a change in procedures for policy change to

---

1. We once titled a convention paper "Shepsle Meets Schattschneider" to emphasize our attempt to add a dynamic to Ken Shepsle's important notion of "structure-induced equilibrium."

occur. We thought it missed the dynamic process by which the system adjusted to new information though the process of issue definition.

Agenda setting is part and parcel of the process that allows stability and incrementalism to be such an important part of the functioning of American national institutions. As we have stressed throughout this book, and as we emphasized in *Agendas and Instability* as well, these are different parts of the same process. Looking back to our figure on the distributions of policy changes reflected in the budget over the past fifty years, presented in chapters 4 and 7, we have argued throughout this book that the extreme central peak (representing the strong status quo bias and the inherent conservatism of American political institutions, the negative feedback system that keeps them in equilibrium most of the time) would not be possible without the fat tails (representing the surprisingly common dramatic reversals, expansions, and abandonments of policy initiatives). Our system produces equilibrium-based outcomes most of the time. But the analysis presented in this book should convince our readers that these equilibria are by nature partial, in the sense that they are temporally instable. They are periodically, if episodically, shaken by punctuations. In fact, the punctuations are driven by the self-same process of attention shifting that makes the equilibria possible in the first place. So, agenda setting, attention shifting, and status quo bias are part of a single process.

The vast majority of American policy institutions have not mastered their policy environments, producing a thermostatic policy response perfectly in balance with the input streams, reacting seamlessly to it. Rather, each is at one of many possible equilibria that they could have reached, based on incomplete policy responses to a variety of inputs that are incompletely incorporated into the response. This inefficient solving of problems exists because of the disjoint and episodic nature of attention allocation and the strong reinforcement of the status quo once a new policy settlement is reached. Inputs change but they are ignored, because no institutions have global, comprehensive purviews over the issues with which they deal. Therefore, when we see a smoothly functioning institution, we note that it is probably only a matter of time before that equilibrium is broken or substantially adjusted by the inclusion of some new dimension of debate, some new set of participants, or some new definition of the underlying problem. The stability belies an underlying potential instability. A full understanding of the process requires that we understand the entire policy change distribution; the tails of the distribution, we have shown, are not just random outliers; they are important and substantial portions of the process.

By conceiving of cognitive processes and institutional procedures as adding "friction" to decision making, we have linked institutions and agenda
setting in a single model. American national institutions, with their complex
interacting requirements for concurrent majorities on policy matters, act to
make some parts of the policy process easier to change than others. Gaining
access to the formal agenda through legislation and congressional hearings is
subject to political and attentional dynamics, but institutional barriers at this
stage are relatively low. On the other hand, passing a statute or achieving
a major budgetary increase or decrease involves both the "cognitive friction"
of gaining attention to the matter and the "institutional friction" of overcoming the concurrent majoritarian requirements of American democracy. Both
imply policy punctuations.

Incrementalism and Disproportionate Information-Processing

We showed in chapters 4, 5, and 6 that incrementalism as a decision-
making strategy is consistent with proportional information processing
where there are numerous "noisy" information sources that must be combined into a single index and a choice made based on that index. Incremental decision making is updating from the status quo based on a proportionate
adjustment to a basket of indicators. Incrementalism and proportionate information processing imply virtually no punctuations, and a normal distribution of changes in policy choices over time. But if information is processed
disproportionately, as would be the case if decision makers over-rely on a
single source rather than numerous sources, then the result is the pattern of
punctuated equilibrium, with mostly stable, incremental decisions but an occasional burst of activity indicated by its signature leptokurtic policy change
distribution.

In politics the decision maker is often not free to combine indicators sen-
sibly, because public opinion may become mobilized, or an extremely visible
event may be publicized in the media, or the party balance may become altered in Congress. So disproportionate processing is a characteristic of individuals, organizations, and political systems. But that does not change the
implications: incrementalism is a special case that emerges from our single
model of decision making under diverse flows of information. Because the
information-processing approach requires an appreciation of the whole policy process, an additional benefit from this perspective is that V. O. Key's
(1940) old question of why there is no theory of budgeting is answered: there
cannot be a theory of budgeting, because it must be embedded in a theory of
the policy process.

The stable, central peak of a typical policy change distribution implies at best incremental change. Indeed, it is *too* incremental—that is, it implies not an adjustment to multiple information sources, but a closed system in which there is no adjustment save a drifting along with the general tide that has raised the typical agency budget over the postwar years. This is consistent with the early incrementalists' verbal arguments about incrementalism, but does not comport with Padgett's (1980) model of incrementalism as a random walk. It resembles more closely Larkey's (1979) error accumulation model of municipal budgeting, in which decision makers completely ignore signals from the environment. This allows the mismatch between policy and the environment to get further and further out of adjustment—errors accumulate, leading to punctuations somewhere down the road. Larkey's model, which is really "less than incremental," was a real breakthrough, and with Padgett's (1980, 1981) work all the tools were in place to solve the budget decision-making quandary. While we are puzzled that no scholars recognized this, we are pleased to put forward a model that does solve these long-running conundrums.

Representation

Political scientists have lavished extensive attention on questions of representation—how more or less fixed opinions of the public get translated into public policy, especially through the mechanisms of elections and the various linkages between elected officials and the public. Representation, of course, is a core function of a democracy and an important value in itself, and we have no quarrel with this.

Embedding representation in a framework of information processing shifts the focus away from representation as a core value to representation as an instrumental value. It is a problem-detection and prioritization device. As a problem-detection device, it is not infallible, whereas representation as a core value must be treated as such. It is likely that democracies operate better than autocracies in substantial part because of the central role that representation—conceived not as an end value but as an instrumental value—plays. Treating representation instrumentally means that other key components of democracy—free expression, assembly, and rights of individuals—must be respected in order to achieve proper signal detection. These components are critical to allow one to learn about the opportunities for pursuing one's goals, as has traditionally been recognized. But they are also critical to the process of detecting, prioritizing, and solving problems.

Well-functioning democracies must involve not only representation as a valued end but also as a means to problem solving. This involves informa-tion processing, communication, and the ways in which public preferences are created and influenced by government policies and through collective at-tention dynamics associated with public agenda setting. Far too little atten-tion has been paid to how we focus our attention on some issues rather than others. This is a puzzle at the individual level as well as a fundamental as-pect of representation and governmental functioning. Why does government try to solve this problem rather than that one? Given attention to one problem rather than another, why do we limit our consideration of alternatives to a few rather than to the panoply of reasonable options? Given the alternatives under consideration, why do political parties and elected officials react to them in predictable and predetermined fashions, when the underlying prob-lems are typically more complex than any single problem depiction could possibly capture? These questions merit significantly more attention, and they force us to take public opinion, social movements, media coverage, and government activities all as dynamic elements in a process in which they each affect the other. This is a far more complex empirical and theoretical task than evaluating the degree to which relatively fixed public preferences are re-flected or not in the actions of public officials.

Stochastic Processes

Stochastic process methods have been powerful allies in exploring the theory of information processing we have developed here. These are based on distributional analyses rather than on individual case studies of policy development or regression models. We certainly do not expect, nor would we propose, that scholars discontinue their traditional focus on longitudinal analyses of single cases of public policy. Often, we want to know how a pro-gram works and how it may be expected to evolve over a relatively short time span. However, we have harnessed the power of the stochastic, distributional, approach because no single theoretical perspective allows us to understand the dynamics of public policy across a great range of policies. Theories de-veloped to explain crime don't work to explain what goes on in the case of foreign aid. Those that help us understand what occurs in energy don't work in the case of health care. And so on. On the other hand, our distributional analysis revealed important insights about the processes that affect all poli-cies across the entire government. Distributional analyses provide no value whatsoever in explaining what may occur in a given case in a given year; they do not provide "point predictions." Traditional regression-based and longi-tudinal analyses are best for that. But the stochastic approach has enough complementary value that this way of thinking should be added to the toolkit of all those working in the area of American politics and public policy.

Implications for Governance and Institutional Design

Finally, we examine some implications for judging the performance of the U.S. government, and democratic governments more generally. Like any system, it has its imperfections. But how should we judge it? Not, we believe, from some standard of ideal and complete rationality. It does not and cannot react efficiently to new problems, where efficiency is understood as we have used the term in this book, that is, in proportion to indicators of change in input variables. Rather, like any system, it allocates attention to those issues that command attention. How do issues rise to that level, and what happens to them when they are below that threshold? Basically, how well does it prioritize information and solve problems, given that governments are rooted in human nature, and must as a consequence suffer the limitations of human nature? These are key questions in evaluating government performance.

Systems for problem-solving in advanced democracies involve three aspects of the policymaking process: the supply of information, the prioritization of information, and the selection of alternatives once a problem has been detected. Decentralized systems characterized by jurisdictional complexity encourage the supply of information, while centralized systems limit that supply. Monopoly suppliers of information, such as occurs in the classic policy subsystem of deference to experts, have motive to supply information only favorable to the interests incorporated in the subsystem. This is not necessarily due to guile. Information is multifaceted, and ignoring some facets in a complex policymaking situation is to be expected. Entire subsystems are often designed around single perspectives on a given issue, so it is no surprise when the information they provide tends to come from a certain perspective. No one expects the Pentagon to focus on issues of human rights; that is some one else's problem. Military officers have a greater focus on other areas of expertise. So when decision makers rely on single institutions for their supply of information, there can be no surprise when that information tends to be limited in its scope and range of perspectives; things could hardly be otherwise.

Decentralized systems may be expected to supply a greater range of information, but they are not very efficient at weighting and prioritizing that information. If parts of the system can solve problems without reference to central authority, then no damage is done. Federalism builds in the capacity of states to act even in the absence of a national consensus on policy action, for example. If policy must be cleared through a central policymaking body, however, then the supply of information will detract from priority setting. Then policy priorities are set through the dynamics of collective attention and agenda setting.

Even if an issue reaches high agenda status, it is not a foregone conclusion that government will act. That depends both on the nature of the proposed solutions, where consensus often breaks down, and on the nature of the institutional rules governing action. In the United States, laws must be passed by concurrent majorities in two legislative bodies and then be approved by the president. These rules guarantee that supermajorities must be assembled for action to take place. In essence, the policymaking system is "fixed" such that type II errors—failing to act when action is required—are very likely.

Some have criticized these rules as leading to policy deadlock and the denial of majoritarian democracy. But the system was designed not solely to promote representation but also to deal with the balance between error types. The framers were as concerned with the protection of liberty as with the promotion of representation. This criticism also ignores the effect of such a system on the flow of information: it has the effect of strengthening signals from outside, as policy proponents know they must transmit signals about the need to act that will encourage the concurrent majorities needed to form.

If policymakers understood perfectly the problems with which they were faced (and those that might face them in the future), they might be able to devise a system of information gathering designed to gauge relevant signals from the environment on a regular basis. There would certainly be no need for duplication and redundancy; a single well-designed institution would be the best design under this scenario. But what if people either do not truly understand the issues that face them or if they have fundamental disagreements about how to address them? In this case a single jurisdictionally monopolistic institution may still be the most efficient in the short term, but a disaster in the long run. In complex environments, competition and diversity of opinions are fundamental to ensure that new information always has the potential to enter the system. Close this off, and you lose potential adaptability in the long run. On the other hand, this adaptability comes at the cost of short-run efficiency and will always be the object of complaint by those people who would gain more power through clearer lines of jurisdictional authority. We have shown that the U.S. government is not efficient as it responds to problems. Further, it becomes increasingly less efficient as we move from those institutions that essentially monitor social inputs to those that actually generate outputs. But is this system broken? Its limitations are human cognitive limitations, for the most part. Future research will tell how efficiently institutions can be designed, and even how efficient different institutions that currently exist are, beyond those that we have studied in this book. But as we think about the standard against which these institutions should be compared, perfect efficiency is not a reasonable reference point. There are important benefits that come from the inefficiencies that we have noted here. To note them is not to decry them; rather, it is to better understand them.

Institutional Design

We cannot say if this line of reasoning can lead to better governmental designs, whether for democratic state building in developing nations or agency creation in advanced liberal democracies. But we can say that often the wrong aspects of democracy are urged on developing societies, just as many of the wrong complaints are lodged against our own system of governance. If democracies are about representation, then elections are key, because they represent mass opinion. Elections are central in democratic information processing, because they ensure sensitivity of politicians to mass opinion. But within wide parameters, democracy does not rise or fall on the nature of the particular electoral system that is employed. At present, we simply do not know whether parliamentary democracies or presidential ones work better, because the wrong questions are being asked.

Democracies are information-processing systems that only partially anticipate the consequences of policy actions. Because of this organizational and individual fallibility, they must also be error-correction systems. In order to be effective error-correction systems, they must be able to detect problems. Many of the elements of government design that appear to lead to greater efficiency in government operations, such as specialization of labor, unification of control, and reduction in redundancy and overlap, probably have significant negative impacts on many of the elements that we have argued to be absolutely central to effective decision making. They lead to an ease of prioritization but imply monopoly suppliers of information; given the imperfections of human decision makers, this is a recipe for disaster.

We have assumed throughout this book that information will be supplied freely in American politics. Yet this happens not because it is invariable, but because American institutions—including both political and social institutions—are designed to encourage it. Perhaps not all countries can afford the overlapping, conflicting, confusing, and frustrating set of separated institutions sharing power that the United States has developed over the years. But it is worth considering some of the arguments of the framers of our own system of government when evaluating the functioning of that system today. In the *Federalist Papers*, Hamilton, Madison, and Jay focused on the need to ensure competition and overlap in the institutions of government in order to ensure that no single institution would accumulate too much authority. The accumulation of power in a single government institution, they wrote (*Federalist* No. 47), is "the very definition of tyranny." Their ideas about separation of powers inevitably also had implications for overlap in jurisdictional authority. Let us consider for a moment the value of their arguments as they apply to the accumulation not only of power, but of information (see Bimber 2003 for a related line of thought).

In *Federalist Papers* Nos. 47 through 51, separation of powers is discussed in detail. The authors argue not for a clear division of authority where no institution duplicates the power of any other (e.g., a division-of-labor system), but rather for a complex pattern of overlapping institutions sharing power, with various checks and balances allowing one institution to veto the activities of another, to appoint the members of another, to oversee their activities, but for none to dictate the activities of any other. The framers thought this structure could help deter tyranny. We think today it acts to stimulate the supply of policymaking information. And it generates much conflicting, confusing, and contradictory information.

These discussions are at the level of the three branches of the federal government, for that is their concern: explaining and advocating a separation-of-powers system for the national government. But *Federalist* No. 10 argues the necessity of a federal system to control the mischief of factions—and suggests a theory of information processing as well. The author, James Madison, quickly ruled out controlling of the causes of faction—which in our terms would stifle the sources of information. "Liberty is to faction what air is to fire"; yet Madison refuses to suppress it. "As long as the reason of man continues fallible, and he is at liberty to exercise it, different opinions will be formed." He explicitly rejects methods designed to suppress the free flow of ideas, even if lots of those are wrong or downright obnoxious.

The suppression of faction being worse than the disease, Madison turns to the control of faction. He finds the answer in the republican principle, by which mass passions are filtered, but more importantly, he advocates a large federalist system of government. Madison developed a theory of contagion and containment of bad ideas in such systems. "The influence of factious leaders may kindle a flame within their particular States, but will be unable to spread a general conflagration through the other States." He argues that the supply of information directed at promoting "improper or wicked projects" should not be suppressed. It is the prioritization that is important; he thought that would be accomplished by "extending the sphere" of the republic. Extending the sphere would have the effect of winnowing the bad ideas, but he had no theory of advancing beneficial ones.

Tyranny is precluded wherever power can be made diffuse. Where there are many factions, the opportunity for any single faction to dominate another is diminished, yet the liberty of factions to produce ideas is not impeded. Where there are many institutions sharing power and checking one another, the opportunities for any single agency, branch, or official to accumulate too much power are diminished, as is the ability to act as a monopoly supplier of information. Multiplication of interests, points of cleavage, and diffuse involvement in the affairs of government are the keys to minimizing the chances that any given institution will become tyrannical. Overlap is central.

The *Federalist Papers* contain an implicit theory of information processing, but it seems fair to say the authors conflated the supply of information with its prioritization. The framers thought that the system of supplying information would act to prioritize it—mostly in the form of deterring "improper or wicked projects." Yet the arguments—and we must remember they were advocacy—contained little in the way of guidance for positive government projects. Nor is there a theory of getting rid of bad policies if by happenstance they get enacted.

On the other hand, the modern fascination with considerations of representation at the expense of effective information processing in discussions of the design of government is striking—and this the framers avoided. Some work on the design of governmental structure has addressed questions of improving individual choice through improving the clarity of information (Schneider et al. 1997), but in recent years only Vincent Ostrom (1997) has raised the issue of collective problem solving with sensible assumptions about the capacities of the governed. Any program for improving government must take into consideration the capacities of humans and governments to process information—something the founders did, but most modern theorists do not.[2] This is in large part because modern theorists insist on relying on rational choice as an underpinning for their pronouncements, refusing to consider the behavioral bounds on human facilities and the institutions they advocate.

Human cognition and institutional decision-making patterns assure that

---

2. Madison was clearly a bounded rationalist. On the one hand, he wrote that "as long as the reason of man continues fallible . . . as long as the connection subsists between his reason and his self-love, his opinions and his passions will have a reciprocal influence on each other." On the other hand, he thought that at least some people could transcend those limits—he thought that the passions of the masses can be moderated in representative councils through "enlightened views and virtuous sentiments" (*Federalist* No. 10).

policymaking attention will be selective and incomplete at any given time. The key to effective decision making is a finely tuned problem-detection system and an ability to consider all the relevant dimensions of choice. Our government is by no means as efficient in this process as one could imagine. There are serious informational inefficiencies, as we showed especially in chapters 6 and 7. On the other hand, we should be wary of calls for reform that focus on efficiency, the reduction of overlap, or greater clarity in jurisdictional authority.

The power to make authoritative decisions in matters of public policy is a primary political issue. As the framers recognized, and built in to the system of government, each institution of government tends to approach a given issue from a different perspective than any other institution, none of which is typically complete in its overview of the relevant perspectives and considerations. Indeed, the different constituencies of the president, House, and Senate, and the different mandates and charges of the various committees and agencies of government, are designed to guarantee that each one differs from the others. The U.S. system, built explicitly on the basis of shared, overlapping powers, at least guarantees that monopolies of information and authority may be challenged occasionally by rival institutions armed with equal democratic legitimacy, but with different constituency interests or mandates. No institution can claim sole and unchallenged authority to decide on matters of high controversy. This, more than any other aspect of the separation of powers and federalism, may be what guarantees reaction, error-correction, and democratic responsiveness.

As we have shown throughout this book, this process is messy, inefficient, and costly. Alternatives focusing on greater clarity would be far worse—because they invariably rely on the restriction of information. In politics, information is not produced in the absence of fundamental liberties of free expression and assembly, and it is undersupplied in the absence of a complex jurisdictional structure of overlapping mandates such as what we have. So we come full circle in a discussion of inefficiency: Humans are inefficient because we cannot possibly attend simultaneously to the thousands of things that affect us; we must set priorities and change these from time to time as new crises emerge. Governments similarly are inefficient. One of the ways in which they seem inefficient—the duplication of effort by multiple institutions—also guarantees greater use of diverse sources of information. This particular form of inefficiency in fact is fundamental to the quality of our institutions, and should be encouraged, not stifled. So inefficiency and duplication of effort, as they provide guarantees against monopoly powers, have powerful democratic effects and stimulate the use of more diverse sources of information in the political process. As Madison wrote in *Federalist* No. 10, "But it could not be less folly to abolish liberty, which is essential to political life, because it nourishes faction, than it would be to wish the annihilation of air, which is essential to animal life, because it imparts to fire its destructive agency."

The Policy Agendas Project

The Policy Agendas Project is jointly operated by the University of Washington's Center for American Politics and Public Policy and the Pennsylvania State University's Department of Political Science. Its aim is to produce high-quality datasets that are capable of tracking policy change in the United States since the Second World War within precise policy content categories. Full information on the project may be found at http://www.policyagendas.org/.

The resources of the Policy Agendas Project include the following:

1. Congressional Hearings dataset
2. *Congressional Quarterly* (CQ) Almanac Stories dataset
3. Public Laws (Statutes) dataset
4. Presidential Executive Orders dataset
5. Gallup Most Important Problem Series dataset
6. *New York Times* Index dataset
7. U.S. Congressional Budget Authority dataset

The first five datasets utilize exactly the same topic coding scheme. The *New York Times* Index dataset uses a revised coding scheme based on the one used in the first five (but uses only the major topic categories, not the extensive subtopics, and adds some additional topics not found in the governmental datasets, such as for sports results, weather reports, and other non-policy-related topics). The U.S. Congressional Budget Authority dataset uses a coding system taken from the Office of Management and Budget's budget documents.

The table below presents the complete listing of major topic codes for all the datasets except Budget Authority. Topics 24 through 31 are in the *New*

York Times Index dataset only. The major topics are further subdivided into 226 subtopic categories. A complete listing of subtopics may be found in Baumgartner and Jones 2002; and at http://www.policyagendas.org/.

Table A1.1. Policy Agendas Major Topic Codes

Major Topic	Topic Code
Macroeconomics	1
Civil rights, minority issues, and civil liberties	2
Health	3
Agriculture	4
Labor, employment, and immigration	5
Education	6
Environment	7
Energy	8
Transportation	10
Law, crime, and family issues	12
Social welfare	13
Housing and community development	14
Banking, finance, and domestic commerce	15
Defense	16
Space, science, technology, and communications	17
Foreign trade	18
International affairs and foreign aid	19
Government operations	20
Public lands and water management	21
State and local government administration	24
Weather and natural disasters	26
Fires	27
Arts and entertainment	28
Sports and recreation	29
Death notices	30
Churches and religion	31
Other, miscellaneous, and human interest	99

Budget Authority

Researchers must surmount serious technical difficulties to study budget change.[1] First, budget categories are not consistent across time, with programs and program units moving across agencies and subfunctions as organizational changes and analytical convenience dictate. The problem of temporal inconsistency stems from the tendency of programs to migrate across agencies (a real-world organizational problem) or across budget categories (a problem of the categories used by OMB analysts). When new categories are added, it is necessary to adjust backward, making the previous allotments to categories consistent with the new categories, but the Office of Management and Budget has done this for budget authority only since 1976. Budget outlays are consistent for a longer period of time, but outlays in too many cases do not occur when budget decisions are made. The disjuncture between outlays and decisions enables mistaken inferences about the causes of a budget allocation. In order to surmount these major difficulties, we have constructed a dataset that ensures temporal consistency for U.S. budget authority for the period FY 1947–FY 2003.

The data are tabulated at the subfunction level. The U.S. Office of Management and Budget groups expenditures according to common objectives. At the largest scale are the major functions. Each major function incorporates several subfunctions. A subfunction can include several programs, where the programs are directed at similar ends.

One may object that, in general, budget decisions are made at the program level rather than at the subfunction level; or even at the generally larger agency level. Program data, however, are not available for a consistent time

1. This appendix was drafted by James L. True and Bryan Jones.

series for this length of time; our new subfunction data constitute the lowest level of aggregation available for an extended time period. Agency levels of aggregation are problematic for three reasons: programs can shift agency locales, measures of variability are more unstable on the smaller n's, and agency totals often include offsetting receipts from primarily financial subfunctions.

Domestic subfunctions exclude financial functions and subfunctions as unsuitable for analysis because they consist mainly of net, rather than complete, transactions. The excluded financial subfunctions are: 155, international financial programs; 371, mortgage credit; 373, deposit insurance: 704, veterans housing; 809, deductions for offsetting receipts; 902, interest received by on-budget trust funds; 903, interest received by off-budget trust funds; 908, other interest; 951, employer share, employee retirement (on-budget); 952, employer share, employee retirement (off-budget); 953, rents and royalties on the outer continental shelf; and 954, sale of major assets. Domestic spending includes all remaining subfunctions except for those in function 050, national defense, and function 150, international affairs.

Mandatory and Discretionary Domestic Spending. We further disaggregated domestic spending by assigning its subfunctions to mandatory or discretionary categories based upon our analyses of table 8–5, "Outlays for Mandatory and Related Programs," in the FY 1995, 1996, and 1997 *Budgets of the United States Government.* Details are available from the authors.

Data Sources. The primary sources of the budget authority data are the *Budget of the United States Government,* hereafter *BUSG* (serial, fiscal year 1949 through 1994, in print form published by the Government Printing Office, Washington, DC, and serial, fiscal year 1995 through 2003, on CD-ROM from the Department of Commerce). Secondary sources include the *Report of the President's Commission on Budget Concepts* (Washington, DC: October 1967) and the "Budget System and Concepts" sections of contemporary budgets, which were used in defining the contents of the contemporary budget authority by subfunction. The data were recategorized into the subfunctions extant in the FY 1995 *Budget* and converted into constant dollar form. Thus, this dataset uses contemporary budget records to extend the OMB historical tables from FY 1976 back to FY 1947.

Budget Authority. Budget authority consists of appropriations and reappropriations, borrowing authority, and contract authority. It should not be confused with budget authorizations. Legally, BA constitutes specific authority to make obligations that will result in immediate or later outlays. The present Office of Management and Budget definition of budget authority includes both federal funds and trust funds. The data presented in this book consist of actual budget authority figures from contemporary *Budgets,* which have been adjusted to conform to the current definition and corrected for inflation. The data are composed of appropriations, borrowing authority, and contract authority for both on- and off-budget federal entities from FY 1976 through FY 2003; of appropriations, borrowing authority, and contracting authority for on-budget entities from FY 1967 through FY 1975; of administrative appropriations and trust fund budget authority from FY 1962 through FY 1966; of new obligating authority and trust fund expenses from FY 1949 through FY 1961; and of appropriations and trust fund expenses from FY 1947 through FY 1948. We omit data from the three months of the transition quarter between FY 1976 and FY 1977.

Current and Constant Dollar Figures. We converted the contemporary actual budget figures into constant calendar-year dollars by using the implicit price deflators for the U.S. gross domestic product (GDP) transformed from calendar year to fiscal year. The deflator removed the effects of inflation for the fiscal year in which the new budget authority was available for obligations by government agencies, i.e., the FY 1955 deflator was used on the FY 1955 data, although an argument can be made for using the inflation rate in effect while Congress is considering budgets for the coming year (White 1995). The source of the deflators was the *National Income and Product Accounts of the United States* (Washington, DC: U.S. Department of Commerce, 1990) and the National Income and Product Tables of the *Survey of Current Business* (Washington, DC: U.S. Department of Commerce) (serial).

Subfunctions. The primary sources of the current subfunction categorization were the *Budget of the United States Government for Fiscal Year 1995* and OMB technical staff paper FAB 79-1, *The Functional Classification in the Budget,* dated February 22, 1979. Criteria for functional classification may be found in "The Budget System and Concepts of the United States Government" in the FY 1995 *BUSG* and from the *Budget of the United States Government* (serial, fiscal years 1948 through 2003).

Macrofunctions. We further assigned the data captured in these budget subfunctions to macrofunctions of mandatory domestic spending, discretionary domestic spending, national security spending, and financial aggregates. These macrofunction aggregations parallel but do not exactly duplicate the definitions outlined in the Budget Enforcement Act of 1990. Subfunction categorization was based on our analysis of table 8-5, "Outlays for Mandatory and Related Programs: 1962–2002," in the *Budgets* for FY 1995, 1996, and 1997. Financial functions and subfunctions were excluded from these analyses, because they consist mainly of net, rather than complete, transactions. The domestic category consists of all of the subfunctions in the mandatory and discretionary macrofunctions as explained below.

Domestic Mandatory Spending. OMB defines mandatory spending or direct spending as a category of budget authority and outlays provided for in entitlement authority, law other than appropriations acts, and budget authority for the food stamp program. We have operationalized that definition to capture whole subfunctions associated primarily with direct spending programs. The subfunctions herein included in the domestic mandatory macrofunction are:

- 351 Farm income security
- 502 Higher education
- 551 Health care services
- 571 Medicare
- 601 General retirement and disability
- 602 Federal employee retirement and disability
- 603 Unemployment compensation
- 605 Food and nutrition assistance
- 609 Other income security
- 651 Social Security
- 701 Income security for veterans
- 702 Veterans education, training, and rehabilitation
- 901 Interest on the public debt

Domestic Discretionary Spending. This macrofunction contains budget authority which is usually provided in annual appropriations acts. The domestic discretionary macrofunction excludes subfunctions assigned to the mandatory, national security, and financial macrofunctions. The subfunctions included in the domestic discretionary macrofunction are:

- 251 General science and basic research
- 252 Space flight, research, and supporting activities
- 271 Energy supply
- 272 Energy conservation
- 274 Emergency energy preparedness
- 276 Energy information, policy, and regulation
- 301 Water resources
- 302 Conservation and land management
- 303 Recreational resources
- 304 Pollution control and abatement
- 306 Other natural resources
- 352 Agricultural research and services

- 372 Postal service
- 376 Other advancement of commerce
- 401 Ground transportation
- 402 Air transportation
- 403 Water transportation
- 407 Other transportation
- 451 Community development
- 452 Area and regional development
- 453 Disaster relief and insurance
- 501 Elementary, secondary, and vocational education
- 503 Research and general education aids
- 504 Training and employment
- 505 Other labor services
- 506 Social services
- 552 Health research and training
- 554 Consumer and occupational health and safety
- 604 Housing assistance
- 703 Hospital and medical care for veterans
- 705 Other veterans' benefits and services
- 751 Federal law enforcement activities
- 752 Federal litigative and judicial activities
- 753 Federal correctional activities
- 754 Criminal justice assistance
- 801 Legislative functions
- 802 Executive direction and management
- 803 Central fiscal operations
- 804 General property and records management
- 805 Central personnel management
- 806 General purpose fiscal assistance
- 808 Other general government

National Security Spending. This macrofunction consists of spending associated with national defense (function 050) and international affairs (function 150), except for the financial subfunction 155 (International financial programs). The subfunctions included in the national security macrofunction are:

- 051 Department of Defense-Military
- 053 Atomic energy defense activities
- 054 Defense-related activities

- 151 International development and humanitarian assistance
- 152 International security assistance
- 153 Conduct of foreign affairs
- 154 Foreign information and exchange activities

Financial Subfunctions. These subfunctions reflect large amounts of credit activity, offsetting receipts, or government-wide contra-accounts. Such subfunctions were excluded from programmatic analyses because of their broad use of net, rather than complete, transactions and offsetting receipts. The subfunctions included in the financial macrofunction are:

- 155 International financial programs
- 371 Mortgage credit
- 373 Deposit insurance
- 704 Veterans housing
- 809 Deductions for offsetting receipts
- 902 Interest received by on-budget trust funds
- 903 Interest received by off-budget trust funds
- 908 Other interest
- 951 Employer share, employee retirement (on-budget)
- 952 Employer share, employee retirement (off-budget)
- 953 Rents and royalties on the outer continental shelf
- 954 Sale of major assets

Constructing the List of Major Statutes

Our system relies on content coding of *Congressional Quarterly* stories and of statutes passed in its annual review volume. We noted whether *CQ* covered the act in the body of its annual volume. For those included, we weighted the statutes by the amount of *CQ* coverage on the major topic area of the statute. We did this on available data, which was for 1948–94 at the time the work was done. This procedure rank ordered the 5,026 statutes that were covered, but cannot, of course, distinguish among those that received no coverage. Of the 5,026 statutes with coverage, 2,719 received 100 lines of coverage or more; 1,045 received 500 or more, and 432 received 1,000 or more. Somewhat arbitrarily, we chose the top 500 laws enacted between 1948 and 1994, inclusive, as "most important." This included all statutes receiving more than 800 lines of coverage.

The *Congressional Quarterly* had less capacity to cover legislation before 1961. In that year, the *Congressional Quarterly* reached a capacity that has remained reasonably stable. So we adjusted for variation in the capacity of the *Congressional Quarterly* by using weights that adjusted the capacity of earlier volumes to that of the 1961 volume, and we inflated the major statute count in earlier years to reflect the 1961 volume. This yielded 536 laws for the period.

When new data became available, we updated by noting the cutoff point used to rank the 536 statutes (800 lines of coverage) and applied the same standard to the laws passed in the 1995–98 period. This yielded 576 laws for the period 1948–98. This procedure will allow easy updating in the future.

Here is a review of our steps:

Step 1: Rank 500 laws based on *CQ* lines of coverage, 1948–94 (the available data at the time). This included all laws with more than 800 lines of coverage.

Step 2: Make adjustments based on *CQ* undercoverage, 1948–61.

Step 3: Determine minimum lines of coverage associated with Step 1 (= 800).

Step 4: Apply to the laws, 1995–98.

Total = 576 laws

The table below presents a summary of lawmaking in the postwar period.

Table A3.1. Laws Passed, 1948–98

Category	Number of Laws
All statutes	17,044
Statutes with some *CQ* coverage	5,255
Statutes with 100 lines of coverage	2,858
Major statutes	576

REFERENCES

Alley, Richard B. 2000. *The Two Mile Time Machine*. Princeton: Princeton University Press.

Anscome, F. J., and William J. Glynn. 1983. Distribution of the Kurtosis Statistic b2 for Normal Samples. *Biometrika* 70:227–34.

Bak, Per. 1997. *How Nature Works*. New York: Springer-Verlag.

Balanda, K. P., and H. L. MacGillivray. 1988. Kurtosis: A Critical Review. *American Statistician* 42:111–19.

Bartels, Larry M. 1988. *Presidential Primaries and the Dynamics of Public Choice*. Princeton, NJ: Princeton University Press.

Baumgartner, Frank R., and Bryan D. Jones. 1993. *Agendas and Instability in American Politics*. Chicago: University of Chicago Press.

———. 2002. *Policy Dynamics*. Chicago: University of Chicago Press.

Baumgartner, Frank R., Bryan D. Jones, and Michael C. MacLeod. 1998. Lessons from the Trenches: Quality, Reliability, and Usability in a New Data Source. *Political Methodologist*.8 (2):1–10.

———. 2000. The Evolution of Legislative Jurisdictions. *Journal of Politics* 62:321–49.

Becker, Gary S. 1991. A Note on Restaurant Pricing and Other Examples of Social Influences on Price. *Journal of Political Economy* 99 (5):1109–16.

Berry, William D. 1990. The Confusing Case of Budgetary Incrementalism: Too Many Meanings for a Single Concept. *Journal of Politics* 52:167–96.

Bikhchandani, Sushil, David Hirshleifer, and Ivo Welch. 1992. A Theory of Fads, Fashion, Custom, and Cultural Change as Informational Cascades. *Journal of Political Economy* 100:992–1026.

Bimber, Bruce. 2003. *Information and American Democracy*. Cambridge: Cambridge University Press.

Bish, Robert. 1973. *The Public Economy of Metropolitan Areas*. Chicago: Markham.

Breunig, Christian. 2004. Distribution of Budget Changes in Germany, the United

Kingdom, and the United States. Portland, OR. Paper presented at the Western Political Science Association meetings.

Brunk, Gregory. 2000. Understanding Self-Organized Criticality as a Statistical Process. *Complexity* 5:1–8.

Buchanan, James M., and Gordon Tullock. 1962. *The Calculus of Consent.* Ann Arbor: University of Michigan Press.

Burstein, Paul, and Marie Bricher. 1997. Problem Definition and Public Policy: Congressional Committees Confront Work, Family, and Gender, 1945–90. *Social Forces* 76:135–78.

Burstein, Paul, Marie Bricher, and Rachel Einwohner. 1995. Policy Alternatives and Political Change: Work, Family, and Gender on the Congressional Agenda, 1945–90. *American Sociological Review* 60:67–83.

Campbell, John, Andrew Lo, and A. Craig MacKinlay. 1997. *The Econometrics of Financial Markets.* Princeton, NJ: Princeton University Press.

Carmines, Edward, and James A. Stimson. 1989. *Issue Evolution: Race and the Transformation of American Politics.* Princeton: Princeton University Press.

Cefis, Elena, Matteo Ciccarelli, and Luigi Orsenigo. 2001. The Growth of Firms: From Gibrat's Legacy to Gibrat's Fallacy. European Pharmaceuticals Regulation and Innovation System working paper.

Chong, Dennis. 1991. *Collective Action and Civil Rights.* Chicago: University of Chicago Press.

Clarke, Richard A. 2004. *Against All Enemies: Inside America's War on Terror.* New York: Free Press.

Cobb, Roger, and Charles D. Elder. 1983. *Participation in American Politics: The Dynamics of Agenda-Building.* Baltimore: Johns Hopkins University Press.

Cobb, Roger, and Marc Howard Ross, eds. 1997. *Cultural Strategies of Agenda Denial.* Lawrence, KS: University Press of Kansas.

Cohen, Michael, James G. March, and Johan P. Olsen. 1972. A Garbage Can Theory of Organizational Choice. *Administrative Science Quarterly* 17:1 25.

Cootner, Paul, ed. 1964. *The Random Character of Stock Market Prices* Cambridge: MIT Press.

Dalaker, Joseph, and Bernadette Proctor. 2000. *Poverty in the United States, 1999.* Current Population Reports, Series P60-210. Washington, DC: U.S. Census Bureau.

Davis, Otto A., M.A.H. Dempster, and Aaron Wildavsky. 1966. A Theory of the Budget Process. *American Political Science Review* 60: 529–47.

———. 1974. Towards a Predictive Theory of Government Expenditure: U.S. Domestic Appropriations. *British Journal of Political Science* 4:419–52.

DeLeon, Peter. 1999. The Stages Approach to the Policy Process: What Has It Done? Where Is It Going? In *Theories of the Policy Process,* ed. Paul A. Sabatier, 19–34. Boulder, CO: Westview.

Dodd, Lawrence C. 1991. Congress, the Presidency, and the American Experience: A Transformational Perspective. In *Divided Democracy,* ed. James A Thurber. Washington, DC: Congressional Quarterly.

Dole, Robert. 2000. *Great Political Wit*. New York: Broadway Books.

Dow Jones and Company. 1996. *100 Years of Dow Data*. Chichopee, MA: Dow Jones.

Downs, Anthony. 1972. Up and Down with Ecology: The Issue-Attention Cycle. *Public Interest* 28: 38–50.

Eldridge, Niles, and Stephen J. Gould. 1972. Punctuated Equilibria: An Alternative to Phyletic Graduation. In Thomas J. M. Schopf, ed., *Models in Paleobiology*, 82–115. San Francisco: Freeman, Cooper.

Erikson, Robert S., James A. Stimson, and Michael MacKuen. 2002. *The Macro Polity*. New York: Cambridge University Press.

Erikson, Robert S., Gerald C. Wright, and John P. McIver. 1993. *Statehouse Democracy: Public Opinion and Policy in the American States*. New York: Cambridge University Press.

Fama, Eugene. 1970. Efficient Capital Markets: A Review of Theory and Empirical Work. *Journal of Finance* 25: 383–417.

Feeley, T. Jens, Bryan D. Jones, Heather Larsen. 2001. *Public Agendas: Annualized Most Important Problem Polling Data, 1939–2001*. Seattle, WA: Center for American Politics and Public Policy, University of Washington.

Fenno, Richard F. Jr. 1966. *The Power of the Purse: Appropriations Politics in Congress*. Boston: Little, Brown.

Finucan, H. M. 1963. A Note on Kurtosis. *Journal of the Royal Statistical Society*, ser. B. 26:111–12.

Gerber, Alan, and Donald Green. 1999. Misperceptions about Perceptual Bias. *Annual Review of Political Science* 2: 189–210.

Gist, John R. 1982. "Stability" and "Competition" in Budgetary Theory. *American Political Science Review* 76:859–72.

Granovetter, Mark. 1978. Threshold Models of Collective Behavior. *American Journal of Sociology* 83:1420–43.

Groeneveld, Richard A. 1998. A Class of Quintile Measures for Kurtosis. *American Statistician* 51: 325–29.

Hall, Billy. 1997. *A Legal Solution to Government Gridlock*. New York: Garland.

Hall, Peter, ed. 1989. *The Political Power of Economic Ideas : Keynesianism across Nations*. Princeton, NJ: Princeton University Press.

Hall, Richard. 1996. *Participation in Congress*. New Haven: Yale University Press.

Hammond, Thomas, and Gary J. Miller. 1987. The Core of the Constitution. *American Political Science Review* 81:1155–74.

Hayes, Michael T. 1992. *Incrementalism and Public Policy*. New York: Longman.

Hinich, Melvin, and Michael Munger. 1994. *Ideology and the Theory of Political Choice*. Ann Arbor: University of Michigan Press.

Hirshleifer, David. 1995. The Blind Leading the Blind: Social Influence, Fads, and Informational Cascades. In *The New Economics of Human Behavior*, ed. Mariano Tommasi and Kathryn Ierulli, 188–215. New York: Cambridge University Press.

Huntington, Samuel P. 1981. *American Politics: The Promise of Disharmony*. Cambridge: Belknap Press of Harvard University.

Inhofe, James. 2003. Global Warming: The Worst of All Environmental Scares. Human Events Online. http://www.humaneventsonline.com/article.php?id=1385. (accessed August 6, 2003).

Ijiri, Y. and Herbert A. Simon. 1977. *Skew Distributions and the Size of Business Firms.* Amsterdam: North Holland.

Jackson, John E., ed. 1990. *Institutions in American Society.* Ann Arbor: University of Michigan Press.

John, Peter, and Helen Margetts. 2003. Policy Punctuations in the UK. *Public Administration* 81:411–32.

Jones, Bryan D. 1994. *Reconceiving Decision-Making in Democratic Politics: Attention, Choice, and Public Policy.* Chicago: University of Chicago Press.

———. 1996. Attributes, Alternatives, and the Flow of Ideas: Information Processing in Politics. Presented at the annual meeting of the American Political Science Association, San Francisco.

———. 2001. *Politics and the Architecture of Choice.* Chicago: University of Chicago Press.

———. 2003. Bounded Rationality in Political Science: Lessons from Public Administration. *Journal of Public Administration Theory* 13: 395–410.

Jones, Bryan D., and Frank R. Baumgartner. 2005. A Model of Choice for Public Policy. *Journal of Public Administration Research and Theory* 15:1–27.

———. 2004. Representation and Agenda Setting. *Policy Studies Journal* 32:1–24.

Jones, Bryan D., Frank R. Baumgartner, and James L. True. 1998. Policy Punctuations: US Budget Authority, 1947–95. *Journal of Politics* 60: 1–30.

Jones, Charles O. 1975. *Clean Air.* Pittsburgh: University of Pittsburgh Press.

———. 1994. *The Presidency in a Separated System.* Washington, DC: Brookings.

Jordan, Meagan. 2003. Punctuations and Agendas. *Journal of Policy Analysis and Management* 22:345–60.

Kelly, Sean Q. 1994. Punctuated Change and the Era of Divided Government. In *New Perspectives on American Politics,* ed. Lawrence C. Dodd and Calvin Jillson, 162–90. Washington, DC: CQ Press.

Key, V. O. 1940. The Lack of a Budgetary Theory. *American Political Science Review* 34: 1137–44.

———. 1961. *Public Opinion and American Democracy.* New York: Knopf.

Kiel, Douglas, and Euel Elliott. 1992. Budgets as Dynamic Systems: Change, Variation, Time, and Budgetary Heuristics. *Journal of Public Administration Theory* 2:139–56.

Kingdon, John W. 1984. *Agendas, Alternatives, and Public Policy.* New York: Harper-Collins.

———. 1989. *Congressmen's Voting Decisions.* Ann Arbor: University of Michigan Press.

———. 1995. *Agendas, Alternatives, and Public Policies.* 2nd ed. Boston: Little, Brown.

Kirman, Alan. 1993. Ants, Rationality, and Recruitment. *Quarterly Journal of Economics* 108 (1): 137–56.

Kotz, Samuel, and Saralees Nadarajah. 2000. *Extreme Value Distributions: Theory and Practice.* London: Imperial College Press.

Krasner, Stephen. 1984. Approaches to the State: Alternative Conceptions and Historical Dynamics. *Comparative Politics* 16: 223–46.

Krehbiel, Keith. 1991. *Information and Legislative Organization.* Ann Arbor: University of Michigan Press.

———. 1998. *Pivotal Politics: A Theory of U.S. Lawmaking.* Chicago: University of Chicago Press.

Kruskal, Joseph. 1964. Multidimensional Scaling by Optimizing Goodness of Fit to a Nonmetric Hypothesis. *Psychometrika* 29:1–27.

Kuran, Timur. 1989. Sparks and Prairie Fires: A Theory of Unanticipated Political Revolution. *Public Choice* 61: 41–74.

Laherrère, Jean, and Didier Sornette. 1998. Stretched Exponential Distributions in Nature and Economy. *European Physical Journal* B 2: 525–39.

Larkey, Patrick. 1979. *Evaluating Public Programs.* Princeton, NJ: Princeton University Press.

Lindblom, Charles. 1959. The Science of "Muddling Through." *Public Administration Review* 19: 79–88.

Lux, Thomas. 1998. The Socio-Economic Dynamics of Speculative Markets. *Journal of Economic Behavior and Organization* 33: 143–65.

Maikel, Burton. 1996. *A Random Walk down Wall Street.* New York: Norton.

Mandelbrot, Benoit. 1963. New Methods in Statistical Economics. *Journal of Political Economy* 1: 79–106.

———. 1964. The Variation of Certain Speculative Prices. In *The Random Character of Stock Market Prices,* ed. Paul H. Cootner, 307–32. Cambridge: MIT Press.

———. 1997. *Fractals and Scaling in Finance.* New York: Springer.

———. 1999. *Multifractals and 1/f Noise.* New York: Springer.

Marcus, George E., W. Russell Neuman, and Michael MacKuen. 2000. *Affective Intelligence and Political Judgment.* Chicago: University of Chicago Press.

Mayer, Kenneth. 2001. *With the Stroke of a Pen: Executive Orders and Political Power.* Princeton, NJ: Princeton University Press.

Mayewski, Paul Andrew, and Frank White. 2002. *The Ice Chronicles.* Hanover, NH: University Press of New England.

Mayhew, David. 1991. *Divided We Govern.* New Haven, CT: Yale University Press.

Mills, Terence C. 1995. Modelling Skewness and Kurtosis in the London Stock Exchange FT-SE Index Return Distributions. *Statistician* 44: 323–32.

Moors, J.J.A. 1988. A Quantile Alternative for Kurtosis. *Statistician* 37: 25–32.

Mortensen, Peter. 2003. *Policy Punctuations in Danish Local Budgeting.* Aarhus, Denmark: Institut for Statskunskab, University of Aarhus.

Nardulli, Peter. 1995. The Concept of a Critical Realignment, Electoral Behavior, and Political Change. *American Political Science Review* 89: 10–22.

Natchez, Peter B., and Irvin C. Bupp. 1973. Policy and Priority in the Budgetary Process. *American Political Science Review* 67: 951–63.

Newell, Allen. 1990. *Unified Theories of Cognition.* Cambridge: Harvard University Press.

North, Douglass. 1990. *Institutions, Institutional Change, and Economic Performance.* New York: Cambridge University Press.

NSC-162/2. 1953. Review of Basic National Security Policy. In *Pentagon Papers,* Gravel ed., vol. 1, pp. 412–29.

Ostrom, Vincent. 1997. *The Meaning of Democracy and the Vulnerability of Democracies.* Ann Arbor: University of Michigan Press.

Padgett, John F. 1980. Bounded Rationality in Budgetary Research. *American Political Science Review* 74: 354–72.

———. 1981. Hierarchy and Ecological Control in Federal Budgetary Decision Making. *American Journal of Sociology* 87: 75–128.

Page, Benjamin I., and Robert Y. Shapiro. 1992. *The Rational Public: Fifty Years of Trends in American's Policy Preferences.* Chicago: University of Chicago Press.

Peters, Edgar F. 1991. *Chaos and Order in the Capital Markets.* New York: John Wiley.

———. 1994. *Fractal Market Analysis.* New York: John Wiley.

Peterson, David, Lawrence Grossback, James Stimson, and Amy Gangl. 2003. Congressional Response to Mandate Elections. *American Journal of Political Science* 47: 411–26.

Pierson, Paul. 2000. Path Dependence, Increasing Returns, and the Study of Politics. *American Political Science Review* 94: 251–67.

Plott, Charles, and Shyam Sunder. 1982. Efficiency of Experimental Security Markets with Insider Information: An Application of Rational-Expectations Models. *Journal of Political Economy* 90: 663–98.

Poole, Keith, and Howard Rosenthal. 1997. *Congress: A Political-Economic History of Roll Call Voting.* New York: Oxford University Press.

Redford, Emmette. 1969. *Democracy in the Administrative State.* New York: Oxford University Press.

Report of the President's Commission on Budget Concepts. 1967. Washington, DC.

Reinhard, Michael, and Fabio Rojas. 2002. Rhetoric, Dimension, and Disjoint Policy Change: "The End of Welfare as We Know It." Paper presented at the Midwest Political Science Association, Chicago.

Riker, William. 1996. *The Strategy of Rhetoric.* New Haven, CT: Yale University Press.

Robinson, Scott. 2004. Punctuated Equilibrium, Bureaucratization, and Budgetary Changes in Schools. *Policy Studies Journal* 32: 25–39.

Rochefort, David, and Roger Cobb, eds. 1994. *The Politics of Problem Definition.* Lawrence, KS: University Press of Kansas.

Rose, Richard, and Phillip Davies. 1994. *Inheritance in Public Policy: Change without Choice in Britain.* New Haven, CT: Yale University Press.

Rubin, Irene. 1988. *New Directions in Budgetary Theory.* Albany: State University of New York Press.

Rundle, John B., Donald L. Turcotte, and William Klein, eds. 1996. *Reduction and Predictability of Natural Disasters.* Reading, MA.: Addison-Wesley.

Sabatier, Paul A., and Hank Jenkins-Smith, eds. 1993. *Policy Change and Learning.* Boulder, CO: Westview.

Samuelson, Paul. 1965. Proof That Properly Anticipated Prices Fluctuate Randomly. *Industrial Management Review* 6: 41–49.

Schaller, Huntley, and Simon van Norden. 1997. *Fads or Bubbles?* Working Papers 97-2. Montreal: Bank of Canada.

Schattschneider, E. E. 1960. *The Semi-Sovereign People.* New York: Holt, Rinehart, and Winston.

Schelling, Thomas C. 1972. A Process of Residential Segregation: Neighborhood Tipping. In *Racial Discrimination in Economic Life,* ed. Anthony H. Pascal, 157–84. Lexington, MA: D.C. Heath.

Schick, Allen. 1988. An Inquiry into the Possibility of a Budgetary Theory. In *New Directions in Budget Theory,* ed. Irene Rubin, 59–69. Albany: State University of New York Press.

Schlesinger, Arthur M. Jr. 1986. *The Cycles of American History.* Boston: Houghton Mifflin.

Schneider, Mark, Paul Teske, Melissa Marschall, Michael Mintrom, and Christine Roch. 1997. Institutional Arrangements and the Creation of Social Capital. *American Political Science Review* 91: 82–91.

Shepard, Roger. 1962a. The Analysis of Proximities: Multidimensional Scaling with an Unknown Distance Function I. *Psychometrika* 27:125–29.

———. 1962b. The Analysis of Proximities: Multidimensional Scaling with an Unknown Distance Function II. *Psychometrika* 27:219–46.

Shiller, Robert J. 2000. *Irrational Exuberance.* Princeton, NJ. Princeton University Press.

Simon, Herbert A. 1947. *Administrative Behavior.* New York: Macmillan.

———. 1983. *Reason in Human Affairs.* Stanford: Stanford University Press.

———. 1996. *The Sciences of the Artificial.* 3rd ed. Cambridge: MIT Press.

———. 1997. Managing in an Information-Rich World. In Herbert A. Simon, ed., *Models of Bounded Rationality.* Cambridge: MIT Press.

Skocpol, Theda. 1992. *Protecting Soldiers and Mothers: The Political Origins of Social Policy in the United States.* Cambridge: Harvard University Press.

Sornette, Didier. 2000. *Critical Phenomena in Natural Sciences.* Berlin: Springer.

———. 2003. *Why Stock Markets Crash.* Princeton, NJ: Princeton University Press.

Soroka, Stuart. 2001. *Question Wording, Number of Responses, and the Most Important Problem.* Oxford: Nuffield College.

———. 2002. *Agenda-Setting Dynamics in Canada.* Vancouver: University of British Columbia Press.

Sparrow, Bartholomew. 1996. *From the Outside In.* Princeton: Princeton University Press.

Stimson, James A. 1999. *Public Opinion in America: Moods, Cycles, and Swings.* 2nd ed. Boulder, CO: Westview.

———. 2004. *Tides of Consent.* New York: Cambridge University Press.

Stimson, James A., Michael B. MacKuen, and Robert S. Erikson. 1995. Dynamic Representation. *American Political Science Review* 89: 543–65.

Stone, Deborah. 1997. *Policy Paradox and Political Reason.* New York: Norton.

Thurmaier, Kurt. 1995. Decisive Decision Making in the Executive Budget Process: Analyzing the Political and Economic Propensities of Central Budget Bureau Analysts. *Public Administration Review* 55: 448–60.

True, James L. 1999. Attention, Inertia, and Equity in the Social Security Program. *Journal of Public Administration Research and Theory* 9: 571–96.

———. 2004. *Converting Contemporary National Budget Records to the Present Functional Categorization.* Seattle: Policy Agendas Project, Center for American Politics and Public Policy, University of Washington.

———. 2004. Has the National Government Begun a New Era of Robust Growth? Paper presented at the Midwest Political Science Association, Chicago.

True, James L., Bryan D. Jones, and Frank R. Baumgartner. 1999. Punctuated Equilibrium Theory. In *Theories of the Policy Process,* ed. Paul A. Sabatier, 97–115. Boulder, CO: Westview.

U.S. Bureau of Labor Statistics. 2003. Consumer Price Index, Current Series.

U.S. Bureau of the Census. 1970. *Historical Statistics of the US: Colonial Times to 1970.* Washington: U.S. Government Printing Office

U.S. Department of Commerce. Survey of Current Business (Washington, DC: U.S. Department of Commerce) (serial).

U.S. Department of Commerce. 1990. National Income and Product Accounts of the United States. Washington, DC: U.S. Department of Commerce.

U.S. Office of Management and Budget. *Budget of the United States Government* (serial, fiscal years 1948 through 2004).

U.S. Office of Management and Budget. 2003. *Budget of the United States Government, Fiscal Year 2004: Historical Tables.*

Wanat, John. 1974. Bases of Budgetary Incrementalism. *American Political Science Review* 68: 1221–28.

Webber, Carolyn, and Aaron Wildavsky. 1986. *A History of Taxation and Expenditure in the Western World.* New York: Simon and Schuster.

White, Joseph. 1995. (Almost) Nothing New under the Sun: Why the Work of Budgeting Remains Incremental. In *Budgeting, Policy, and Politics: An Appreciation of Aaron Wildavsky,* ed. Naomi Caiden and Joseph White, 111–132. New Brunswick, NJ: Transaction Publishers.

Wildavsky, Aaron. 1964. *The Politics of the Budgetary Process.* Boston: Little, Brown.

Wills, Christopher. 1993. *The Runaway Brain.* New York: Basic Books.

Wlezien, Christopher. 1995. The Public as Thermostat: Dynamics of Preferences for Spending. *American Journal of Political Science* 39: 981–1000.

———. 2003. *On the Salience of Political Issues.* Oxford: Nuffield College.

Worsham, Jeffrey. 1997. *Other People's Money.* Boulder, CO: Westview.

Zahariadis, Nikolaos. 1999. Ambiguity, Time, and Multiple Streams. In *Theories of the Policy Process,* ed. Paul A. Sabatier, 73–96. Boulder, CO: Westview.

Zebroski, Ernest. 1997. *Perils of a Restless Planet.* New York: Cambridge University Press.

Abu Ghraib in implicit index construction, 133
Adler, Scott, 182n
agenda, public, 211, 213, 251–53
agenda congruence. *See* congruence
agenda correspondence. *See* correspondence
agenda crowding, 24, 52–53, 213, 259
Agendas and Instability, vii, ix, 278, 279
agenda setting, ix, x, 38–40, 92, 278; distributions, 197; equation, 209, 215, 227
agenda size problem, 178–80
agenda space, 263–67
agency missions, and decision making, 48, 51
agriculture policy, 103
Aid to Dependent Children, 79
Aid to Families with Dependent Children, 81, 82
"alarmed discovery," and overreaction, 52, 55, 56, 76, 133
Alley, Richard B., 2
al-Qaida, and agency missions, 51, 52
alternatives, 35–36, 66–67; as stage in decision making, 34. *See also* solutions
ambiguity, and decision making, 7, 13–14, 90–91
Anscome, F. J., 181n
Arrow, Kenneth, 42
Ashcroft, John, 15

attention, in decision making, 16, 18, 19, 20–21, 26, 61, 88, 135; intensity of, 244–45; public, 211; shifting, 126, 137, 275
attention allocation, 10, 92, 205, 208, 210, 232; to government, 232–37; inefficiencies in, 44–45, 231–32, 279, 288; to issue components, 242–44; to issues, 237–42
attribute intrusion, 55, 63–64, 68, 69, 76–78
attributes, in problem characterization, 14, 62, 64, 66

Bak, Per, 149–50
Balanda, K. P., 181n
Bartels, Larry M., 141
Baumgartner, Frank R., 4, 19, 23, 68, 70, 84, 123n, 127, 265, 278; on information, x, 5, 9; and the Policy Agendas Project, 21, 201, 292; on punctuations, 19, 140, 141, 142, 143, 156, 278
Bayes' rule, 17
Becker, Gary S., 141
behavioral organization theory, 18
Berra, Yogi, 141
Berry, William, 123
bias, 3, 7, 59
Bikhchandani, Sushil, 141
bills, congressional, 172, 176
Bimber, Bruce, 286